CRIMEAN BLUNDER

By the same author:

A FLAG FOR THE MATABELE
DEATH OF THE LAST REPUBLIC

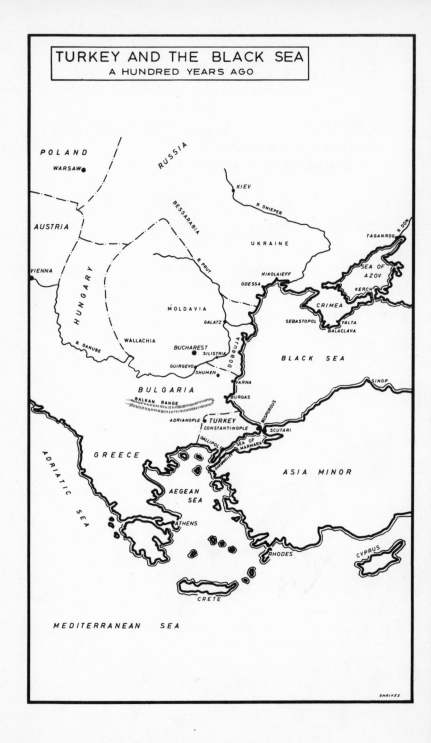

CRIMEAN BLUNDER

The story of war with Russia a hundred years ago

by

PETER GIBBS

"You cannot have a little war."
—*The Duke of Wellington*

HOLT, RINEHART AND WINSTON, INC.
NEW YORK

To my brother-in-law
Brigadier Cyril Collier Duchesne, O.B.E., M.C.,
who likes to call himself
a simple soldier

Contents

	Page
Foreword	11
Introduction	13
Chapter One	35
Chapter Two	45
Chapter Three	54
Chapter Four	62
Chapter Five	75
Chapter Six	93
Chapter Seven	108
Chapter Eight	123
Chapter Nine	141
Chapter Ten	160
Chapter Eleven	178
Chapter Twelve	195
Chapter Thirteen	225
Chapter Fourteen	245
Chapter Fifteen	260
Bibliography	291
Index	293

Illustrations

Facing page

Field-Marshal Lord Raglan   32

General Pélissier with Lord Raglan and Omar Pasha   33

A wharf at Balaclava   48

Balaclava harbour in 1855   49

Lieutenant-General Sir George Brown and his staff   128

General Bosquet and his staff   129

A quiet day in a French mortar battery   144

The interior of the Redan   145

Looking down on Balaclava plain   192

A private in full marching order   193

A group of the 47th Regiment in winter dress   208

Officers and men of the 8th Hussars   209

Maps

Turkey and the Black Sea 100 years ago   *Frontispiece*

	Page
"Crim Tartary": The Crimean Peninsula	109
Marshal St. Arnaud's plan for the Battle of the Alma	133
The Battle of the Alma	139
South-West Crimea	169
The Battle of Balaclava	197
Mount Inkerman	227
The Sebastopol Defences	269

Foreword

ALTHOUGH the Crimean War was fought over a hundred years ago it was nearer in time to my parents when they were teenagers than the World War of 1914-18 is to the teenagers of to-day; and I have a friend—admittedly he is in his eighties—who complains that when he was a boy his father was always talking about his experiences in the Crimea at breakfast.

People probably talked about their wars more in those days, but they certainly wrote less. Apart from Kinglake's *Invasion of the Crimea* in eight substantial volumes—which describes the war, virtually shot by shot, with a delightful garrulity and with a flowery sentimentalism that irritates at first and then, after a few volumes, grows positively endearing—the only complete story as a historical narrative, in English, that I have found has been General Sir Edward Hamley's *The War in the Crimea*. All the other books I have come across deal with particular phases, or with particular persons or military units. Hamley served throughout the war as a comparatively junior artillery officer; his book is straightforward and attractively written with none of the stiltedness common to so many of the writers of the last century. But although it was not published until thirty-five years after the war, in 1891, that was still a long time ago and our perspectives have changed considerably since then. That is my justification for writing the story over again, looking on the events as the ordinary person, claiming to be neither a historian nor an authority on military affairs, would be more likely to look on them to-day.

Professor Trevelyan, in his *English Social History*, has said, "We were not engaged in any great war for a hundred years after Waterloo. The Crimean War was no exception. It was merely a foolish expedition to the Black Sea, made for no sufficient reason, because the English people were bored by peace." That is clear enough to us to-day, and is another reason why the story can now be written again because the writers of the nineteenth century saw it quite differently. What Professor Trevelyan would class as a "great" war he himself would perhaps find it difficult to define with any exactness. Certainly it would not be one that, although it went on for more than a year, was concerned solely with the capture of one town. But if the Crimean War deserves no label of greatness it cannot be dismissed as altogether negligible as wars go, if only because it cost nearly three hundred thousand lives.

The story which I have told is of events in Turkey and the Crimea and on the shores of the Black Sea, and so that this story may have continuity I have purposely omitted any mention of an excursion to the Baltic which the allies made early in 1854. As soon as Britain and France had declared war on Russia they sent a British naval expedition under Sir Charles Napier, together with a French landing force, to confound the Russians by attacking Kronstadt and Helsingfors. But nobody had taken into any account the strength of these fortresses and although the French made a landing the expedition was signally unsuccessful and had no effect on the main current of the war at all; so I have disregarded it.

I have not attempted to document the narrative because my purpose has been to tell a plain story rather than to pretend a formal history. My sources are contained in the bibliography at the end of the book.

Once again I owe a debt, gratefully incurred, to Brigadier John Deedes, my indispensable mentor on military subjects, for reading the manuscript of this book and advising me on it so patiently. My thanks are due also to Mr. and Mrs. Gernsheim for kind permission to use a number of Roger Fenton's photographs taken in the Crimea during the war—fine specimens of early photography.

Bulawayo,   PETER GIBBS
Southern Rhodesia.
April, 1959

Introduction

THE chain of events which by 1854 had induced Britain and France to embark, with no small degree of enthusiasm, on a full-scale war with Russia had started with a dispute between a handful of monks in Jerusalem about the keys to certain doors of the Church of the Holy Sepulchre. It seems that three keys were involved; the key of the main church door and one for each of the two doors leading to the sacred manger. There was also some dissension over the powers of the main doorkeeper to exercise a right of admission to the church.

The argument arose in the course of what Lord Clarendon, Britain's Foreign Secretary, described as "rival Churches contending for mastery in the very place where Christ died for mankind." At the time when the dispute came to a head it was the Greek monks who were enjoying access to the church although rivalry over rights in the Holy Places between the Greek Orthodox and Roman Catholic Churches had been going on for centuries. To add insult to the injury complained of by the Latins, the porter who sat at the main doorway of the church was a Mohammedan, an infidel, and they accused him of showing an unworthy favouritism by restraining Christians of their denomination from entering the church except at certain hours, and allowing the Greeks right of access at any time of the day. That was one of the reasons why they wanted a key for themselves.

The Mohammedan porter was quite entitled to his authority. He was appointed by the Governor of Jerusalem, who was a loyal pasha of the Sultan of Turkey. Palestine had been part of the Ottoman Empire since 1516—and was to remain so until General Allenby entered it four hundred and one years later—and the Turkish sultans, dedicated Mohammedans as they were, had embraced so much of the old empire of Greece that they even numbered among their subjects many Christians of the Greek Church. By the middle of the nineteenth century, at the time of the trouble about the keys in Jerusalem, there were fifteen million Orthodox Christians in the Turkish Empire.

Compared with this formidable influence the number of Roman Catholics in Palestine was almost negligible. But there had ever been a stream of pilgrims, of both Churches, to the Holy Places—a practice that was such a rewarding source of income to Turkey that she would have been foolish to discourage it. In fact, a hundred years before, the then Sultan had entered into an agreement with Louis XIV's government that Catholic pilgrims to the Holy Places, whether French or of other nationalities, should enjoy in Palestine the protection of the French flag. The agreement was involved in one of those "capitulations", as they were called, into which Turkey made a habit of entering with various foreign countries, and which over the years were to cause her so much embarrassment. The principle of a capitulation was based on the theory that the sovereignty of a state could only apply to its own subjects, and that foreigners, visiting or even living in the country, should still be governed and protected by the laws of their own country whence they came. The Turks saw nothing humiliating in the idea—no suggestion that their visitors might be behaving patronizingly towards them; in fact, far from resisting the arrangement they welcomed it because in their view the privilege of Turkish citizenship was much too good to be extended to foreigners.

The first capitulation had been given to France in 1536, and she had appointed consuls in Constantinople who exercised their authority over the French people there. In 1583 England had also been given a capitulation by Turkey but hers was a more remote control and in theory Englishmen in Constantinople were answerable to Queen Elizabeth in far-off London. The result was that England had made little real use of the privilege and when, fifty years later, France claimed to be the official protector of all Catholic foreigners in Turkey, no matter what their nationality, she raised no objection.

The subsequent agreement with Louis XV, made over a hundred and fifty years later in 1740, had been a renewal of the

14

capitulation to France, and it particularly mentioned that French protection would be available to all Catholic visitors to the Holy Land. But, by the end of the eighteenth century, the French Revolution had tended to divert that country's attention from Holy Places, and by the time it was over any rights granted by the capitulation of 1740 might well have been regarded as surrendered by default.

For in France, after the Revolution, the Directory had followed the Commune; Napoleon Bonaparte had risen and fallen; the monarchy had been restored. The Second Republic had come and gone, and in its place the Second Empire had arisen with someone who called himself the third Napoleon at its head.

Prince Louis Napoleon had found that something more than a family name, and a few spasmodic cries of "Vive l'Empereur," were necessary to consolidate an imperial position which had not been attained too scrupulously. The people of France, having acquired a new Emperor a little unexpectedly, now needed an Empire, and their notion of empire had been prescribed for them by their first Emperor on an ambitious plane. The prescription required a successful war. So Louis Napoleon set about kindling one, and as a first spark in the conflagration that in the end was to involve Paris, London and St. Petersburg he fanned the almost extinguished embers of dissension between the Greek and Latin monks in Jerusalem. He knew that, remote as the Holy Places were, any interference there would annoy Russia, and there was nothing that would make him more acceptable to his at present unconvinced subjects than if he were to stage a revenge for 1812.

So Louis Napoleon's ambassador at Constantinople was instructed to present to the Turkish government at the Sublime Porte a formal demand for the restitution to the Catholics of all their rights in the Holy Places. The ambassador did so, requesting that in earnest of their good intentions the Turks should hand over duplicates of the three keys that were causing all the trouble, and instruct their porter to spread his favours more equitably among Christians of both denominations. The authorities in Constantinople, who were a little uncertain of what the trouble was all about, suggested appointing a commission of enquiry. The suggestion had the added merit of avoiding an immediate decision, which was always an attraction to the Eastern mind. On instructions from Paris the French ambassador agreed to an enquiry, but only on the understanding that no documents that were dated later than the capitulation of 1740—that is to say, over a hundred years before—would be admissible as evidence to the commissioners.

Nicholas the First, the Tsar of Russia, was equally interested in the Holy Places, although so far everything had been working there to the benefit of the Orthodox Christians and he had not up to now been concerned with the little storm in the Jerusalem tea-cup. Besides holding the office of Emperor of All the Russias, he was the acknowledged champion throughout the world of the Greek Orthodox Church, whose practice of Christianity had been upheld many times during the last centuries by the might of Russian arms. Through his own ambassador at Constantinople he heard of the attempt by the French to upset the happy state of affairs that had prevailed at Jerusalem for some time, and how it was proposed to beguile the commission of enquiry by confining the evidence before it to information that was a hundred years out of date. Of course, Louis Napoleon had never wanted the Tsar to acquiesce in this, and he was not to be disappointed.

So the Turkish government at the Porte was treated to successive notes from Paris and St. Petersburg, one demanding a supply of keys, and the other hotly protesting that these should not be handed over. It may be that the French demands were more insistent, or more telling; or it may be that Turkey's age-long antagonism to Russia prevailed. Whatever the reason, the Porte at last announced, in a formal note to the two powers, that the Catholic claims to equal rights in the Holy Places were valid. In effect, the note laid down a pious expression of principle about which it deftly avoided undertaking to do anything.

The note drew a heated remonstrance from the Tsar, whose Christian principles balked at any toleration of a sister Church. The Sultan, who was having trouble with his army organization and could not afford at the time to disregard Russian remonstrances altogether, hurriedly drew up a proclamation, known as a "firman," ratifying the old exclusive privileges enjoyed by the Greeks and thereby virtually revoking his acknowledgement of their claims which he had so recently given to the Latins. When it came round inevitably to the French turn to remonstrate the Turks got over this new difficulty in truly oriental fashion by promising not to read the firman in Jerusalem, so that in effect the people whose privileges it feigned to ratify need know nothing about it. However, the Turks were impartial enough to make a concurrent promise to the Russians to instruct the Governor of Jerusalem not to give any keys to the Latins. In the Sultan's view the wishes of both sides had been acceded to, so everybody ought to be satisfied.

The duty of giving effect to these involved undertakings fell to one Afif Bey, a calm Mohammedan who had little concern for the squabbles of Christianity. He was sent by the Sultan to Jerusalem where he first paid friendly visits to the Greek and Latin patriarchs, avoiding any dangerous discussion with them about keys and porters. He subsequently invited them to meet him under the great dome of the Church of the Resurrection, in front of the Holy Sepulchre itself. Here they assembled expectantly with their followers, the representatives of each Church savouring the prospect of the discomfort to be administered to their respective rivals. Afif Bey began by impressing on them at some length the desire of the Sultan to gratify all his subjects no matter what their religion. This sounded ominous to the Greeks and hopeful to the Latins. Then he abruptly terminated the proceedings and strode away, inviting them to meet him later in the Church of the Virgin, near Gethsemane.

After these artless delaying tactics he felt it at last incumbent on him to produce and read a proclamation by the Sultan. But it was not the firman the Greeks had been waiting for and expecting. It was an inspired document intended to gratify both sides while still avoiding the subject of keys and porters. In it, the Sultan proclaimed that the Latins would be permitted to celebrate mass in the Church of the Holy Sepulchre once a year, but that on those infrequent occasions the Greek altar and ornaments must remain undisturbed. It was not an arrangement that held much appeal to either side. The Catholics, in the view of the Greeks, would desecrate the Orthodox altar, and for themselves they would be expected to celebrate mass, as Kinglake the historian has described it, "on a schismatic marble slab with silk and gold covering, instead of plain linen, among schismatic vases, and before a crucifix with feet separated instead of one nailed over the other". Having read the proclamation, Afif Bey wisely withdrew under cover of the clamour he had caused. He was subsequently visited in his lodgings by an angry Russian consul-general who demanded that the Sultan's promised firman be read officially to the Latin monks—that proclamation that was to put the Latins in their place by impressing on them that the long-established monopolies of the practice of formal Christianity in the Holy City were to remain a privilege of the Greeks. Afif Bey at first protested an affected ignorance of the existence of any such firman; then blandly informed the consul-general that he had not brought a copy of it with him. Finally, having calmly produced the original firman itself, he lamented his inability to read it publicly as he had received no formal instructions from the Sultan to do so. In fact, throughout his mission, Afif Bey faithfully honoured his master's equivocal undertakings to both France and Russia.

The effect on the Tsar could not have been more promising for Louis Napoleon. Moved presumably by the highest motives of Christianity, Nicholas sent two army corps to the Turkish frontier and a special envoy, with instructions to adopt a bullying attitude, to Constantinople. Antagonism between Russia and Turkey had flourished for nearly three hundred years. In fact, the history of the two empires was a series of mutual wars, patched-up truces and wars again. Once, in 1833, the Turks had shown an unusual amity towards Russia by calling for help when an army of Egyptian rebels—Egypt, of course, was then part of the Ottoman Empire—had reached the very gates of Constantinople. The Russians had been only too happy to answer the call, welcoming such a heaven-sent chance to march their own troops into the city. England and France had hurriedly intervened, as they had no intention of permitting Russian expansion southward across their vital line of communication with India and the East. And it was the happy presence of Turkey, lying athwart the narrow channel of the Bosporus and Dardanelles, that kept Russia safely locked up in the Black Sea and out of the Mediterranean—a lucky geographical accident that won for the Sultan such fond and influential friends in western Europe.

Mohammed Ali, the rebel Egyptian governor who at the time had driven his Turkish overlords through Palestine and Syria right back to the very outskirts of their capital, had been bought off with a profusion of hereditary governorships of minor Turkish provinces on Mediterranean shores, and Russia had consented to withdraw her armies from Constantinople—after having forced a secret treaty on Turkey which allowed the Tsar to send warships through the Dardanelles to the Mediterranean and to land troops on any Turkish shore he might choose. This had been the discredited treaty of Unkiar Skelessi, which, when its secrets came to light, had caused no little consternation in Europe, for it left Turkey virtually at Russia's mercy and perpetuated the Russian threat to their communications with the East which it had been the whole concern of the western European powers to avoid. By 1840, Britain had felt constrained to take some steps to upset this ominous arrangement and she had called a conference in London. By what proved to be a happy chance, France had then been in the doldrums of the Restoration and had not taken any part in the proceedings. Thus it had been virtually left to Britain to come to a settlement with Russia.

The Tsar had gone to London, and while there he had advanced the imaginative proposal that the two countries should carve up the Ottoman Empire between them. Britain could take Crete and Egypt, Constantinople would be a free city—whatever that was intended to imply—and Russia would have the rest. This easy solution having been rejected a shade arbitrarily by Britain, the Tsar showed a remarkable docility by accepting a British counter-proposal that the Dardanelles should be closed, during times of peace, to warships of all nations. He also agreed that the shameful treaty of Unkiar Skelessi was to be regarded as a dead letter.

Thus there existed an uneasy truce between Russia and Turkey at the time when, in 1853, Tsar Nicholas, driven to extremes by what he regarded as un-Christian agitations in the Holy Places, sent his special envoy to Constantinople and moved two army corps to the Turkish frontier. Of course he had not abandoned altogether his hope of one day sharing out the Turkish Empire with England—that is, if he were unable to take it entirely for himself. At a court reception in St. Petersburg early in 1853, when his envoy must have already left for Constantinople, he had taken the British ambassador, Sir Hamilton Seymour, to one side, and had spoken to him a little wistfully about the prospect of the Turkish Empire breaking up altogether. "We have on our hands a sick man," he said, "a very sick man." Then, like an affectionate nephew distressed at the thought of his beloved rich uncle dying intestate, he added with troubled concern, "It will be a great misfortune if one of these days he should slip away from us, especially before all the necessary arrangements have been made."

The Tsar's choice of envoy to Constantinople fell on Prince Alexander Menshikov, great-grandson of a certain favourite of Peter the Great who had once wielded tremendous influence in Russia. The younger Menshikov was now nearly seventy himself. He had been brought up as a soldier, had fought against Napoleon, and had retired nearly thirty years before, although he was yet to command a Russian army in the Crimea. Now he was a Serene Prince, a High Admiral, and a one-time Governor of Finland, and he came to Constantinople with a full awareness of the awe in which the Turks should hold him. He himself held the Turks in even greater contempt than he held the French, and the Tsar could rely on him to browbeat the Sublime Porte into a sensible acquiescence of Russian demands to keep the Latins out of the Holy Places. The Tsar relied on him also to take this opportunity, afforded so encouragingly by the presence of the two army corps on the frontier, to demand of Turkey a more effective protectorate by Russia of all the Orthodox Christians in the Ottoman Empire. In theory the Tsar was already the nominal protector of these people by virtue of the old capitulations, but he was really hoping for something more rewarding—something more on the lines of the protectorate over Poland which the Empress Catherine had achieved in the previous century, and which she had so adroitly turned into complete Russian domination of that unhappy country.

Prince Menshikov came to Constantinople on the last day of February 1853, accompanied by an entourage whose military complexion tended to belie its ostensible purpose of settling a monastic dispute in Jerusalem. It included the commander-in-chief of the Russian fleet and the chief-of-staff of the Russian Army, and arrived in two men-of-war. The warships, coming from the Black Sea port of Odessa, had had no need to defy the prohibition of passage of the Dardanelles to which the Tsar had agreed in London, and to revoke which Menshikov had every intention of prevailing on the Sultan. When the Prince with his warlike staff landed at Constantinople and drove in state to his headquarters in the fashionable suburb of Pera, Greeks lining the streets hailed him as their liberator—a demonstration which inclined to confirm the lurking suspicions held by some of the other ambassadors in the city that Russia was aiming a little higher than mere protection of her privileges in the Holy Places.

At the time this formidable mission was sailing into the Bosporus from the Black Sea, the British ambassador was away from Constantinople, on leave in London. He had been away for two years. His name was Stratford Canning, he was a cousin of the statesman, and he had recently attained a peerage as Viscount Stratford de Redcliffe. He had been in and out of Constantinople for the last fifty years and could claim to know something about the Turks and their troubles. As early as 1808 he had been first secretary to the then ambassador, and in 1824 he had become the ambassador himself. After that he had tried politics in England— he was elected to Parliament by one of the rotten boroughs—but he had not achieved much success there. Even so, he was still acknowledged the prime authority on Turkish affairs and was sent repeatedly to and from Constantinople. In 1833 the then Prime Minister, Lord Grey, had chosen him as ambassador to the court of St. Petersburg, but as he had been mainly instrumental in Britain's sharp reaction to Russia only a few months before, at the time when the armies of both Russia and Egypt had threatened Constantinople, it was not very surprising that the Tsar refused to have him. So far as it is reasonable to pretend to trace historical cause and effect, the refusal was probably one of the contributory causes of the Crimean War twenty years later. For through the closer intimacy of the embassy, Canning, as he then was, might well have made some more receptive contact with

Tsar Nicholas. As it was he went back to the embassy at Constantinople, and the two men glared at each other across Europe in mutual antagonism for nearly a quarter of a century—an antagonism that had much to do with the uncompromising stand taken in 1853 by both Menshikov, at the Tsar's prompting, and the newly-created Viscount de Redcliffe.

When the British government heard of Menshikov's intention to descend on Constantinople with some apparently aggressive intent they hurriedly packed de Redcliffe off, back to his post. He actually left England on February 25th, but he was not in Constantinople until April 4th, having called at Paris and Vienna on the way that he might have some idea how the other European powers were reacting to Russia's behaviour. He found Louis Napoleon more than satisfied; in fact it was with some difficulty that the Emperor was restrained from ordering the French fleet forthwith through the Dardanelles. In Vienna he found the young Austrian emperor, Francis Joseph, in something of a dilemma, because, not five years before, the Tsar had come to his help by suppressing a revolt against him in Hungary—not the last time that Hungarians, rising to recapture their ancient liberties, were to be crushed by the intervention of Russian bullets. But the possibility of Russian domination of the Bosporus was an ever-present nightmare to Austria, to whom any such outcome spelt dangerous encirclement, and the instinct of national preservation was unlikely to give ground to the demands of mere gratitude. However, for the time being at any rate, Francis Joseph was groping cautiously.

De Redcliffe arrived at last at Constantinople to find that Menshikov had made a considerable impression, if by ways that were a shade unconventional in oriental diplomatic circles. Menshikov, having staged his arrival with some effect, stayed in his quarters in baffling seclusion for three days. Then, having proposed himself for a formal reception by the Grand Vizier he turned out in a plain, informal frock coat without any decorations. As a representative of a foreign power, etiquette demanded of him that he should first present himself to the Foreign Minister who was waiting for him expectantly in the next apartment to the Grand Vizier with ceremonial pipes and sherbet. Menshikov disdainfully rejected these attractions and chose to go direct to the Grand Vizier with whom, however, he did condescend to smoke a calumet. Stung by such an outrageous affront the Foreign Minister offered his resignation. He was confident that the Porte would be in honour bound to refuse it and to demand from Prince Menshikov a suitable apology. But the Porte, impressed by Menshikov's obvious aggressiveness, accepted their own minister's resignation with an unflattering alacrity.

By the time that de Redcliffe arrived from England, Menshikov had impressed his demands on the Porte to the stage of insistence. The demands were clear enough now and showed the real purpose of Russia's display of latent force; for not only did they include the maintenance of the Orthodox Church's privileges in the Holy Places, which was really what the dispute had started about, but they also insisted on an effective Russian protectorate over all the Christians throughout the Turkish Empire. In return, Russia had graciously proposed to renew the treaty of Unkiar Skelessi, by which, if only the Turks would appreciate it, the Tsar undertook to come to Turkey's help if ever she needed it. Of course, according to Russia, effective help could only be offered if Russian ships could pass through the Dardanelles, and Russian troops could land on Turkish shores, even out in the Aegean Sea. From western Europe's point of view de Redcliffe had arrived back in Constantinople none too soon.

Despite the long and frequent interruptions of his embassy, de Redcliffe had enjoyed the confidence of the Sultan and his ministers for a long time. His influence at Constantinople was not due solely to the happy accident that he represented one of the strong European powers; he was a man of imperious bearing, and to whomever he happened to be talking he gave the frightening impression that while he was disposed to be perfectly friendly and polite he was only just managing to keep his temper under control. The Turks had for long looked on him as a stern father who might perhaps have their happiness at heart but was never one to be ready to romp with them. When he arrived back among them, the Grand Vizier hesitated for some days before confessing to him what demands of Menshikov he had been listening to. The Grand Vizier's reticence is unlikely to have been prompted by any delicacy about disclosing to the British ambassador what a Russian envoy had told him, no matter how confidentially; that would have been of little concern in the local diplomacy of the time. Rather was he ashamed to confess that he had allowed himself even to listen to such naughty proposals. But at last he blurted out the truth—or, at least, most of it—and de Redcliffe assumed his most pained parental manner.

De Redcliffe was not one to brush lightly over the surface of a subject. Like a catechizing father he soon had out of the Grand Vizier the full story of Turkish equivocations over the monks in Jerusalem. It was clear in what deep water the Turks had engulfed themselves in their dealings with Russia. The Tsar had obviously felt himself thwarted over Jerusalem, so that, stung into active remonstrance, he had now increased his demands. De Redcliffe warned the Turks that if they continued behaving unreasonably towards Russia they stood to lose the sympathy and protection of Britain. He put it so censoriously that they believed him. He advised them to tell Menshikov that the two subjects—the Holy Places, and the general protectorate—must be discussed quite separately, and the issues of the one must not be allowed to cloud the other. If this was clearly understood then he, de Redcliffe, saw no reason why they should not give the Russians what they wanted in the Holy Places. It would cost the Turks nothing and it would serve to make France more intractable to Russia. De Redcliffe knew well enough that Louis Napoleon had never really wanted to win this minor issue. In any case, Christian toleration in the Holy City was a secondary consideration to keeping open the road to the wealthy East. Not that the British ambassador was openly sympathetic to the French Emperor's well-known proclivity to produce a war. But it was neither to Britain's nor France's interest, in fact it was to their deadly peril, that Russia should gain the foothold of an effective protectorate in Turkey.

So, at de Redcliffe's insistent prompting, the Turks conveyed to Menshikov that the Tsar's wishes in Jerusalem would be conceded and that the long promised firman would be read and given effect to. But, with unwonted resolution, backed by a comfortable knowledge of Britain's implied support, the Porte rejected the Russian demand for a protectorate. No reference was made at the time to the proposal to renew the Unkiar Skelessi treaty because even the Grand Vizier had not brought himself to confess to de Redcliffe about that. However, one refusal was enough for Menshikov, and on May 7th he announced to the Turks that he would give them three days to reverse their decision. He issued no ultimatum; he merely demanded acquiescence. The Grand Council of the Porte met, and, supported by de Redcliffe's fatherly encouragement, rejected the Russian demands by forty-three votes to three. As a result of that decision Louis Napoleon was to have his war and the British were to share its tragic horrors with him.

So Prince Menshikov and his admirals and generals left Constantinople, having failed to bully Turkey into submission. As a token of their disgust at the intractability of the Turks they took away with them all the members of their permanent embassy, and removed the Russian eagles from the Grand Palace where they had been housed. Their two battleships coasted back along the western shores of the Black Sea to the shelter of Odessa harbour, whence the Prince set out on the long overland journey to St. Petersburg to report to his impatient master.

The abortive negotiations in Constantinople had taken eleven long weeks, and now Lord Stratford de Redcliffe had been left there virtual champion of the diplomatic lists. Nobody seemed yet to have realized fully how in fact Britain had been drawn, quite unwittingly, into the serious commitment of a defensive alliance with Turkey against Russia, even though such an arrangement had never been openly suggested. The process had been insidious. The British Government had started off merely by instructing its ambassador to advise Turkey not to be browbeaten by the Tsar. Then, for the sake of a diplomatic advantage, de Redcliffe had persuaded the Turks to give way over the Holy Places. By doing so, against their own real inclinations, they had immediately put Britain under an obligation to them. The obligation became even stronger when de Redcliffe next took it upon himself to advise them to reject the Russian demands for a protectorate, when the implications of his advice had not received even the briefest consideration of the British cabinet. Now Prince Menshikov had gone back to tell the Tsar that, encouraged by Britain, Turkey had defied him. At the end of May the British Foreign Secretary Lord Clarendon, somewhat concerned that his government had apparently become enmeshed in an altogether unexpected and explosive situation, hurriedly sent a despatch to St. Petersburg enquiring anxiously what next move Russia had in mind, and "in what manner and to what extent the dominions of the Sultan and the tranquillity of Europe" were likely to be threatened.

The man who would decide what Russia's next move would be might seem to all superficial appearances quite capable of making that decision wisely. As Emperor of All the Russias he held as despotic a power as has ever been enjoyed by a dictator, but he claimed that his own standards of conduct were modelled on the English gentleman, of whose urbanity he had a consuming envy, and he was fully convinced that in his personal behaviour he closely resembled the recently lamented Duke of Wellington. Tsar Nicholas was a big man, with a commanding presence; his people held him in fitting awe, and kept their distance. It was fortunate for him that his unassailable position required them to do so, as otherwise they might have more readily noticed, as foreigners who were able to approach him with a greater intimacy never failed to observe, that he had a remarkably poor intellect. He was an indefatigable inspector of troops. He had a room in his palace filled with toy soldiers—they were wooden in those days—and their intricate movements across the floor, of which he never tired, constituted his entire concession to the study of military tactics. On the strength of this qualification he had in the past assumed full command and direction of his own real army without ever troubling even to consider, and certainly not to plan for, any commissariat or medical services which his wretched troops might need. Twenty-five years earlier, in 1828, he had led his armies in person in one of Russia's traditional invasions of the Danubian provinces of Turkey, at a time when Turkey had been without an ally and her own army had been in a state of utter disintegration. Thanks to the Tsar's insistence on directing the whole campaign himself the Russians had been beaten by hunger and sickness, and Turkey, quite undeservedly, had survived.

Another mistake, admittedly more excusable, which the Tsar was to make in 1853 was to believe that the British people were so wrapped up in their money-making that they would never agree to go to war. Even his own Foreign Minister, Count Nesselrode, had once said to the British ambassador at St. Petersburg, "My dear Sir Hamilton, you have lived away from your country so long that, forgive me, you do not know its condition and temper. We do." When Sir Hamilton Seymour had assumed a sceptical expression, Nesselrode had added, "Pardon me for saying so, Sir Hamilton, but your country is notoriously engaged in commerce." It was a theory which the British Prime Minister, Lord Aberdeen, had done nothing to discourage by his own repeated expressions of personal aversion to war.

When Menshikov reported on his return to St. Petersburg, Nicholas immediately gave orders for the two Russian army corps to cross the frontier. Count Orlov, one of his few confidants, heard of this and came hurrying to him, crying, "This is war!"—an opinion which seemed greatly to surprise the Tsar.

The Russian armies had been waiting for four months on the banks of the Prut. The Prut is a tributary, in fact it is all but an equal partner of the Danube and it joins it at the head of the delta through which in partnership the two rivers split and flow through marshland into the Black Sea. The Prut rises in the Carpathian Forest and drains the southern slopes of the Ukrainian plateau, running generally from north to south. It forms a right angle with the Danube and enclosed in the angle is that country which to-day is Roumania, but in the middle of the last century held a number of principalities whose allegiances, whether to themselves or to other contenders, had been long in doubt. The two chief principalities were Walachia and Moldavia, which had at one time been dependencies of Hungary; at another they had recognized the suzerainty of the King of Poland. Now they boasted a nominal independence—an independence with certain reservations, and certain frustrating complications. Their princes were appointed by Turkey and removable by Russia; and although the Sultan of Turkey now exercised a nominal suzerainty, the Tsar enjoyed some form of protectorate over their Orthodox subjects. But the Russian frontier was unquestionably the Prut, and an advance of Russian troops across the river could hardly be construed as of peaceful intent.

Nevertheless it surprised the Tsar to hear that anyone should believe otherwise and he was at pains to make the situation clear to the world. He sent a circular letter to the European powers explaining that he intended to press his demands on Turkey "by force but without war" although, disappointingly, he kept to himself how he intended to effect this paradoxical conception. His occupation of the principalities, he declared, was mere security for the Sultan's compliance with his wishes. In a manifesto to the Orthodox Church he said, "We have no intention to commence war. But if blindness and obstinacy decide for the contrary, then we shall call God to our aid, leave the decision of the struggle to Him, and march forward for the Church." Surely nobody could twist such words into a declaration of war; so it was left to Turkey to remedy the omission and make the declaration herself.

But before she had a chance to do so the leaders of the western powers, realizing at last the pitfalls into which the British ambassador in Constantinople had led them, hurriedly gathered in Vienna and asked Russia to send a representative to meet them. Turkey, whose fate was to be decided, was not invited to take part in this belated conference. But Louis Napoleon had already sent the vanguard of his fleet to the eastern Mediterranean and allowed no doubt of how warlike his intentions were—a factor which more than balanced in her favour Turkey's absence from the conference table. However, Russia concurred in an attempt to avoid actual war—because the attempt was obviously so inept—by joining with the other powers in sending to Turkey what became known as the Vienna Note. The Note was neither fish nor fowl, and when Turkey received it she blandly agreed to its terms on condition that certain amendments were made which she well knew Russia could be relied on to reject. Russia obliged by rejecting them; and so on October 23rd, 1853, convinced as he was of western European support, the Sultan declared that a state of war existed. The Tsar hailed the declaration with some relief and told the world that "Russia is challenged to fight, and nothing remains therefore but to have recourse to arms." The excitement in Constantinople nearly touched off a Muslim rising against the Christians there, and the pacific British Government, drawn inexorably into this game of warlike neutrality, sent its fleet into the Dardanelles with the manifestly innocent purpose of assisting the Sultan to maintain order. Louis Napoleon's ships followed with alacrity.

On the southern shores of the Black Sea, on the Turkish coast of Asia Minor, there is a little town with a long history named Sinop. For more than two thousand years it has stood at the end of a great caravan route from the East, linking the headwaters of the Euphrates with the Black Sea coast; a route that labours northward from the Syrian desert on to the high Turkish plateau and drops down suddenly to the little town lying on the narrow littoral. The town stands on a flat isthmus that sweeps away from the mainland to form a sheltering bay, the only winter harbour on the long coast-line.

Late in November 1853, a month after the Sultan had declared war, a Turkish naval squadron sailed into the harbour, driven to shelter by a seasonable gale. The squadron consisted of six frigates, two corvettes and a sloop, all sailing vessels, and two of the new-fangled steamers whose main job in those days was restricted to towing the sailing ships in calm weather—eleven ships in all. They had hardly anchored when another fleet of two- and three-deckers, formidable ships of the line for those days in that part of the world, loomed out of the murky, spray-lashed sea and stood off the entrance to the bay, obviously waiting for the weather to moderate; five line-of-battle ships with two frigates, and three steamers. This was the Russian fleet from Sebastopol, Russia's naval port a hundred and eighty miles across the Black Sea, on the Crimean peninsula.

The Russians waited outside the bay for three days, and the Turks in the harbour, subdued by the knowledge that their government had been rash enough to declare war on Russia, knew there was nothing they could do to save themselves. Once the weather had abated the Russian fleet with its heavier armament could approach near enough to bombard them mercilessly and still stay outside the range of their own guns. And so it came about, at noon on November 30th. The five Russian men-of-war stood in to the town, leaving the frigates and the steamers outside the bay to cut off any Turkish ships that might try to escape. As it was, one Turkish steamer did slip away—the only survivor of the holocaust that followed, although the Russians saved one frigate and took it away as a prize. First, the Russians shot away the masts and yards of the Turkish ships; then they lowered their sights and bombarded the wooden hulks with broadsides from their sixty-eight pounder guns. In desperate attempts to escape the carnage, the Turks slipped their cables and their ships drifted ashore or on to each other, in flames. The slaughter went on for an hour and a half, and of four thousand men in the Turkish crews nearly three thousand perished.

Then the Russians turned their guns on to the town whose defence batteries were as outranged as the Turkish ships had been. The Governor of the town had wisely saddled his horse as soon as the Russians had first been sighted, and when they started firing he mounted and rode away. After the Russians had drawn off he returned to the town, quite unabashed, and his prudent flight was later rewarded by removal from his post, and, with a truly oriental sense of fitness, by appointment to a more highly coveted governorship.

The Turkish steamer, the *Taif*, the only vessel which had managed to elude the Russian trap, sailed into Constantinople with news of the disaster on December 2nd just as the victorious Russian fleet was returning to Sebastopol. The British and French fleets were now in the Bosporus, and when their admirals heard what had happened they agreed at once to send two ships with doctors and provisions to succour the wretched survivors of the slaughter. Even so, their situation was difficult because there was no actual intelligence that the Russians had left the scene, and a collision with the Russian Navy, particularly at the scene of a recent battle, might have been embarrassing, even though Britain and France were still technically neutral. For that reason they refused to allow any Turkish ships to accompany their steamers— the *Retribution* and the *Mogodar*—which duly sailed to Sinop on December 4th. They did, however, relax their security measures to permit one Turkish officer to sail in the *Retribution* on the clear understanding that should they meet the Russians while at sea he would avoid any possible embarrassment to the British by removing his fez.

The British and French surgeons, and scores of sympathetic bluejackets, clambered ashore at Sinop over the burnt-out hulks on the beach and searched out the cafés and hovels of the town for the terribly mutilated men who lay where they had fallen, or whither they had crawled, dying agonizingly for want of attention. Wounds were painfully and inadequately dressed, and limbs crudely amputated. Those lucky enough also to survive tetanus were at last carried aboard the ships and brought back to Constantinople. At the request of the Turkish authorities the hundreds of wounded were taken ashore during the night in an attempt to conceal from the people of the city the shocking extent of the disaster.

But it would never really have been in the interests of Turkey to try to hide from the world what had happened at Sinop. For public opinion in western Europe could well be relied on to forget that it was Turkey who had made the actual declaration of war and had thereby presented Russia with convenient legal sanction for any violence she might choose to commit. Even so, the wave of popular indignation which followed the Sinop slaughter did not spring exclusively from sympathy for the victims of a bully. There were other, less abstract implications of an easy Russian conquest of Turkey. From the moment the news spread across Europe—as it soon did despite any misguided attempts by the Porte to suppress it—the people of Britain, as well as of France, were convinced of the righteousness of embarking on war with Russia.

But whatever may have been the French Emperor's intentions towards Russia, the British Government's declaration of war when it came some months later was no outcome of a reasoned, calculated policy. Ever since de Redcliffe had taken it upon himself to imply Britain's support for Turkey, the unacknowledged militant alliance between the two countries had matured insidiously until it had now become an awkward reality from which there was no hope of withdrawal. If ever Britain drifted rudderless towards war she did so in the first months of 1854, and she was finally to be wafted into the imprisoning current by an unexpected puff of ill wind from Austria.

For while the people of Britain were clamouring to send their navy to punish the Russian bully in the Black Sea, the Austrians were more concerned with their old bogey of encirclement implied by the presence of the two Russian army corps in the Danubian principalities. On February 22nd the Austrian Emperor sent a message to the British Government through its ambassador in Vienna asking Britain to name a date by which hostilities would commence if the Russian armies had not evacuated the principalities. The message implied Austria's belief that Britain had already made up her mind to fight, while the only hint it contained of Austria's own intentions was that "the Cabinet of Vienna would support the summons."

The suggestion that the burden of sending an ultimatum to Russia—to redress a threat to Austria—should rest on Britain came as something of a surprise to Lord Clarendon, who understandably sought some clarification from Vienna as to whether, if Britain was being asked to fix a date for going to war, Austria actually intended to go with her. The only answer he received was a repetition of the ambiguous promise that Austria would "support the summons."

On the part of Louis Napoleon and his government they were unconcerned whether they would be supported by Austria or not and they fastened with some avidity on the proposal for an ultimatum. The British cabinet, caught between French persistence and their own people's mounting enthusiasm for war, were carried farther than ever along the course of drift. The French proposed an actual date, March 31st, when the ultimatum should expire. The British Government demurred but was finally prevailed on to agree to April 30th. The ultimatum was drafted, and signed by the representatives of Britain and France. It followed the time-honoured practice of intending belligerents to infer that the final rupture had been made by the other side, demanding as it did that if, within six days of receiving it, the Russian government had not replied with a written undertaking to withdraw the troops from the principalities before the end of April the omission would be looked on as a declaration of war.

The messenger carrying this joint ultimatum to St. Petersburg travelled via Vienna, possibly in order that the British ambassador

He lost a lot of battles, but he won a lot of hearts; Field-Marshal Lord Raglan.

(All the photographs in this book were taken by Roger Fenton and are reproduced by courtesy of the Gernsheim Collection)

He brought to the councils of the allied generals an executive ability that had long been lacking; General Pélissier (*right*) with Lord Raglan and Omar Pasha.

there, Lord Westmorland, might at least obtain the Austrian Emperor's written endorsement of his country's participation—which Britain had never doubted—in the concerted action by the powers that was now proposed; although, at the time, Lord Westmorland's instructions from his government had only been to express the hope that the ultimatum would meet with Austrian approval. No reference was made to the rather vital question of whether or not Austria really intended to join with Britain and France in their undertaking to remove the threat to her safety—an undertaking which Britain, at least, had embarked on mainly at Austria's instigation and with her implied practical support. No reference, at this stage, seemed necessary because it was obvious that as the subject of differences between Russia and the western powers contained in the ultimatum had been confined to the occupation of the Danubian principalities—while Turkey and Sinop had not even been mentioned—Austria was the party mainly involved. But now that Francis Joseph had found such accommodating friends in Britain and France, who had declared themselves ready to take up his cause for him and to drive the Russian threat away, he was able to recover his sense of gratitude to the Tsar and he forbore to go to war against the people who had once come to his rescue and might one day be needed to help him again.

So it was only Britain and France who were committed to war with Russia, and on March 19th, 1854, Count Nesselrode informed their ambassadors at St. Petersburg that the Tsar had no intention of answering the ultimatum. Louis Napoleon promptly showed the righteous distress expected of a national leader by saying, "To avoid a conflict I have gone as far as honour allowed. Europe knows that if France draws the sword she has been constrained to do so." The British Government which, after all, consisted of gentlemanly democrats, found it a little more difficult to ascribe a valid reason for the pass to which they had allowed themselves to drift. But when war is declared, some explanation to the people is usual, and on the advice of her government the Queen declared that she had felt impelled to take up arms, in alliance with her friend the Emperor of France, in defence not only of Turkey but of the whole of Europe, from a power which had violated the faith of treaties. The actual treaties, whose violation was complained of, were necessarily left unspecified.

The Tsar had no doubts of where he stood. "Russia," he declared, "fights not for the things of this world, but for the Faith. England and France have ranged themselves on the side of the enemies of Christianity, against Russia fighting for the orthodox faith." The little squabble over the keys in Jerusalem was not to be allowed to be forgotten.

I

WHEN the 1st Battalion Coldstream Guards left St. George's Barracks at midday on February 14th, 1854, to march to Waterloo Station, crowds packing the London streets cheered with delight. It was a particularly happy occasion, for it was the first time England had been at war for nearly forty years. Only the elderly could remember clearly what it had been like for the country to be at war and their impressions were apt to be coloured by encouraging memories of Waterloo. For the others, who had merely heard their fathers talk vaguely of the days when England had been in a perpetual state of conflict with Napoleon, the prospect of war was exciting and glamorous. They were agreeably unaware of its inconveniences and profoundly unconscious of its miseries and tragedies.

They were of a generation which had been brought up in an entirely new England, and, in truth, the whole life of the country had changed since the turn of the century. In less than fifty years England had moved into the Victorian age, and in entering it she had passed through as complete a revolution as the one through which she was to pass, half a century later, when she moved out of it. When at last the first half of the twentieth century was to come and the modern world as we know it to-day was to emerge, the changes—rapid, cataclysmic, undreamt of as they were—really needed two major wars to bring them about. The sciences of the new world are the children of war and destruction. A hundred years ago, when the eighteenth century had given way to the nineteenth, a revolution was born of peace, and even scientific changes, startling as they were at the time, had needed no war to spur them on.

For scientific progress had not been idle since the time of Waterloo when troops had still marched on their occasions across

England, or any other country in Europe for that matter, because there was no other means of transporting them. Now, in the fifties, after nearly forty years of unaccustomed peace, hundreds of miles of railways already criss-crossed Britain. The great trunk roads, those ancient highways of romance, along which for so long so much of England's life and history had been lived, had fallen almost into disuse. Not until the day of the motor-car were they to come into their own again. Mail coaches, postilions, posting inns, all were fading away into history—as already had the highwayman, and with him had gone the lively spirit of an era. Now, everybody whose business took him about the country travelled prosaically by train, and the four-in-hand had given way to the dog-cart which merely took the family to the station.

Indeed, during those forty years of peace since England had last gone to war, her whole social life had changed. The industrial revolution had created entirely new towns and had transfigured most of the old ones into unsightly travesties of their past. Now, more than half the people of England lived in the towns and cities, many of them in unspeakable slums. The revolution had divided the country, as she had never been divided before, into classes of rich and poor living not only on different economic levels but in physical segregation as complete and rigid as any colour bar. For the people in the happier circumstances—their numbers, also, had been growing over the years—a new way of life was emerging; a way of life that was to become typically English—house parties, shooting, hunting, gentlemanly involvement in politics—albeit that it was but a modest imitation of the habits and pleasures that for centuries had been reserved for the very few. But the upper middle class was already becoming a power in the land.

Politically, too, the turning point had come when the mantle of power and decision had begun to slide from the shoulders of aristocratic authority, its weight to be transferred, little by little over the next hundred years, to the broader back of democracy. Already, in the towns, shopkeepers were taking over from noblemen, as mayors and councillors gravely took up their new civic responsibilities; and the struggle for parliamentary reform was at its height. Perhaps the change was not yet so noticeable in the country where the squire was still the magistrate and the gentlemen Justices of the Peace still exercised their ample authority. But a new age was dawning, and although privilege was still to flourish for many years to come it was already beginning to lose its exclusiveness and was spreading into unaccustomed social spheres.

Paradoxically, throughout this era of peace, the greatest personal influence in England had been that of a soldier. The Duke of Wellington, having disposed of the Napoleonic menace to Europe, had turned to statesmanship. His first post after Waterloo had been nominally military—commander-in-chief of the Allied army of occupation in France—but it had made him virtual political master of Europe for three years. From his headquarters in Paris he had commanded an army of a hundred and fifty thousand men with no battles to fight, an army that included Russians, Austrians, Germans as well as Britons. Each of the allies had made him a marshal of their own army; he could have enjoyed little authority over his command without such profusion of rank. But there had been no fighting and few military duties, and he had been kept occupied disposing of peace treaties and distributing the rewarding benefits of French reparations, almost exclusively by his own prescription. He had proved a powerful and effective statesman.

When his task in Europe was over he had come back to England, still only fifty years old. Even before the Waterloo campaign, after his Peninsula victories, he had been made a duke, and a Knight of the Garter, and had been presented with a gratuity of half a million pounds; and after Waterloo itself his fellow-countrymen had thankfully added another two hundred thousand. Now that he was back from France once again, having settled their affairs in Europe, there had been little they could offer him that would not seem out of scale and he had had to rest content with a junior cabinet post. But some years later, thanks to a timely political hiatus, he had more fittingly assumed the Prime Ministership.

For two years thereafter the Duke of Wellington had led the government of the country and for the next five years his had been an essential influence, if not exactly the decisive power, in

English politics. On one occasion, when King William IV had found himself in an embarrassing situation when neither Whigs nor Tories could form a government, the Duke had come to the rescue of the country and for three weeks had served England as Prime Minister, First Lord of the Treasury, Home Secretary, Foreign Secretary, Secretary at War and Secretary of the Colonies, all at once. But during those earlier periods when he had held office in more orthodox circumstances—besides Prime Minister he had served as Master-General of the Ordnance, Commander-in-Chief and, for a short time, Foreign Secretary —he had not been the unqualified idol of the people into which he was later to blossom. He had shown rabid opposition to the popular cry for parliamentary reform, for he loathed mobs, and to him the English crowds clamouring for the vote were no different from the mobs of France who had shouted half a century earlier for equality, and who, in the end, had marched servile behind Napoleon. For he could not forget that he had spent the best part of his life fighting the French for the sake of these people who now seemed unaccountably to want to follow in their footsteps. He loudly opposed reform, and for his pains he was threatened, even stoned, by the London crowds. The windows of his house at Hyde Park Corner suffered repeated attention from the factious so that in the end he had to cover them with iron shutters. Once he was followed by a hostile mob all the way from Hyde Park Corner to the City and back to Apsley House. The day had been an actual anniversary of Waterloo—"an odd day to choose" as the Duke put it—but the incongruity of the date was due more to coincidence than design, for on the day before he had made a speech in the House of Lords, condemning the idea of reform, an action which was unlikely to endear him to the masses at that particular stage in history.

But in 1832 the Reform Act had at last become law; five years later the young Queen had come to the throne and the more placid days of the Victorian era were dawning. The Chartists with their strikes and threats of revolution, more effective in their implications than in their reality, had had the wind taken out of their sails when the Corn Laws had been repealed without any need for revolutionary excesses, and Lord Shaftesbury's long campaign to persuade the masters of industry to treat their workers, particularly the children, as human beings was already having some grudging effect. As England moved on towards comparative contentment the Duke assumed the aura of an elder statesman. When old age settled on him and his sixties gave way to his seventies, and then to his eighties, the people came to recognize a little belatedly that the common sense of the Duke, which had been his most effective attribute as a soldier, was their greatest political asset. Soon, from high and low, they were referring nearly every matter of public importance for his sage opinion—matters ranging from choosing a Prime Minister to ridding the great exhibition in Hyde Park of hordes of sparrows which had been trapped inside the monstrous glass building and were incontinently befouling the exhibits.

The Duke had died in 1852 in his eighty-third year, and the people, who had now happily forgotten his opposition to their struggle for emancipation twenty years before, preferred rather to recall the long catalogue of his victories over Napoleon, and that, within the freshness of their more recent memories, he had been their oracle and their universal mentor. They had stood in their hundreds of thousands in the rain of a November morning watching him take his last ride, in a hideous funeral carriage which had been designed in the awful fashion of the day and which had sunk to its monstrous axles in the mud of the Mall and had needed twelve dray horses and fifty burly policemen to drag it out again. Three thousand infantrymen, three squadrons of horse and three batteries of artillery, in splendid martial columns, had followed in his wake down the puddled streets, and the people had been spontaneously reminded that the real glory of Wellington, which he had bequeathed to England, had been built on military achievement, even though its practice had lain sadly dormant for nearly forty years.

So when, but fourteen months later, they saw their soldiers marching down the same streets, but this time really off to a war, they cheered with some fervour. This was the army on whose banners were woven not only Waterloo, but names like Talavera, Salamanca, Vittoria; and a few people in the crowd could still remember what those names had once meant to England. It was axiomatic that the British Army marching off to war must be destined for more such victories. But people were apt to overlook that those battles had been won forty years and more ago and that very few of the men who had fought in them were still alive and even fewer were still in the army, and that those who were had passed the prime of their lives by now and were hardly likely to have retained their full measure of martial vigour. Certainly, not many such veterans could be found among the rank and file even though they did seem to survive fairly tenaciously among the generals and their staffs. The commander-in-chief, Lord Hardinge, had lost a hand at Ligny and was sixty-nine; Lord Raglan, who was destined to command in the Crimea, had lost a whole arm at Waterloo and was already sixty-six; and many of the generals who were soon to take over divisions and brigades, although perhaps they could not all claim experience on active service and still had most of their limbs intact, had already passed the more lively period of their lives.

But in essence it was still the same army as that of half a century before, a fact that was more of a shortcoming than an asset. Not a single aspect of its military character had been changed and it had survived nearly fifty years without anybody suggesting innovations of any sort, to the intense relief of those who were responsible for keeping it in being. After finally catching up with Napoleon the country had turned hungrily to the more rewarding pursuit of money, so that public opinion had been out of sympathy with anything that begat taxation and not a few people had been ready to doubt the need for an army at all. For that reason the Duke of Wellington had been at pains to keep it well out of sight. He had sent as many men as he could away to the colonies, where the British taxpayer could not see them, and he had paraded the home army before the public as seldom as possible. To suggest improvements in its organization, or ideas for bringing it up to date which could only have involved expense, would have been to invite trouble. In fact it was only by a process of natural evolution, so natural that it was almost unnoticeable, that in the late eighteen-thirties percussion caps had begun to replace flint-locks on the British soldiers' muskets—a change of fashion in firearms which had started at least thirty years before and had been almost universal outside the British Army. In the safe remoteness of South Africa, during the Kaffir War of 1851, the British had tried out some of the new French Minié rifles, and after that a small number had been distributed among chosen individuals in a few regiments. But even these were muzzle-loaders and the bullets had to be forced down the barrel with a ramrod and, because they needed to fit tightly in the rifling, had to be hammered home with a mallet—a procedure which was not only risky but which was so protracted that it tended to impair the rifle's usefulness at the height of a battle. Fortunately, some-body was soon to invent a bullet with an expanding tail-cap which relied on the force of the firing charge to open it out so as to engage the rifling; this could be pushed more comfortably down the barrel and the alarming process of hammering it home against a charge of gunpowder could be dispensed with. But the day of the breech-loading rifle was still a long way off and even by 1854 the soldier who enjoyed the doubtful privilege of carrying a muzzle-loader was still the exception. The Coldstream Guards, marching so impressively down the Strand with sloped muskets that February afternoon, were armed no more formidably than their predecessors who had marched to Malplaquet under Marl-borough a hundred and fifty years before.

Nor had they enjoyed any training for the more practical aspects of war. Discipline they had in abundance, and discipline was the one and only attribute that was to keep them together as an army through the war to which they were marching. They could put on magnificent displays of disciplinary precision which were not to be without their military value in confounding the enemy. But in the science of war not a man, from a general to a private, had been given any training whatever. The nearest approach to military exercise, as distinct from pure drill, which any of the soldiers had enjoyed in the last forty years had been occasional firelock competitions which the officers had organized quite unofficially so that they could lay bets with each other on the elementary marksmanship of their men. The target was usually a crudely shaped representation of an oversize French grenadier, and the officers would invite their men to stand never more than a hundred yards away and try to hit it with ball shot from their muskets. Nobody pretended that the sport was a form of battle training because, as everybody knew, the musket was a notoriously inaccurate weapon and soldiers were not meant to waste their powder firing single shots. If practical training for war had been the purpose, men and powder would have been better employed practising controlled volleys, which was all that would be expected of them if they did happen to go into battle.

So in their scarlet jackets with gold trimmings, tight blue trousers and heavy black bearskins—their legs, arms and muskets in impeccable alignment—the Coldstream Guards marched across Waterloo Bridge as they had been trained so assiduously to march before their sovereign on parade, on their way to fight the Russians on the bare steppes of the Crimea. Unfortunately, for all their brave show, which tended to move the tens of thousands lining the streets to exhibitions of immoderate enthusiasm, they had not been supplied with any greatcoats, and as it was still only February even a journey on the South-Western Railway could have its discomforts. But they had one additional item of uniform, and it was the only one, hidden in the baggage wagons which were rumbling over the cobbles along the back streets well out of public view. This was the forage cap which had been designed so thoughtfully by the Prince Consort to save the men from having to wear their bearskins all day. Otherwise the baggage was limited to the equipment which each man, when he came to the field of battle, would be expected to carry himself. There were no tents, no proper stores, and there were certainly no medical supplies. Following the wagons, also in the decent obscurity of the back streets, a sparse but miscellaneous collection of camp followers shambled along—decrepit old pensioners whose ostensible purpose was to remove the wounded from the battle-field, but who were more likely to be in need of assistance them-selves long before they got there. There were some women too, of not particularly prepossessing appearance. They also had an ostensibly administrative purpose but in practice their part in the campaign was unlikely to be confined to cooking and washing.

In the next few weeks, in London and in towns up and down the country, there were to be many such brave displays of Britain's soldiers striding off so magnificently to war. Out of barracks at Windsor marched the 1st Scots Fusiliers; from Manchester came the 1st Royal Fusiliers. Wherever these majestic battalions marched through the towns to the railway stations the crowds waxed delirious with enthusiasm. Britain's was a volunteer army and, as everybody knew, it was more than capable of defeating the Russians—who were unwilling conscripts, most of whom carried only dummy muskets, and, so it was reputed, had to be driven on to the battlefield by their officers at pistol point. So there was no danger, not even a suspicion, that the realities of war might intrude on the people themselves. There were eighty thousand men in the army and it would be absurd to suggest that they could not deal with two or three times as many Russians. Nobody knew, of course, how many British soldiers were actually off to the war and no one in authority had made up his mind how many ought to be sent. Nor had anybody, from the commander-in-chief downwards, any idea of the size of the Russian Army which Britain was so keen to fight. Intelligence services were not an accepted part of the country's military organization. As Kinglake the historian of Crimea has so engagingly put it, "The gathering of knowledge by clandestine means was repulsive to the feelings of an English gentleman."

The troop trains clattered along the new iron roads to converge at Winchester, where the battalions were formally inspected, again amid scenes of fulsome public enthusiasm. Thence they passed on to Portsmouth where ocean-going transports awaited them. There was no brigading of the troops nor any suggestion of making them up into army formations. Nor was there any decisive opinion about where they should go. Some said they should land on the Gallipoli peninsula; others that they should go through to the Black Sea and land at the mouth of the Danube. In the event they all went to Malta, and the decision on where the war was to be fought was conveniently postponed.

The atmosphere on embarkation confirmed those high hopes which the cheering crowds had held of the splendid spirit of their soldiers. The expedition was but a light-hearted and glorious adventure. There were no senior officers with the troops because it would obviously be inconvenient for these to arrive in Turkey, or wherever it was finally decided that the battles were to be fought,

43

before the men had settled themselves ashore. The junior regimental officers and non-commissioned officers could see to all the tiresome business of disembarkation, and in any case there was a string of receptions and banquets at home which still must be attended by every officer of responsible rank. So at Portsmouth the troops went aboard the transports under the charge of their junior officers, some of whom brought their wives with them, for the whole expedition was to be a picnic, and to the great appreciation of the soldiers some of the wives even brought their ladies' maids. Flowers, hothouse fruits, cases of vintage wines, were hoisted up the ships' sides and spread lavishly through the officers' cabins, and the British Army, with its boisterous assortment of followers, sailed away to enjoy the war.

2

SHORTLY after Nicholas the First had become Tsar of Russia in 1825 he had said, "Revolution stands on the threshold of Russia, but I swear it will never enter Russia while my breath lasts." He was already speaking from some experience, for the Russian Revolution—which, when it came at last, had been inevitable for hundreds of years—nearly broke out on the day he was proclaimed Tsar. The spark was struck, the fuse was lit, and if he had not taken drastic means to douse it himself the explosion might well have been set off there and then.

His elder brother Alexander had reigned before him as Tsar since 1801. Alexander, who had found an unexpected place in history as the nemesis of Napoleon Bonaparte, had pretended a liberalism towards his subjects which he had successfully avoided. In private life his liberalism had been just as confused, for he had lived in permanent separation from his Empress, which had tended to impair her ability to produce an heir to the throne, but had fathered several children of the Polish wife of a court official. So the imperial succession had been left to his brothers, of whom there were two—Constantine, who was the elder, and Nicholas. Alexander died on December 1st, 1825—a fateful month. He died at Taganrog, on the shore of the Sea of Azov, where with an unwonted consideration he had actually gone to visit the Empress because she was ill, but it was he himself who succumbed. The legend grew in Russia that he had not really died then at all but had retired to a hermitage in Siberia, and the story was enhanced a hundred years later when the Bolsheviks, in the course of their depredations, opened up his tomb and found his coffin to be empty. But if Alexander had really embraced the life of a hermit at forty-nine it would have been quite out of character.

Brother Constantine, the heir apparent, shared Alexander's

45

taste for Polish ladies. He had first married a German princess, a match which would in no way have disqualified him from the tsardom. But later he had succumbed to the charms and determination for respectability of one Johanna Grudzinska, and he had treated the lady as honourably as he could by marrying her morganatically and returning to live with her in her native Warsaw. It was perhaps a little hypocritical of Alexander, who had shown no aversion himself to a Polish amour, to object to his brother's unorthodox liaison and to insist that because of it Constantine should renounce the succession; but brother Constantine had thankfully and very sensibly complied, and had added his own endorsement to a manifesto drawn up by Alexander which named young Nicholas heir to the throne. This vital document was sealed up and hidden carefully away so that nobody else knew that it even existed, and its purport was just as carefully concealed from the unsuspecting Nicholas himself.

In the leisurely tempo of the day the news of Alexander's death took some time to reach St. Petersburg. When Nicholas heard it he loyally swore allegiance to his elder brother Constantine in Warsaw. More time elapsed while the couriers continued their journey to Warsaw where they were a little taken aback when Constantine reacted to the news by swearing allegiance to his brother Nicholas in St. Petersburg. In all it took two weeks for the confusion to be sorted out during which the imperial throne of Russia was unoccupied by tsar or regent, and it was not until December 14th, that fateful day, that Nicholas the First was proclaimed to be the Tsar.

Alexander's pretensions to liberalism during his reign, which in effect had done nothing to relieve the traditional tyranny of Russian imperial rule, had sown more fecund seeds of revolt than had been generated throughout the previous reign by the excesses of his father Paul who had been an unusual despot even for a Russian tsar, and had been murdered for his pains. And the seeds which were now germinating had been sown, not in the stolid hearts of the peasants who had no comprehension of, and so no striving for, a different order, but in the impetuous minds of the young nobility—that privileged stratum of society in the nineteenth-century Russian imperialist system which the Soviets have so successfully copied in their twentieth-century bureaucracy. These young men, driving Napoleon back to Paris, had seen something of the outside world, and the world had revealed to them the promise of more rewarding prospects even than the carefully ordained privileges, generous as they might be, which were enjoyed exclusively in Russia by the fourteen ranks of the nobility—each rank with its particular privileges neatly classified.

The nobility were graded in rank not by birth but by their occupations, although of course it was the sons of the families already in the nobility for whom the more fortunate occupations were in practice reserved. Among these unlikely people, enjoying the best of their own world, the seeds of revolt germinated, fed by the revolutionary ardour of a distinguished soldier, Paul Pestel, whose leadership emphasized the rebels' social standing, for he himself was the son of the governor-general of Siberia. Pestel had no time for the proposals for a constitutional but still monarchial government for which most of his friends were plotting covertly. Even that starry ideal might have needed for its fulfilment a formidable and bloody enough revolution. But Pestel preached almost openly the gospel of the republic, whose attainment implied as a matter of course the murder of the Tsar and the imperial family; and for ten years he worked with an extraordinary lack of secrecy through revolutionary minded bodies whose disarming labels, such as the "Union of Welfare" and the "Society of the True and Faithful Sons of the Fatherland," did little to cloak their real intentions. Pestel rashly committed his gospel to paper—although events prevented him from actually completing the task—under the title "Russkaya Pravda," the Russian Truth, which outlined in remarkable detail the real revolution which was to follow nearly a century later. The whole movement was so open that Alexander was quite aware of what was going on, but the only security precaution he took was to have Pestel moved south to the army in the Ukraine. Perhaps he really did recognize the inevitable, and perhaps there was after all some valid motive for retirement to a Siberian hermitage.

The uncertainty about the succession following Alexander's death offered a chance for action which was too-tempting for the revolutionaries, although they were entirely unprepared for an organized revolt. The "Union of Welfare" in St. Petersburg, after Pestel had been packed off to the south, had changed its name to the "Northern Society" in an unavailing attempt to enhance its anonymity, and its leadership had been assumed by the poet Ryleyev. The members of the society met daily during the exciting confusion of the interregnum, although like most inflamed revolutionaries they were quite unable to agree on any practicable action. They had never discussed any plans for setting off a popular revolt; they had spent the years in talking instead of organizing, which in those days was a typically Russian failing marking the generic difference between the Slav and the western European. The most provoking way they could think of to incite a disturbance was to induce some of the regiments of the army to proclaim their allegiance to whichever of the two brothers, Constantine or Nicholas, turned out to be the one not chosen for the succession.

On December 14th Nicholas acknowledged the tsardom and was formally proclaimed by the Senate. When the army was paraded that morning to take the oath of allegiance to him the officers in command of the three thousand men drawn up in the Senate Square, in the shade of the mounted statue of Peter the Great, induced them to shout for Constantine, whom the troops had no reason to suppose was not their new tsar anyway. Most of the soldiers would have been quite unconcerned, of course, which of the two brothers was to become their overlord; they knew that the familiar tyranny would still go on so long as Russia was ruled by a tsar.

The ten thousand troops in the next square, the Admiralty Boulevard, whose officers apparently were not members of the Northern Society, although they probably had often indulged in the same revolutionary dreams, went through the routine of taking the oath of allegiance to Nicholas as the newly-proclaimed tsar dutifully enough. So the army in St. Petersburg stood divided, quite arbitrarily, in its professed allegiances, three-fourths assembled in one street and committed to supporting Nicholas, the rest, drawn up not a couple of blocks away, shouting quite uncomprehendingly for Constantine. The conspirators of the Northern Society imagined, if without much justification, that Russia's hour of liberation had come. They believed it was only

The whole of Britain's war effort was to be poured into this harbour; a wharf at Balaclava.

The camps were now well hutted; Balaclava harbour in 1855, with the Genoese fort overlooking the harbour mouth.

necessary now to touch off the spark of real revolt and the country would be in flames. Unfortunately for the cause of revolution, none of the revolutionaries had given any thought to what was to happen next. For a whole day, in the bitter northern cold of December, the unrehearsed insurgent troops stood stamping their feet and dutifully calling for Constantine, who, happily unaware of this sudden surge of popularity, was hundreds of miles away in Warsaw enjoying the demure company of his Polish wife. The revolutionary leaders—some of them soldiers, some civilians—came and went in the Senate Square throughout the day or stood about irresolutely with no idea how to continue the revolution; thousands of spectators stood watching them, merely curious to see what would happen next. The three thousand soldiers, with muskets loaded, who had deferred taking their oath of allegiance to the Tsar, had now tested the excitement of something quite beyond their understanding and were not averse to continuing to behave defiantly. The only missing actor in the drama was the man who had been chosen to be the dictator of the republic. His name was Trubetskoy and he might have made history, but he was a timid man and while there was still some doubt of whether the revolution would be successful he felt it wiser to stay at home.

Late in the afternoon, after long dragging hours of intense inaction, somebody got killed, and this only through a misunderstanding. The victim was General Miloradovich, the military governor of St. Petersburg. He had ridden into the Senate Square to try reasoning with the refractory troops; and Prince Obelenski, one of the revolutionary officers—who, like most of his colleagues, was intent on avoiding any violence—had caught the bridle of the general's horse to hold him back from possibly dangerous proximity to the soldiers who were growing, quite understandably, a little restive. The gesture was interpreted by many who watched it from the ranks as a timely assault on the general—such as they were now quite ready to make themselves, if only to relieve the inactivity—and one man who could no longer contain his impatience raised his musket and shot the general dead.

Had Miloradovich not been shot the whole affair might have

fizzled out and December 14th as a date might never have achieved its notoriety in history. But at last Nicholas decided the time had come to act and he ordered up cannon to fire on and disperse the troops in the Senate Square. Once the firing had started it went on for an hour. The three thousand alleged insurgents, still woefully ignorant of the part they were supposed to be playing, not unnaturally put up some resistance when they found themselves attacked. But it was a one-sided battle and Nicholas had no need to use anything but the cannon themselves, except the force of his imperial discipline to keep the gunners firing on their comrades. The casualties were inevitably heavy and were enhanced by shots which passed right over the square to fall on the frozen Neva, so that the thick ice was broken and many hundreds of people crowding on the river to watch the fun were drowned.

Away to the south, in the Ukraine, Pestel had been able to organize something more positively insurgent. His plans were for nothing less than an ambitious attempt to take over the city of Kiev and there to declare a republic. But Pestel himself had long been suspect and the authorities had been watching him—for there was still an overwhelming body of officialdom with vested interests in the preservation of the imperial régime—and the day before Nicholas was proclaimed Tsar, Pestel was arrested as a wise precaution. A fellow officer, Sergey Muraviev-Apostol, took over the leadership, and just at the time when the bewildered troops at St. Petersburg were shouting ineffectually for Constantine, Apostol was marching at the head of a regiment advancing to the gates of Kiev. But it was an ill-managed affair and such plan as there was had been disclosed when Pestel was arrested, so that the insurgent force was easily overcome. Apostol was taken prisoner and he and Pestel were brought to St. Petersburg to share the fate of two hundred and thirty-eight others who had been arrested as ringleaders of the débâcle in the Senate Square.

Nicholas, as the first duty of his reign, personally took over the interrogation of the arrested revolutionaries. For months he carried on his inquisition, the conduct of which appealed to his narrow intellect far more than the pressing responsibilities of his position. Fundamentally he was a poseur and he liked to feel that he was impressing everybody by his grasp of affairs. Each of the two hundred and forty were brought one after another into his presence in the Winter Palace to be questioned, and there they were induced to make fulsome confessions of their guilt by methods which would have done credit to the Soviets. He worked on each of the prisoners for hours at a time. He had so narrow an understanding of men's minds that it was impossible for him to see the logic of any opinion but his own, and while he pretended to be sympathetic he was able, from their very protestations of innocence, to extract the incriminations he wanted. Then, having selected his victims from their own confessions, he handed over a hundred and twenty to a court which he specially picked for the purpose, whose members merited the confidence he placed in them by sentencing five of the leaders, including Pestel, Ryleyev and Apostol, to death by quartering; thirty-one others to the less disagreeable fate of decapitation; and seventeen more to civil death, which meant that they went through in public the token procedure of placing their heads on the block, which was apt to be nerve-wracking, and then suffered banishment for life to Siberia, which was worse. The remainder and less blatantly revolutionary of Nicholas's chosen victims were sentenced to imprisonment, with loss of nobility—which was more effective and lasting—and banishment for twenty years to Siberia or the Caucasus.

Strangely enough, despite the age-long tyranny of tsardom, actual execution by any method had rarely been applied in Russia during the last hundred years—the wastes of Siberia offered just as effective a means of liquidation—and of course the sentences drew a storm of protest from the western nations. To the Duke of Wellington, who voiced Britain's concern, Nicholas said, "I will surprise the world by my clemency", and to prove his sincerity he spared the five leaders the more grisly part of their sentences and merely had them hanged—which incidentally was considered by the soldiers as a more degrading fate even than quartering. Like every other undertaking in Russia the hangings were bungled, all the ropes broke and three of the victims fell to the ground still alive; when the ropes had been re-knotted and the wretched, half-strangled men had regained a certain degree of composure they were strung up again. To impress the world as he had promised, Nicholas also commuted the thirty-one sentences of decapitation to banishment to Siberia which merely made the fate of the victims longer drawn out. And so the Decembrist revolutionaries became martyrs, and on their martyrdom were laid the foundations of the real Russian Revolution which was to come nearly a hundred years later.

Like all stupid men vested with unjustified power Nicholas was convinced of his own intellectual superiority. He was certain that the way he had handled the Decembrists by dealing himself with each case individually and in the minutest detail had saved Russia from revolutionary ruin, and that nobody else could have managed the situation so competently. From that certainty sprang the inference, which he was constantly at pains to make, that he was the only one capable of handling any affairs at all, and when a stupid man with unlimited authority gets that idea into his head life is apt to become difficult for his subordinates. It was quite beyond his grasp to recognize that one man is unlikely to be able to conduct in detail the affairs of fifty million people. Nicholas certainly found that the attempt needed the help of some special agencies—which would not abrogate his own prerogatives but would wield their power under his direct orders—and early in his reign he started turning Russia into as effective a police state as it had ever been, even in the days of Ivan the Terrible; and as it ever was to be, even in the days of Stalin.

In the second quarter of the nineteenth century, at the time when Britain was moving through her placid revolution to the brighter prospects of reform, the promise of liberalism in a Russian imperial régime, which Alexander had at least hinted at even if he had firmly avoided, was shattered by Nicholas for ever. There was an ominous spirit moving throughout the land and even the peasants, driven by an insatiable land hunger, were becoming faintly articulate. During the first few years of Nicholas's reign there were literally hundreds of scattered peasant risings and most of them had to be put down by military action. Nicholas regarded them not as symptoms of a need for reform but as a cause for sterner discipline, and the measures he took earned him the at least distinctive nickname of Nicholas Palkin—Nicholas the Flogger. A new tyranny, harsh even for Russia, swept the country, and martial regimentation and summary police action took control of every walk of life. Nicholas, directing it all through the relentless bureaucracy of which he was tremendously proud, even found time to design compulsory uniforms for everybody—officials, students, shopkeepers, and all the rest; at the same time, in pursuance of a throttling censorship which he imposed on anybody who was sufficiently educated to write, he personally censored Pushkin's work because, as he said, he could trust nobody else to do it properly. Inevitably, as a very product of suppression, there emerged a new literary force in the land, and the reign of Nicholas was to see the burgeoning of those great Russian novelists—Gogol, Turgenev, Dostoevsky, Tolstoy—who might otherwise never have been driven to tell the intrinsic stories of their time.

So during the twenty-nine years of his reign Nicholas had built up in Russia an all-pervading influence of military discipline. This was the Russia against whom Britain and France had arbitrarilo declared war. The Russian armies might be ill-led, ill-officered, ill-trained and ill-equipped—all these they were—but they were made up of a solid, almost inexhaustible mass of enslaved soldiery whose lives had been a constant regimentation and most of whom had been flogged into ensuring that they would fight heroically for their country.

3

VIEWED offshore from the Black Sea a hundred years ago the Russian seaport of Odessa enjoyed an unfortunate resemblance to Brighton. Nor was the resemblance merely physical, although the rolling steppes behind Odessa could sometimes, after a little rain, evoke a reminder of the Sussex downs; and the town itself, with its young ladies' schools and rows of storeyed houses facing the waterfront had the inimitable stamp of the nineteenth-century fashionable holiday resort. But it was in civic endowments that Odessa was mainly comparable with Brighton, for although it had not enjoyed the patronage of actual royalty it had blossomed from a pretty little fishing hamlet—as, too, had Brighton—and had been forced into unlovely maturity under the inspiration of a fully-fledged duke.

Soon after the French Revolution the Duc de Richelieu, who had been of the court of Louis XVI, had been fortunate enough to escape the fate of many of his contemporaries and to extract from the National Assembly a passport to Russia. Russia always had room and prospects for full-blooded aristocracy and de Richelieu was welcomed to assume the vacant governorship of Odessa, from which he later graduated to the governor-general-ship of the whole province along the Black Sea shore, which included the Crimean peninsula and which, at the time of his elevation, had assumed the promising title of New Russia. That was fifty years before, in the first few years of the century, and before he died the duke had done as much for Odessa by sound municipal administration as George IV when Prince of Wales had done for Brighton by staying there with Mrs. Fitzherbert. The Royal Pavilion at Brighton was rivalled by the Imperial Lyceum at Odessa, and both towns were lit extensively by gas. In fitting expressions of municipal gratitude they had both erected statues to their benefactors, and in 1854 the bronze figure of the Duc de Richelieu looked patronizingly out to sea from Odessa across an exhausting flight of two hundred granite steps leading up from the harbour.

On Odessa, the fashionable bathing resort, was to fall the questionable honour of experiencing the first assault on Russia in the new war with Britain and France. Beside bathing beaches and other holiday attractions of the highest gentility the town had considerable harbour facilities and, hidden away behind the wharves, most of the squalor that goes with a seaport; and it was in fact the only Russian port except Sebastopol of any consequence on the Black Sea coast. Not that it boasted any dockyard facilities, and the Russian fleet, after its diverting excursion to Sinop, had gone back to its base in the safe fastness of the natural harbour at Sebastopol. As soon as war had been properly declared by Britain and France, their fleets had sailed out of the Bosporus, where they had been so conveniently waiting, into the Black Sea, and had trailed their boats provocatively across its waters hoping that the Russian ships would be so imprudent as to come out again.

Meanwhile a naval steamer, H.M.S. *Furious*, was sent to Odessa to bring away the British consul. The *Furious*, which bristled with guns and looked fittingly provocative, did not anchor offshore but kept under way, cruising in the offing. A boat displaying a flag of truce was lowered from the steamer and was rowed to the mole flanking the town's harbour. A Russian quarantine officer came forward to meet the boat as it touched alongside the mole and to him was delivered a letter addressed to the British consul. It can be assumed that the letter asked the consul to prepare himself to be picked up later, for without any further ceremony the boat turned away and was rowed back to the steamer. As she neared the *Furious* a couple of shots from a shore battery fell into the sea uncomfortably close; the boat's crew scrambled aboard in some haste, and the steamer made off out of range and hurried back to the fleet at sea to report the insulting behaviour to which she had been subjected. Although history is silent about the fate of the consul, he was presumably abandoned and left to spend the rest of the war among his country's enemies.

The story that the dastard Russians had fired on a flag of truce could not have been more acceptable to public opinion in England, and there was an enthusiastic clamour for retaliation. No one came forward to remind the people—because no one would have been thanked for doing so—that it was hardly the custom, or even sensible, for a belligerent to send a boat to an enemy shore, even carrying a flag of truce, without making some prior arrangement for the conditions in which its business was to be carried out. The proper procedure, of which the captain of the *Furious* could hardly have been unaware, would have been for the crew of the boat to have waited at a respectable distance from the shore and there to have rested on their oars until the enemy had sent out another boat to meet them, also under a flag of truce. If it had been essential for the British boat to go all the way to the mole to achieve its innocent purpose it would at least have been reasonable for it to wait for the Russians to come out and escort it in, as they would have been quite entitled to do. It was hardly surprising that the Russians took some offence at a British boat entering their harbour and rowing off again without so much as a by-your-leave, having had a grand view of enemy dispositions and even a chance, had it wished to take it, to plant some lethal instrument. So far as the Russians were aware the English gentleman's repugnance to clandestine activities was not shared by the lower deck of the Royal Navy. In subsequent recriminations the Russians explained that they had not fired at the boat at all but at the *Furious* herself whose head was pointing provocatively towards the shore, and which appeared to be in need of a warning not to come any closer. In actual fact the Russians had no need to put themselves on the defensive over their action, for they had every right to fire at an enemy boat in their waters which might well have been bent on some sinister purpose under cover of a white flag. Not that the British public would for an instant have accepted that any foreigner had the right to suspect British integrity.

The British naval commander, Admiral Sir Dean Dundas, decided on reparation, if not actual retaliation, for the shocking incident. He sailed to Odessa with a strong force of British and French ships, not with the idea of affecting any strategic purpose but with the sole intention of teaching the Russian governor a lesson. The war had only just started, and if it was going to be the satisfying diversion everybody was looking forward to, the Russians would have to understand that it must be played according to the rules. For the purpose of chastisement he took a formidable squadron which included twenty sailing ships of the line, five of them with auxiliary screw propellers, and a dozen paddle-driven steam frigates. Among the line-of-battle ships was H.M.S. *Queen*, a magnificent three-decker with a hundred and sixteen guns. The lesson was to be a salutary one.

At daylight on Thursday, April 20th, this considerable fleet anchored off Odessa, the ships cleared for action, and all guns were loaded with shot. The British and French admirals met together in the *Queen* to consider the penalty they would impose on the governor of the town. They hammered out the draft of a note which required him, as a form of ransom for firing on a British boat, to send away the neutrals from the harbour and to surrender all the Russian ships there and also to dismount and surrender all the guns from the shore batteries. After some hours' discussion the draft was toned down and the demand for the shore batteries was dropped "on consideration of the improbability of a general parting with his guns", as one chronicler has naïvely put it; as if a general might not have equal aversion to parting with anything else.

So it was finally agreed that the demand should be reduced to the release of neutral ships and surrender of Russian vessels. A formal note would be sent ashore to the governor next morning if nothing aggressive on the part of the Russians had occurred during the night. At four o'clock that afternoon the ships hoisted their battle ensigns as a blatant provocation to the shore batteries, but the gunners wisely refused to be drawn. Next morning, on the Friday, a little French steamer, the *Caton*, armed with the comforting knowledge that she was covered by the guns of the fleet, sailed blithely into the harbour with the admirals' demands to the governor and with the intimation that he would be given until sunset to comply with them. The governor replied, artlessly enough, that he was not aware that the countries were at war.

Count Osten-Sacken, the governor of Odessa, must have been a courageous man. There was a formidable naval squadron mounting some hundreds of guns lying offshore and he could not have been altogether unmindful of the recent fate of Sinop in very similar circumstances and of the repeated expressions of British and French determination to revenge it. Not only was he brave but he was considerate; he had little doubt of what would happen on the morrow if he defied the admirals, so he released the neutral ships in the harbour and allowed them to escape an undeserved fate. He might well have kept them in the harbour in the hope that their presence would serve as some guarantee of protection for his own ships. He believed there was little hope of avoiding a massacre of the hundred thousand inhabitants of the town. The French, particularly, were known to support the theory that belligerent fleets not only could, but should, bombard enemy seaside resorts. Not many years before, the Prince de Joinville, a French admiral and one of Louis Philippe's surviving sons, had gone some way to re-establishing royal popularity in republican minds by publishing an article declaring his intention, if ever France were at war again with England, to bombard Brighton and other south coast towns. With something of this sort in mind most of the people of Odessa very sensibly withdrew into the hills.

On the Saturday morning six steamers stood in from the fleet, and started to bombard the harbour and seafront. The new-fangled paddle-steamers, with their clumsy paddle-boxes spreading from each beam, came ponderously into their own, for they were of shallow draught and able to move well inshore, keeping cunningly out of the field of fire of the batteries which had been set up to deal with more conventional attackers in the bay. The first shot was fired by H.M.S. *Samson*, a little six-gun paddle-steamer, and she and H.M.S. *Tiger*, which boasted all of sixteen guns, operated close inshore, immune from the enemy's fire. However, H.M.S. *Terrible*, with twenty-one guns, was unlucky enough to receive twelve round shot; one of her crew was killed and four wounded and the damage to her decks was such that next day eight carpenters from the *Queen* took all day to repair it. She was the only allied ship to suffer casualty or damage of any note during the action.

But it was the sailing frigate, H.M.S. *Arethusa*—fifty guns—

who stole the morning's show. She was in the tradition of Nelson's navy with no nonsense about paddles or screws to encumber her. Under full sail she stood in for the shore, holding her fire until within short range despite attention from the Russian batteries. There was a mortar battery on the heights to the west of the town and it was the purpose of the *Arethusa's* captain to get within range and destroy it. His manœuvres were classic. He sailed in until the battery was abeam and fired a broadside from his port guns. Then he tacked, and as his bow guns came to bear on the target he fired again. Then he hove about and discharged a starboard broadside; and as he went around he followed with his stern guns. He repeated the manœuvre three times and the old sailors watching in the fleet purred their admiration. It was the last occasion in history when a sailing frigate was to bombard a shore target. Having destroyed the battery, the *Arethusa* swung out to rejoin the ships anchored in the bay, her only damage her captain's gig shot away.

There was a sixteen-gun battery at the feet of the Duc de Richelieu which was well served by the Russians during the early part of the morning but by ten o'clock it had been blown up by the inshore steamers. Then the British admiral sent in his rocket-boats—precursors of our modern method of waging war, primitive as they were. The little boats were inadequate targets for the shore guns and they managed to get close enough to discharge their fireworks with marked effect on the Russian ships in the harbour, where several vessels were soon in flames and fires were started in the more crowded part of the town near the wharves. At one time the Russians managed to send four field-guns to the rescue, their horses clattering along the mole with gun-carriages and limbers; from the end of the mole they were able to fire more directly at the rocket-boats whose range of action was limited to a few hundred yards and which perforce had to enter the very mouth of the harbour. By then the other allied ships had wisely withdrawn into the bay, out of range of their own rocket-boats—whose aim, thanks to the unsteadying effect of wind and tide, was apt to be a trifle unpredictable. Faced by this unexpected artillery menace the rocket-boats, for their part, had the wisdom to withdraw too; those that had fired away their rockets could well leave the scene of the action anyway, while the others, still encumbered with their dangerous fireworks, were a little vulnerable.

In any case it was already noon and time for the whole squadron to dine so the ships withdrew out of range of the shore guns. But although it was evident that the fires in the docks were uncontrolled and spreading, Admiral Dundas was still not satisfied that the lesson had been as complete as it might have been. As soon as dinner was over he signalled to the commodore, "Can you destroy any more?" and the commodore replied that he would be only too happy to try. So at three o'clock that afternoon the bombardment was opened again and the waterfront and harbour works were peppered with more round shot until, in all, four thousand projectiles had been pumped into Odessa by the allied guns before the sun started to go down and the squadron finally withdrew.

The civilian casualties in the town do not appear to have been recorded; probably they were negligible if the people had had the sense to keep away from the seafront. The Duc de Richelieu, in his exposed position, received a glancing blow from a round shot, which, in other circumstances might have had an unfortunate effect. In the despatch which Admiral Dundas wrote following the action he was at some pains to emphasize how humane he had been to spare Odessa from destruction. But later he found public opinion in England to be unappreciative of his forbearance and the Press was outspokenly critical of his failure to destroy Odessa and its people altogether. From the people in England the scene of war was comfortably remote and in those days there were none of the deterrents to civilian ferocity which in this nuclear age tend to make us more charitable to our enemies. So, in the following year, when Dundas returned to England he determined to clear himself of this imputation of unmanly sentimentality. He persuaded a friend in Parliament to establish it clearly in debate that on a subsequent occasion, six months later in fact, he had strenuously sought to return to Odessa to finish off the job of complete destruction, and had only been prevented from doing so by an unreasonable reluctance shown by the commander-in-chief to spare the fleet from its duty of guarding the army, which by then was in an uncomfortable position on the Crimean peninsula.

But the squadron which had gone to punish Odessa was not to

depart wholly unscathed. As night came down after the ships had withdrawn from the bombardment, a thick fog descended. For days the fleet groped blindly back and forth, and H.M.S. *Tiger*, one of the paddle-steamers which had operated inshore, finally went aground on the Russian coast, not six miles from Odessa. Her commander, Captain Henry Giffard, hoping to lighten his ship so that she would float off with the tide, lowered his boats and cast them adrift and threw all but one of his guns overboard. As soon as he had done this the fog inconsiderately lifted, to reveal the awkward presence on the cliff overlooking him of a battery of Russian artillery which had been waiting hopefully for such a turn of providence. The ensuing fight between the battery and the solitary gun was one-sided as the gun could not be given enough elevation to reach the enemy at all. Both of Captain Giffard's legs were shot off and a midshipman and two seamen standing beside him were killed. The ship's crew had no option but to surrender. They were made prisoners by the Russians and Captain Giffard was carried painfully to Odessa where Madame Osten-Sacken, who might well have been forgiven for feeling little sympathy towards him, received him into her house and tried her best to save his life. His own wife was in Constantinople with the other ladies who had come out from England to enjoy the war. So, a week or more later, a boat from a British man-o'-war, showing a flag of truce, once again approached Odessa—cynically enough the ship was named H.M.S. *Retribution*—and Mrs. Giffard went ashore among the prioners, but she was too late to see her husband before he died. So she was rowed back to the ship in the bay and H.M.S. *Retribution* sailed away once more from Odessa, this time a little less exultingly. The incident of the consul's boat, and the two shots fired at it, had shifted somewhat out of perspective and the balance sheet of the events rising from it left some doubts as to which side had been punished most; Odessa had certainly been peppered with round shot, the town's batteries had been put temporarily out of action, and some Russian ships, none of which were men-o'-war, had been destroyed; while a British man-o'-war had been lost, her captain and three others had been killed, and the rest of her ship's company had been ignominiously taken as prisoners by the Russians.

4

THE British army had had a pleasant voyage to Malta. Once clear of the Bay of Biscay—where there had been much distress among the horses, inadequately haltered in the holds of the transports so that they had been thrown from side to side of the ships and many had had to be destroyed—the sun had come out, the sea had been delightfully calm, and the spirit of a Mediterranean cruise had prevailed as one happy ship after another had sailed into Valetta Harbour. The sojourn at Malta that followed confirmed the promise that the war was to be one long holiday; although after the first few weeks, during which the army had been living largely on the delicacies provided by the people who had been so eager to see it go away, the commissariat arrangements began to fall somewhat short of perfection. There were, of course, still no senior officers with the army. The first troops had arrived on March 2nd and by April 15th there was still hardly a colonel to be seen, although it was confidently expected that Lord Raglan, the general who had been appointed to command the expedition, would arrive any day.

The man on whom had fallen the honour of leading the British army against the Russians had spent the active service part of his career—and it had been but a small part—fighting the French, who were now to be ranged alongside him as an ally. It was a complication which was to beset him throughout the war and he never altogether abandoned the habit, which tended to embarrass everybody but himself, of referring to the enemy as the French even when conferring with French generals. Lord Raglan, born Fitzroy Somerset, had started life with some advantages. He was the youngest son of the Duke of Beaufort and his mother's father had been the renowned Admiral Boscawen who had fought the French on most of the high seas. From Westminster School young Somerset had entered the Army at sixteen and but three years later he was on Wellington's staff at Copenhagen, when the Duke was still Sir Arthur Wellesley. When Wellesley went to Portugal in 1808 young Fitzroy Somerset went with him as aide-de-camp, and he served with the great man, as aide-de-camp or military secretary, throughout the Peninsula War. Few young soldiers have experienced such a distinguished apprenticeship even though Somerset was never actually to hold a command of any sort during the first forty-seven years of his career. It was said of Somerset that, when the walls of Badajoz had been breached by Wellington's siege train, he had been the first to mount the breach, and that it had been his energetic example which had led the English troops to surge forward into the citadel before the French had had time to concentrate their defence where the wall had been broken down. He saw the war right through—always close to the Duke although that was no guarantee of immunity from danger—and when Napoleon went to sojourn on Elba he followed Wellington to Paris as secretary to the British embassy. During the lull in fighting the French he consolidated his own strategic position by marrying Emily Wellesley, the Duke's niece. Then Napoleon was on the march again, and Fitzroy Somerset, who was only twenty-seven and had been on active service for eight years, was once more trotting behind Wellington at the height of the battle of Waterloo. Near Le Haye Sainte he received a bullet through his right arm and the arm had later to be amputated. But the loss of a hand had no effect on his secretarial capacity and he was soon back in Paris with the Duke. When Wellington came back to England and entered politics so did Somerset. He entered the House of Commons as member for Truro, a seat held once upon a time by grandfather Boscawen. When Wellington became Master-General of the Ordnance, and later Commander-in-Chief, Somerset stayed close beside him through the years as his military secretary. When at long last the Duke retired Somerset became Master-General of the Ordnance himself—so that the administration of the Army was unlikely to be anything but conservative—and he was created Baron Raglan. And now, in 1854, this man who had served his country as a soldier all his life, and had never commanded a platoon, and had spent the last thirty-five years of his career in and out of the offices at the Horse Guards, was to lead the British army to war against Russia.

Nevertheless Lord Raglan was a romantic figure for all his sixty-six years. His clear-cut features showed little sign of his age —perhaps this was because he had never carried the actual responsibility of command despite the tremendous variety of his military experience. He wore his hardly greying hair in the fashion of the time, brushed back from the brow and swept forward again in a tress over each ear. The fashion usually went with side-whiskers, and while others who affected it were apt to look over-hirsute and unshorn Raglan was handsome enough to carry it off. His friendly mouth and square stubborn chin were clean-shaven except for a narrow grey tuft of moustache under his nose, but not even the determined set of his jaw could detract from his good-humoured expression.

On April 11th, when his soldiers had been waiting for him for more than a month in Malta, Lord Raglan arrived in Paris. At the Tuileries he was received by Louis Napoleon—who was an old friend, for the exiled prince had lived for many years in London —and the Emperor introduced him to the man who was to command the French army which was to fight alongside his own in the war. This was Achilles St. Arnaud, the Marshal of France who had started life as Jacques Arnaud Le Roy and whose outstanding accomplishment so far had been to betray the régime he was being paid to defend. Early in life, Le Roy had canonized himself by changing his name to St. Arnaud, and adopting the surprising first name of Achilles, but sometimes he is still referred to by the historians as Jacques Le Roy St. Arnaud. The truth is that Jacques Le Roy, while still quite a youngster, had found it convenient to discard both names. He had been born in Paris in 1801 and like Raglan had become a soldier at sixteen, but by then Napoleon was already on St. Helena so he had never fought against the English.

Not that the first part of St. Arnaud's military career had been a pronounced success. He rose no higher than sub-lieutenant in ten years—and that in a democratic army—and then he left the service abruptly for causes which seem to be shrouded in some mystery. Certainly he was heavily in debt, but in the French

64

Army of those days debt was not necessarily a handicap to the pursuit of a career. There was some scandalous background to the story, unpalatable even to the French, about which the historians have been strangely reticent, and for four years St. Arnaud found it prudent to remain outside the country. He was an enterprising young man—he was still under thirty—and he wasted none of his enforced exile. He stayed for some time in England and learnt to speak English well, and he travelled in other countries—by some undisclosed financial means, although one historian suggests that he was involved in the more disreputable class of travelling theatre—and returned to France in 1831 an unusually versatile linguist. Quite unabashed by any past reflections on his integrity he applied for a commission in the Army again, thankfully accepting his previous rank of sub-lieutenant. His new commanding officer, General Bugeaud, who had served Napoleon and was later to make a name in history as the conqueror of Algeria, had recently written a book about military camps. It was not a particularly erudite book but St. Arnaud, with his new facility for tongues, translated it into several languages. Bugeaud was flattered by the implication that so many countries were eager to study what he had to tell them and he took St. Arnaud on to his staff, promoted him captain, and made him one of his aides-de-camp. But St. Arnaud's old habits, whatever they were, persisted and he fell under a cloud again. He was moved to the Foreign Legion and reduced once more to the familiar rank of sub-lieutenant. But it would have taken more than two humiliating episodes to discourage St. Arnaud who sustained himself by the expressed conviction, "I will be remarkable or die." He was certainly to achieve the first alternative despite the inevitability of the second. The Legion was serving in Algeria and thither he went, once again to fall under the command of Bugeaud who fortunately had always been well disposed towards him.

In the less fastidious climate of the Legion, St. Arnaud's besetting failings were not so likely to frustrate advancement in his profession. Within a few years he was a colonel and he had established with those who would one day appreciate it a nice reputation for a disregard of scruples. On one occasion his battalion had trapped five hundred Arabs in a mountain cave. Eleven frightened men had emerged and surrendered to the legionaries. Then St. Arnaud had ordered the entrance of the cave to be hermetically sealed and he had left the rest of the five hundred to die slowly in their tomb. It was an incident which suggested qualifications for work that would be unlikely to appeal to the more scrupulous, such as might not be found among the conventional officers of the French Army.

Louis Napoleon was at that time President of the Second Republic, and was determined to make the republic an empire, and himself its emperor. Unlike his august uncle, or even the megalomaniac dictators of the twentieth century, he displayed no strong pretension to be imbued with a mission to lead his people to better things; he merely had the ambition to be emperor. To achieve this estimable purpose control of the Army was essential, and so he sent a young captain named Fleury to Algiers to find for him a soldier whose conscience would be unlikely to be hampered by niceties. Fleury inevitably found St. Arnaud. But Fleury reported that if St. Arnaud were to be of any use to Louis Napoleon, in the role that was to be thrust upon him no matter how acceptably, St. Arnaud should at least have a popular reputation for military success—a qualification which he so far lacked despite the episode of the Arabs in the cave, reports of which had perforce been withheld from the public. To Louis Napoleon, who was about to engineer an empire, the fabrication of a military reputation presented little difficulty. St. Arnaud was ordered to take his regiment to restore order in the district occupied by the Kabyle tribes of Algeria, who at the time were enjoying a state of remarkable tranquillity. St. Arnaud duly marched into the interior where the startled tribes not unnaturally put up some resistance to this unexpected intrusion. The skirmish that followed gave St. Arnaud the opportunity to establish his brilliance by restoring, with exemplary firmness, that peace which the tribesmen were only too eager to enjoy, and the President saw to it that the success of the campaign was prominently featured in the Paris newspapers. In fact the popular enthusiasm which ensued gave Louis Napoleon all the justification he needed to send for St. Arnaud himself, and as a mark of appreciation of such outstanding military ability to promote him general and give him command of a division. Then, after a barely decent interval, St. Arnaud's genius was appropriated to the post of Minister of War, so that control of the whole Army was now lodged in the hands of a man who could hardly disappoint the President after having had such gratuitous and profuse favours showered upon him.

On the night of December 1st, 1852, there had been a brilliant party at the Elysée. Late in the evening the President, with his Minister of War and the Prefect of Police, had sidled out of the drawing-room, and the little party of conspirators had slipped along the corridor to the President's study where they had made their final arrangements for overthrowing the Republic. The Prefect of Police had undertaken the straightforward and satisfying task of arresting all the political leaders. Louis Naopleon had taken from a locked drawer, and had given to St. Arnaud, ten thousand francs which were to be distributed among the soldiers as the price of betraying France. St. Arnaud had gone out into the misty night and by dawn forty thousand troops had been posted in the Paris streets; when the sun had come up on December 2nd, and the morning had grown light enough for people to read, the Parisians had learnt from the posters, which had been pasted up throughout the city during the night, that the popular assembly had been dissolved and that they were now all under martial law. Thanks to the presence of St. Arnaud's soldiers—who were satisfied, apparently, to overthrow the state for twenty-five centimes each, that is if St. Arnaud ever distributed the money—there was nothing the Parisians could do; and at ten o'clock in the morning Louis Napoleon had ridden through the Arc de Triomphe to the tune of well-organized shouts of "Vive l'Empereur!"—despite the open derision of many Parisians—and St. Arnaud had ridden right behind him sharing his triumph; a triumph which next day was consolidated by St. Arnaud's soldiers who massacred hundreds of peaceful citizens. But the excesses of his men were no bar to his own promotion and soon St. Arnaud was to be a Marshal of France—a fairly rapid ascent from a sub-lieutenancy in the Foreign Legion. By the time war had been declared with Russia, not two years later, the political demand for his particular abilities had fallen away and he had left the ministry to become commander-in-chief, and now his military genius was to be tested, a little unexpectedly, in an actual campaign.

Lord Raglan's sojourn in Paris pursued its leisurely course. While the strategy which the war was to follow still remained undecided he was suitably feasted, and one morning he reviewed with the Emperor thirty thousand French troops in the Champs de Mars. Sitting on a horse beside him was Queen Victoria's cousin, the Duke of Cambridge; and although the Duke was Raglan's military junior his presence as a representative of the English throne tended to divert attention from Raglan himself and helped to ease that natural embarrassment which Raglan, as a mere soldier, could hardly avoid when called on to appreciate the qualities of any army which traditionally was his enemy, even though it was now to fight on his side. The Duke of Cambridge, being a German himself, found it less difficult to reconcile differences in national outlook. He had been born in Hanover, a few months before Victoria—and for those few months he had enjoyed the heir-apparency to the English throne although he had been a little too young to appreciate it—and as soon as he had grown up he had started his chosen career as a soldier in the Hanoverian Army. But within a year cousinly influence had come to his aid and he had transferred to the British Army as a full colonel. Not that this rapid elevation through the ranks was any reflection on him, for in his time he was to become a fine soldier. Ten years later, after service in various parts of the world, he became a major-general and now he was to command Lord Raglan's first division in the war against Russia.

In Paris, after the reviews and the banquets, Louis Napoleon —who was convinced he had inherited his uncle's military genius —took Lord Raglan privately to his study and set before him his grand plan for defeating the Russians. This was not a subject to which the British general had given any serious thought, but Raglan was ever amiable and he allowed the Emperor to expound at some length, confining his own contribution to the discussion to details of how the British and French camps should be set up in relation to each other when, at some later but unspecified stage, it had been decided where the armies were actually going. It was

characteristic of Raglan that he should apply himself to administration and not to strategy; in his experience Wellington had
always dealt with the strategy and he himself had been left with
the administrative details. Louis Napoleon hinted, also, that some
problems might arise over the ever-vexed question of joint
command if British and French troops were to be engaged in the
same battles, but Raglan had a genius for avoiding embarrassing
topics and he deftly turned the conversation back to the safer
subject of cavalry lines.

Having settled nothing in their private discussion the Emperor
and Raglan at last emerged from the study presenting an aspect of
cordial agreement. In the ante-room they joined the Duke of
Cambridge, St. Arnaud and General Vaillant—who had succeeded St. Arnaud as Minister of War—and when the whole party
sat down round a table the strangeness of the alliance was accentu-
ated by the presence also of Prince Jerome, Napoleon Bonaparte's
only surviving brother. General Vaillant, who was an artless
soldier and had the Frenchman's full share of logic, broke dangerous ground immediately by suggesting that they should discuss
how the relations between the two armies were to be handled. St.
Arnaud had his own ideas on this particular subject and had no
intention of revealing them at this stage. He protested engagingly
that the good sense of the allied generals could be relied on to
settle such problems, which were unlikely to arise anyway. Raglan
was only too ready to let it go at that. But Vaillant was a precise
and obtuse thinker and he seemed inclined to labour the point.
However, any need to face the problem was happily averted by
Prince Jerome who seemed quite uninterested in what might
transpire between the British and French but was profoundly
concerned about how they would both get on with the Turks.
Here, at last, the two allies of Turkey were on common ground.
The Turkish commander-in-chief, Omar Pasha, and his troops in
the Danubian principalities, had shown no little valour and had
achieved considerable success in holding up the Russian advance
during the long months while Britain and France had been
completing their laborious preparations to come to their rescue.
The opinion round the conference table, propounded by Prince
Jerome and heartily endorsed by all present, was that these

successes were unfortunate and would serve to give Turkey—which, after all, was an uncivilized country by decent western standards—an entirely false idea of her real position in international affairs and would make her a difficult ally with whom to remain in the proper relation of superiority. Someone formally expressed, and all unanimously agreed, that in the interests of the better prosecution of the war, to say nothing of proper international relations, it would be salutary for Omar Pasha and his men to suffer the discipline of a few wholesome reverses. On this satisfying note, which expressed the limit of joint strategic planning by two great powers embarking on a war against a third, the conference broke up and the two commanders-in-chief, Raglan and St. Arnaud, moved on at last to join their patient armies.

Some of the British troops had already moved from Malta to the Gallipoli peninsula, for despite the absence of any definite plan, and although the enemy was still some hundreds of miles away on the line of the Danube, it was coming to be accepted that the proper role of the British and French armies in this war was simply to defend Constantinople. The notion had been conceived in the mind of Sir John Burgoyne, an engineer officer who had been sent out to Constantinople by a frightened government when it was at last realized that the British ambassador, Stratford de Redcliffe, had implicated his country in possible hostilities. Sir John Burgoyne was seventy-two, a circumstance which possibly inclined him towards caution. Like his younger contemporary, Raglan, who was a mere sixty-six, he had served throughout the Peninsula War, nearly half a century ago, and had been Wellington's commanding engineer. But Burgoyne had been in the Peninsula even before Wellington and had trudged with the rearguard to Corunna—an experience which could hardly have failed to implant in his mind a life-long pre-occupation with last lines of defence. When he had come to Constantinople he had worked out an elaborate line of fortifications, thirty miles long, on an arc round the city—stretching from the Gallipoli peninsula to the Black Sea—and to his intense pride he had been able to incorporate in the line a succession of lakes and marshes which would serve to reduce to a mere nine miles that part along which it would be necessary to position any troops. The plan that he finally propounded with great satisfaction, to concentrate the British and French armies along the front of nine miles and to wait for the Russians, appealed strongly to the common sense of the French Minister of War, General Vaillant, and towards the end of March the French army, fifty thousand strong, started pouring into Gallipoli.

Here they were joined at last by the first drafts of British soldiers who, after a pleasant six weeks' interlude at Malta, had started moving eastward in the latter half of April with their wives and followers, but still without any appreciable complement of senior officers and without any suggestion that they should be made up into any army formations. In charge of the first fifteen thousand British troops who sailed up the Dardanelles was General Sir George Brown, another Peninsula veteran, with but five staff officers and one brigadier-general; even the brigadier was supernumerary as there had as yet been no attempt to compose a brigade. As the British started to arrive, joining the French on the Gallipoli shore, conditions tended to become somewhat crowded, for although Gallipoli is a wide and empty peninsula it is not well watered, and suitable camping ground was limited; and so, later drafts made for a little town on the Asiatic shore of the Bosporous, opposite Constantinople itself, where the troops settled down to enjoy the dubious amenity of accommodation in the bare stone shells of Turkish Army barracks—the Turks, of course, were away fighting the Russians. And thus it was that the British soldier first came to Scutari where in time was to be born the immortal legend of the Lady with the Lamp. Ship after ship came sailing or chugging its way up the Dardanelles, through the Sea of Marmora, dropping anchor in the Bosporus and disgorging hundred upon hundred of British infantrymen. The Scutari barracks were soon filled up and camps sprang up on the grassy plains under snow-capped Olympus, overlooking the lovely waters of the Golden Horn; but there were still no cavalry, no artillery, no military stores, so it was just as well that Sir John Burgoyne had planned for the army to be disembarked two hundred miles away from the enemy. But it was spring, the picture made by the minarets of Constantinople sparkling in the sunshine across the deep blue water could not have been more delightful, and the soldiers were still enjoying their holiday.

At last, on April 13th, Lord Raglan arrived at Scutari and on that day he issued General Order No. 1—marking the official beginning of military operations although the likelihood of meeting the enemy was still as remote as ever. The order duly enjoined maintenance of discipline among the troops, and, in familiar admonishment to soldiers operating in a foreign land, it cautioned against entering "Mosques, Churches and private dwellings of a people whose habits are peculiar and unlike those of the other nations of Europe." But there was a more unusual circumstance about this war, of which the soldiers needed to be tactfully reminded. As the order put it quite bluntly, "The Army will for the first time be associated with an ally to whom it has been the lot of the British nation to be opposed in the field for many centuries." Generously it conceded that "the gallantry and high military qualities of the French Army are matters of history," and Her Majesty's troops were enjoined to be animated by the spirit of Marshal St. Arnaud, who, they were assured, was determined to "cultivate the best understanding with the British Army and to co-operate most warmly with it."

Had it not been for this assurance St. Arnaud's first steps in cultivating such an understanding might well have been misinterpreted. The first ten days after he and Raglan arrived had been spent in establishing camps for the two armies on an apparently permanent basis—an exercise which was close to Lord Raglan's heart—for it seemed that there, athwart the Dardanelles, the allies were to remain and to await the Russians; and if the Turks were to continue their successes on the Danube it might be that the Russians would never come. On May 11th, St. Arnaud crossed from his headquarters in Gallipoli to call on Lord Raglan at Scutari to make the surprising announcement that the Turkish Government had decided to place its army—which was a hundred and fifty thousand strong and was fighting the Russians two hundred miles away—under his command. Raglan knew little about the Turks but he suspected that they would be touchy on the subject of leadership, and it seemed to him a little unlikely that they would make such a sweeping sacrifice of independence, apparently quite voluntarily. It was clear enough to Raglan what was in St. Arnaud's mind. Britain was at present committed to sending only twenty-five thousand men to Turkey; there were already fifty thousand French troops in Gallipoli, and with another hundred and fifty thousand Turks added to them they would make Raglan's own command appear comparatively puny and St. Arnaud could well claim control of the whole campaign. Raglan never entered into an argument if he could help it, so he merely told St. Arnaud that he was sure the British ambassador had no knowledge of this singular proposal, and he suggested that they should cross over to Constantinople, together, to acquaint him of it.

De Redcliffe, who had not met St. Arnaud before, assumed his best inquisitorial manner and soon extracted from the Marshal an admission that, despite what he had told Raglan, no agreement had been made with the Turks nor had anyone actually suggested to them his imaginative plan to subordinate the command of their army to the French. Not that St. Arnaud was the sort of man to suffer any embarrassment in making the admission. He continued to insist, as if it were in the power of the three of them to arrange it, that the Turkish Army should be placed under his command—even, apparently, without Turkish concurrence—as, for some obscure reason which he tried unsuccessfully to explain, he wished to incorporate a Turkish infantry brigade and a battery of Turkish artillery in each of his French divisions. He turned to Raglan and reminded him of what they had both said about the Turks in Paris, and Raglan, whose good humour was unshake-able, found himself in the unfamiliar situation of having to take a positive line of argument, recanting everything he had said previously and stoutly defending Omar Pasha. In fact from now on, for the rest of the war, he was to find himself defending Omar Pasha to the French. But to have taken any other line now would have been to admit the force of St. Arnaud's proposals of whose real implication all mention had been carefully avoided. However, as a trump card de Redcliffe was able to produce a copy of the treaty which had been signed by Britain, France and Turkey when they had entered into their present alliance, and therein it had been agreed that each army should remain under the independent control of its own commander. St. Arnaud was in no way abashed by the weight of argument and circumstance against him and he maintained his case blatantly to the end; but he must have faced considerable opposition, for Lord Raglan, who was not given to over-statement, later wrote, "The Marshal saw that our opinions were stronger than our expression of them."

Undeterred by this lack of understanding shown by his British colleagues St. Arnaud returned to Gallipoli to work out an alternative approach to the end he had in mind. In Paris he had been only too happy to follow Raglan's lead and avoid discussion about the delicate question of command in the event of British and French troops operating together in the same battle. Now he conveyed to the British general how disturbed he was that nothing had been arranged on this account; and he put forward the proposal, which sounded so delightfully simple and sensible, that on any occasion when the troops of the two countries should so operate together the senior officer present, whether British or French, should always assume overall command. He implied, if a little obliquely, that the proposal was intended to apply only on those occasions when small detachments from the main armies might find themselves jointly engaged, but no mention was made of where a line was to be drawn and how it was to be decided that the circumstances were such that the arrangement would no longer apply. The two armies had come as allies all the way to Turkey to fight the Russians and it could be assumed that at some time or other they might find themselves engaging the enemy simultaneously in force; if the precedent had been conveniently established that during joint operations the senior man on the spot was to assume command, then when it came to the big battles Achilles St. Arnaud, being a Marshal of France, would outrank Lord Raglan who was a mere general.

Raglan again fell back on de Redcliffe who once more drew St. Arnaud's attention to the terms of the tri-partite treaty, and for the second time the Marshal was rebuffed. But St. Arnaud showed no resentment—it was not the first set-back he had suffered in his career.

5

FORTUNATELY for the allies their enemy's military machine was as ponderous and slow in getting into motion as their own and the Russian advance through the Danubian principalities hardly fell within the category of a blitzkrieg. A Russian invasion south towards Constantinople had necessarily to be launched from Bessarabia, involving two river crossings. As we have seen, the Prut meets the Danube a hundred miles inland from the Black Sea coast, but along those hundred miles the joint rivers flow eastward and branch out again into a three-pronged fork through a delta which is mostly impassable marshland. Consequently despite their conjunction the two rivers had to be crossed separately, and a Russian army had first to cross the Prut westward into Moldavia, then march south across the steppes of Walachia—the present-day Roumania—and finally turn east to cross the Danube into the principality of the Dobruja, through which it could march comparatively unhindered, at least by natural obstacles, into Turkey.

Russian troops had first crossed the Prut early in July in the previous year, 1853, after Prince Menshikov had failed to bully Turkey into submission to Russian demands. In the unhurried politics of the nineteenth century Turkey had not made any response to this invasion for nearly four months, not until October 23rd in fact, when she had at last declared war on Russia and had started moving her own army towards the Danube. Impelled by no greater consideration of urgency, Britain and France had followed suit five months after that, on March 19th, 1854; so that by the time all three allies had declared war some of Russia's troops had already spent nearly nine months across the first river waiting patiently for their enemies to make up their minds to oppose them.

75

When the British and French declarations finally came the Russians set forth on their incursion into Ottoman territory in greater earnest, crossing the Danube at Galatz—a few miles above its conjunction with the Prut—invading the unhealthy, marshy province of the Dobruja, which is to-day part of Roumania. Here they had their first real battles with the Turks, who gave ground unwillingly, but progressively nevertheless. The Russians advanced southward along the very banks of the Danube, on the Constantinople side, and they fought their way steadily on for two months until the Turks had been driven back to their fortress at Silistria on the south bank of the river. From Silistria the road to Constantinople diverged from the river bank, striking due south through Shumla, another Turkish fortress where Omar Pasha was waiting with the main body of the Turkish Army.

That army, in 1854, was but a recently reformed institution. For centuries the military power of the Ottoman Empire, such as it was, had rested on a body of fighting men known as janissaries, who by 1826—in which year they had been bloodily eliminated—had numbered a hundred and fifty thousand. The janissaries had first been recruited from renegade Christian prisoners, early in the fourteenth century, and a thousand Christian youths had been taken forcibly from their parents each year to train as fighters for their Mohammedan masters. However, by the sixteenth century, for some unaccountable reason impressment into the corps of janissaries had come to be looked on as a privilege and Christian parents were competing for their children to be taken off their hands, until the authorities were compelled to restrict admission to the sons of former janissaries. Not that the terms of engagement appeared to offer much attraction to emergent youth. Janissaries were prohibited from acquiring beards or wives; they were subject to the death penalty for an impressive catalogue of mild offences; and the commander of a deceased janissary was entitled to inherit any property the man might have acquired, so his life was apt to be regarded as readily expendable in battle. In time of war janissaries were expected to provide themselves with their own arms— a military system which was surprisingly successful, for it encouraged a man, if only for his own benefit, to equip himself with the best. The corps of janissaries inevitably became a strong, if boisterous political influence in Turkey. Their traditional form of political protest had been to set fire to Constantinople, and in Sultan Ahmed III's reign in the early eighteenth century the city had been set alight no less than a hundred and fourteen times. Sultan Selim III, in 1806, tried to curb their power and they dethroned him. But his successor, Mahmoud II, was a stronger man, and although it had been traditional for the janissaries to compose the Turkish Army for the last five hundred years—that is to say for five centuries the fighting power of the Mohammedan empire of the Ottomans had been provided exclusively by Christians—he dared in 1825 to raise a rival corps of Mohammedans. Thereupon the janissaries broke into open revolt, but their personal arms were little match for the cannon which the Sultan had had the foresight to provide for his new army. The hundred and thirty-five thousand janissaries were exterminated to a man—shot, burned or, where necessary, hanged—which was an effective, if drastic way of removing their opposition.

The Nizam, as the Mohammedan regular Army which replaced the janissaries was called, was first established in the best traditions of the press gang, and in consequence it was not regarded with any marked respect even by the Turks themselves whose standards of military efficiency were not particularly exalted. Mahmoud II was the first Sultan to favour the westernization of his people and he himself had given a lead by discarding his turban for a fez and dressing himself in European clothes. He introduced French and Prussian instructors into his Army—one of them was a Captain Moltke, who was destined to lead the Prussians into Paris in 1870. When Mahmoud died in 1839 he was succeeded by Abdul-Mejid, who was still the Sultan at the time of the Crimean War, and who intensified his father's drive for modernizing Turkey. Abdul-Mejid introduced a legitimate system of conscription and reduced military service to a limited period, in place of the traditional service for life. He exempted Christians from service altogether, so that the whole relative apposition of the soldiers to the people was reversed and in Mohammedan eyes the profession of a soldier had at last acquired a respectability such as it never could have achieved in the days of the Christian janissaries. As time went on and the Army acquired not much more than the rudest elements of discipline and efficiency, it came to be looked on by the Turks as something of which they were inordinately proud.

The Turk had all the natural attributes of a soldier. He was a fatalist and, as a Mohammedan, obedience to authority was instinctive in him, while the fasts of Ramadan accustomed him to hunger and thirst. No matter what might be the privations of active service they were never worse than he was used to at home. All he asked of his leaders were cartridges and bread and when, as often, he got neither he was still inclined to go on fighting because it never occurred to him that he was being ill-used.

His main handicaps were his officers whose training hardly conditioned them for enlightened leadership. Sultan Mahmoud had introduced naval and military schools as an early innovation, but as the officers had first to be taught to read and write there was little time for any advanced instruction. Not that a lack of elementary education was considered a bar to promotion; in 1853 at the time when the Russians had crossed the Prut and had started their invasion of the principalities, a lieutenant-general, two major-generals and a colonel were struggling with the alphabet in one of the military schools in Constantinople. Admittedly they were still mere youths—all under twenty-one—but they were fortunate enough to have fathers who were ministers of state. As soon as war was declared they hurried off to their responsible duties—the boy lieutenant-general, Mahzar Pasha, taking command of a cavalry division in Bulgaria and achieving, incidentally, a remarkable degree of success.

In addition to the Nizam, Turkey boasted a force of fifty thousand irregulars known, pertinently enough, as the Bashi-Bazouks. These gentry looked like, behaved as and were in fact brigands. They materialized from every part of Asia Minor in little troops of a few dozen or a few score. When war was declared the call went out for their help in what they conveniently imagined to be a holy war and they converged uproariously on Constantinople, requisitioning their supplies on the way in the name of the Prophet and at the point of the pistol. They wore no military uniforms but the assortment of lethal arms with which they draped their persons made their warlike intention unmistakable, and they were well-mounted; their ages ranged from sixteen to sixty, and they swept through Constantinople brandishing their yataghans to the terror even of their fellow Turks. One troop of a hundred who had come all the way from Marash in Kurdistan, near the Syrian border, was led by a middle-aged spinster named Kara Fatima, who was as adept at brandishing pistols and sabres as the male brigands who followed her, and caused some comment among the more conservatively yashmaked ladies of the city. Even the Turkish authorities found the Bashi-Bazouks something of an embarrassment—while the English soldiers who happened to see them were rendered unnaturally speechless—and as these troops of desperadoes rode through Constantinople they were hastened on their way with little ceremony to the fighting front at Silistria and Shumla.

The Russians, who had had some discouraging experience of fighting the Turks in the Danubian principalities twenty-five years before, when the Tsar had insisted on leading them in person, expected the reduction of the fortress at Silistria to involve a prolonged siege and they set about the investment of the town deliberately. The Tsar had at last outgrown his zeal for commanding the armies in the field himself and the invasion had been entrusted to Prince Paskevich who, twenty years before, had captured Warsaw for the Russians and had thus been the instrument of destroying Poland's age-long independence. When Paskevich learnt that Britain and France had joined Turkey as allies he realized the need for some haste if he were to reach Constantinople before them, delayed as their arrival was likely to be, and he tried to make up for the wasted months on the banks of the Prut. He set May 1st as the target date by which Silistria must fall, but the Turkish resistance in the Dobruja had been more determined than he had expected and he only arrived before the fortress on the nineteenth of that month.

The Turks had put a lot of work into the preparation of Silistria as a fortress. They had engaged a Prussian engineer, a Colonel Grach, to assist them, and this gentleman was actually present in the town during the siege although he was meticulous in observing the terms of his contract which required him to provide technical advice only, and he very wisely kept himself away from the fighting. The height of his technical achievement was the construction of an earthwork, known as the Arab Tabia, whose possession by the attackers would apparently serve as a key to the capture of the town. No doubt Colonel Grach had some good purpose for constructing the Arab Tabia, but the sparse evidence available does incline to suggest that if he had never built it the garrison might have been saved some trying weeks preventing it from falling into the hands of the enemy.

By the time the siege of Silistria was opened the British and French commanders in Gallipoli had at last come to the conclusion that their armies might be better employed nearer the seat of war, instead of remaining behind Sir John Burgoyne's last line of defence. Not that any particularly enterprising plans had been made or even discussed. But it was agreed that it might be as well to move some of the troops up the Black Sea coast to Varna, which was the nearest point on the coast to Shumla where Omar Pasha's main army was waiting—so that when, as it was confidently hoped, the Turks had suffered a really salutary reverse the allies would be there to administer the delayed, but much needed lesson of western superiority. So by the middle of May a few, but not many, British soldiers had been moved to Varna; any attempt to move an appreciable number had been frustrated by the besetting lack of such elementary military requirements as commissariat and transport.

Thus it happened that two uninhibited young Englishmen had been able to make their way quite voluntarily from Varna across sixty miles of Bulgarian highlands to Silistria, there to join unofficially but enthusiastically in the defence of the fortress. They were a certain Captain Butler of the Ceylon Rifles, and a Lieutenant Nasmyth of the East India Company's service who had also made a rewarding arrangement with the London *Times* to act as a special correspondent. It may be that holding the East India Company's commissions as they did—which implied some social inferiority, as East India commissions were obtainable by merit only and not, like the more coveted Queen's commission, by purchase—they felt less compulsion to observe those social demands of war which seemed to attract the full attention of the officers from England, most of whom, as soon as they arrived at

Varna, set about testing the sporting possibilities of the district. At Varna, when the first Englishmen arrived, double-barrelled shotguns were more in evidence than muskets while ducks and hares claimed far more attention than Russians.

But Captain Butler and Lieutenant Nasmyth had come to fight the Russians and they slipped away unobtrusively across the intervening country and threw themselves into the battle at Silistria, primitive as were its tactics and its methods. Although they were not meant to be there and although Silistria was garrisoned by a foreign army they soon had the defence of the town entirely under their charge. The fighting was robust enough, if a little unscientific; the small arms used by both sides suffered the besetting inaccuracy of the times and casualties were caused more by chance than marksmanship. When the besiegers attacked the defences, as they repeatedly did, they relied on sheer weight of numbers, and the Turks threw them back in stubborn, hand-to-hand fighting. But although the weapons used in the battle may have been primitive by standards of later wars, both sides used to the full the advanced science of the dynamiter, blowing each other up whole-heartedly, and the fight was inclined to resolve itself into a struggle between the besiegers pushing out saps under the defences, to blow up the earthworks of the Arab Tabia, and the defenders springing mines to the confusion of the sappers. Without holding any official ranks in the Turkish Army, Butler and Nasmyth virtually took over command between them; they achieved a quality of inspired leadership that became a legend among the Turkish soldiery, and even the older commanders in the garrison found themselves compelled by public opinion, and sometimes by more forceful agencies, to comply with their orders. As Nasmyth was later to tell the readers of *The Times*, he had once seen Butler drag a senior Turkish officer from hiding at the height of a battle and deliver him to his post by means of a "peculiar inducement". In the end when Butler was examining a defence work not a few yards from the enemy line he was struck by an unlucky ball shot and he died on June 22nd, just before the siege was over. Nasmyth miraculously survived.

It was on the day after Butler died that the Russians raised the siege of Silistria, utterly dispirited by their lack of success during the five weeks they had been investing the town. They had suffered more than twelve thousand casualties and most of their senior officers, including Prince Paskevich, had been killed or wounded. Their withdrawal from the siege was a virtual admission that their bid to advance on Constantinople had failed and that the main objective of the war could no longer be pursued.

There was, however, another Russian force on the north bank of the Danube at Guirgevo, fifty miles upstream from Silistria; and on the opposite south bank at Rustchuk a considerable Turkish force faced it. Both these forces had thankfully accepted the Danube flowing between them as a decisive obstacle to joining battle, and left to themselves neither would have been likely to conceive any notion of crossing the river. But at Varna the fashion of going unofficially to war had been spreading, and there was now quite a galaxy of British officers with the Turkish Army and as the battle of Silistria was over they had all come to Rustchuk, where the prospect of a fight seemed more hopeful—two Royal Engineers, Captain Bent and Lieutenant Burke, Lieutenant Meynell of the 75th; and Lieutenants Hinde, Arnold and Bullard of the Indian Army. With them at Rustchuk was a General Cannon who had also once been an Indian Army officer but had for some years been attracted by the more picturesque possibilities of foreign campaigns. He had fought in Spain after the revolution of 1820 and now he held the rank of general in the Turkish Army, wherein he was known as Behram Pasha. He had with him a Colonel Ogilvy as his aide-de-camp—seconded to him, officially this time, by the British Army—so that in all there were eight Britishers with the force at Rustchuk, and encouraged by his fellow-countrymen the aptly-named Cannon resolved to lead the Turks across the Danube in an attack on the Russians.

On the night of July 7th, some two weeks after the fall of Silistria, General Cannon and Captain Bent persuaded three hundred Turks, embarked in small boats, to cross the river with them and land on the north bank near Guirgevo. They found themselves virtually on an island, facing a loop in the river which opened out to their front into a considerable pool. But on each flank the loop, where it joined the main stream, was easily fordable, and when the Russians found them next morning they were assailed by bitter attacks. At the same time, some miles downstream, the other British officers had rallied two battalions of Turkish infantry and had led them too across the river. This party had fought its way along the north bank to join up with Cannon and Bent and had suffered heavy casualties, including Lieutenants Arnold, Meynell and Burke, who were all killed. The fighting went on for two days during which more Turks made the crossing until the force on the north bank numbered five thousand, which was too formidable for the Russians to dislodge but was still insufficient to drive them back altogether and permit of a proper bridgehead to be established.

When the third morning dawned the intruders on the north bank noticed with some alarm that an entirely new Russian army appeared to be encamped on the hills overlooking them. The Russian command, after Prince Paskevich had been wounded, had reverted to Prince Gortchakoff, a general who had unsuccessfully besieged both Silistria and Shumla twenty-five years before, the last time the Russians had attacked Turkey. Now, as soon as he had taken over from Paskevich, he had accepted the need to withdraw from Silistria and to remove his troops entirely from the south side of the Danube, and disengage completely from the enemy. If the Turks had not been goaded on by a few young battle-hungry British officers they too might have been happy to accept that situation. But when Gortchakoff heard that an impudent incursion had been made on the north bank he had collected all the troops he had withdrawn from Silistria, and all the others available in the principalities, and he had marched them hurriedly to Guirgevo, sixty thousand strong, in what he felt convinced was overwhelming force. He was satisfied that it was only necessary to launch a determined attack on the little bridgehead and the Turks would be either exterminated, or thrown back across the Danube. Even General Cannon and his surviving colleagues felt some doubt of the ability of their five thousand to withstand the inevitable assault.

At this critical stage there appeared on the turgid waters of the Danube an unusual, almost phenomenal sight in the shape of two British naval gunboats. Admiral Dundas, importuned by his junior officers who showed some envy of the licence being enjoyed by their Army colleagues, had consented that two boats should be sent up the Danube, manned by thirty seamen from H.M.S. *Britannia*, and carrying also thirty sappers. The boats had made the two hundred mile passage up river to time their arrival off Guirgevo, miraculously but quite unwittingly, to coincide with that of Prince Gortchakoff and his army. The effect they had on Gortchakoff's army—considering that the army was exactly one thousand times the strength of those manning the boats—was remarkable. They managed to sail into the loop of the river and thus place themselves between the Russians and the Turks, and while the bluejackets discharged the guns with some effect towards the Russian lines, the sappers collected all the small boats which had been used to bring over the Turkish soldiers, and constructed an effective pontoon bridge across the river over which the main Turkish army, still waiting in Rustchuk, would be able to cross to the north bank.

Prince Gortchakoff, with his army of sixty thousand and the troops already in Guirgevo, would readily have assaulted the five thousand Turks who had first crossed to his side of the river, but when the first formations of the Turkish army—which was over a hundred thousand strong—came streaming over the pontoon he not unwisely retreated across the Walachian plain to Bucharest, and to all intents and purposes the war was over. Turkey had beaten off the menace of Russian invasion without any help from the allies—other than an unofficial contribution by ten British officers and a couple of gunboats—and the threat of Russian domination of the Bosporus, which had brought Britain and France into the war, had been effectively removed.

Gortchakoff's somewhat precipitate retreat had been given an added impetus by the Austrian Emperor, Francis Joseph, who was now coming to the comforting conclusion that the Russian invasion might not be as successful as he had once feared. When Britain and France had declared war on Russia he had been careful to avoid any mischance of becoming involved; but when it seemed obvious, by the middle of June, that the Turks were not going to be pressed back beyond Silistria, he found his loyalty to the Tsar less compelling and he gave the Turkish government a gratuitous undertaking—which the Porte had no option but to accept, if a little grudgingly—that when the Russians were driven out he would send in his own armies to occupy the principalities. And on August 20th, a couple of weeks after Gortchakoff had withdrawn on Bucharest, the Austrians who had been waiting prudently on the frontier until the fighting was over, marched proudly into Walachia, while the Turks, who had spent three exhausting months dislodging the Russians, had perforce to withdraw. Yet Francis Joseph was not able to forget altogether the debt he owed to the Tsar, and after the Turks had fought so desperately, and at such cost in lives, to prevent the Russians from encircling his country, he now showed the measure of his gratitude to them by stepping in with his own troops and protecting the Russians in retreat. He placed his armies between Gortchakoff and the understandably vengeful Turks, and when the allies subsequently decided to shift the war to the Crimea, Francis Joseph's opportune presence allowed Prince Gortchakoff to withdraw his unharassed army safely across the Prut and so be able to hurry off to meet them.

For the allied commanders had at last resolved on a definite plan even though it might not have been based on any profound strategic considerations. In May, before the Russians had reached the gates of Silistria, it had been decided that the British and French armies should be moved to Varna, on the Black Sea coast of Bulgaria—the town was later dignified with the name of Stalin—so that at least that port should be protected if the Russians were to break through to the line of the Danube, and the Light Division under Sir George Brown did in fact sail from Gallipoli on the twenty-ninth. The way in which the campaign was expected to be conducted had been revealed in a regimental order issued at Scutari on the twenty-fifth which stated: "There will be no store of any kind at Varna. Everything not intended for the field must be left here." The troops were to carry on their persons all they needed for a campaign of whose probable length nobody had any idea, and any change of clothing or article of personal convenience which they might be lucky enough to possess was to be packed in a squad bag and left behind. Of course these restrictions did not apply to the officers. An officer lived in a world apart from his men and he was able, at almost any stage

of the war, to acquire facilities for transporting as much para-
phernalia as he could muster, not excluding sporting guns and
tin baths. In fact the same regimental order required that "officers
are to provide themselves with animals for the conveyance of their
baggage without delay." And although the restrictions on kit for
the soldiers might have suggested an intention to be free from
needless encumbrances, concentrating on the minimum necessities
for serious fighting, it did not mean that the wives were to be
left behind. The general practice was to provide two tents with
each battalion for the wives of the regiment—in a situation where
tentage was at a considerable premium. More than a hundred
wives and other female appendages of the army accompanied the
British troops to Bulgaria, and later some of them were actually
to land on the unfriendly Crimea.

As soon as the British Light Division had been sent off to Varna
and this great strategic movement had been set irrevocably in
motion St. Arnaud announced to Lord Raglan that the French
army, still on the Gallipoli peninsula, was not ready to make a
move. He sent this hardly encouraging information at eleven
o'clock one night by a certain Colonel Trochu, whom Louis
Napoleon had recently and quite gratuitously appointed to St.
Arnaud's staff as first aide-de-camp. Now that the Emperor was
faced with the realities of being at war and that there was an
immediate risk of actually meeting the enemy he had begun to
suffer some understandable doubts of his recently promoted
Marshal's experience and ability, and Trochu had been sent to
St. Arnaud's headquarters as a moderating influence. Trochu,
when he arrived with St. Arnaud's message, stayed with Raglan
for two hours, and although the English general maintained his
habitual good humour he left Trochu in no doubts of what he
considered the French army should be doing. At one o'clock
Trochu left having failed entirely to assuage the English general's
quietly voiced displeasure, and after an interval of only a few
hours' sleep Raglan was assailed by St. Arnaud himself, who was
learning rapidly that when it came to challenging an enemy his
Emperor was not prepared to be as bold as he had been in the
face of the unarmed Parisians.

St. Arnaud now announced that despite the plan to move the

allied armies to Varna, on which the two generals had already agreed, he had no intention of moving the whole of his own army there at all; he would send one division only, to match up with the Light Division which Raglan had already sent, and the rest of the French army would move into a defensive line on the Constantinople side of the Balkan Range—a chain of mountains that runs east and west across Bulgaria and separates Turkey effectively from the Danubian plain—and he pressed Raglan to change his plan, too, and send the rest of the British army to join him there. The whole object of the original plan to send the armies by sea up the coast to Varna had been to circumvent these very mountains and to land at a point in Bulgaria on their northern side so that it would be possible to march over comparatively easy country to the Danube. St. Arnaud's new plan—the evident inspiration of Colonel Trochu, reflecting his Emperor's new-found caution—was to establish a line along the southern slopes of the range, its right resting on the sea at Burgas, its entire length safely sheltered by the mountains from any assaults by the Russians. The only difference in strategic conception between the occupation of this line and the occupation of Sir John Burgoyne's last line of defence in Gallipoli was that the new line was a hundred and fifty miles nearer the enemy, which still placed it, however, little more than half-way to the Danube. But there would still be an effective mountain barrier to screen off the real line of battle. And if by any mischance the enemy were to break through the Turkish line—and at this stage the siege of Silistria had not yet been raised—St. Arnaud's grand strategy, if it had come into effect, could well have allowed the Russians themselves to march unhindered to Varna, there to embark and sail down the coast and assault the allies inconveniently from the rear.

St. Arnaud pressed his plan to Lord Raglan with some insistence. During the course of discussion he revealed, quite unashamedly, that he had already set it in motion without any consultation or agreement with his ally, by sending off one division, under a General Bosquet, to march to Adrianople, half-way between Constantinople and the Balkan Range. Raglan was never one to argue and he liked to avoid awkward subjects, so he evaded the main issue and asked St. Arnaud, innocently enough, what was to be the purpose of the two divisions, one British and one French, which St. Arnaud was apparently prepared to concede should go to Varna. Despite St. Arnaud's facility with the English language he found himself for once at a loss to express his answer clearly, and he asked Raglan if he might give his reply in writing, intimating that he would like to write it there and then. Raglan provided him with pen and ink and St. Arnaud sat down in the English general's tent to compose a long thesis. The burden of his argument to support the proposal to move only one British and one French division to Varna was based on the curious theory that it would be injudicious for the allies to become entangled with the Russians before the Turks had had a chance of disposing of them themselves—a theory obviously inspired by the Emperor's new timidity and at some variance from the derogatory opinion of the Turks expressed so unanimously in Paris; and if the allied forces at Varna were known to be too weak to be really effective, public opinion in Europe would hesitate to criticize any reluctance on their part to go to the relief of Silistria. It was a remarkable argument to come from a Marshal of France, particularly as he never revealed how he intended to explain his purpose in sending troops to Varna at all if they were to be too few to be of any effect. But he made one telling point: that both armies were ill-served by their commissariats and for that reason could not yet expect to achieve any great success wherever they went.

Well satisfied with the case he had made St. Arnaud left Raglan with this astonishing document to read at his leisure and the promise that he would send Colonel Trochu to see him next day. Trochu when he came was voluble in his advocacy of the plan and left little doubt in Raglan's mind that he had conceived it himself. Raglan heard him out; but there was no obligation for him even to discuss the plan with Trochu who was his subordinate in rank, so he was spared the need to argue and he simply told Trochu to remind St. Arnaud that the allied generals had already promised Omar Pasha to go to Varna, and that if the French were not yet ready to join the British there he would merely wait at Scutari until they were. Lord Raglan may have suffered from a disinclination to face controversies but it was a shortcoming which often worked to his advantage, because no opinion he formed was ever exposed by discussion to the risk of doubting whether he was right. In any case his constant good humour masked an obstinate determination of purpose and it was unlikely that even St. Arnaud had failed to become aware of this. On June 10th, after a week's delay, a message came to Raglan's headquarters that St. Arnaud was moving the whole French army by sea to Varna, so that the difference of opinion on major strategy had been resolved with remarkable simplicity. General Bosquet's unfortunate division, which had already marched seventy long miles to Adrianople, was faced with another seventy miles over difficult country to the coast, at a time when most of the troops could well have wished that they had no marching to do at all.

For cholera had broken out in the French army. The first cases had been reported during the voyage from Marseilles; and it seems safe to assume that the tragic epidemic which was to sweep through the French and British armies in the next few weeks had its origin in that insalubrious port, rather than in the marshes of Bulgaria which were subsequently to receive all the blame. Not that there was any authentic knowledge in those days of how the illness was spread. In fact the opinion held by the best authorities was that the germs were carried by the wind, particularly if the breeze was damp. At one stage, during the epidemic which was to come, some ships actually fled from port to shake off contact with the scourge, and when, notwithstanding their flight, these ship's companies succumbed while at sea, the pundits were convinced that the infection had been brought by a squall and that it would have been better to have stayed in the shelter of the crowded harbour, despite that people there were dying all around them.

So the French army moved to Varna, bringing cholera with it, and the British army moved in to share the epidemic. The effect on the British troops was tragic enough; eight hundred men died a shocking, repulsive death in a few weeks. In the French army, in the same period, ten thousand men died. And these numbers were not to be the full toll which the disease was to take. But when the soldiers who had sailed so jauntily from England a few months before landed at last at Varna, still in reasonable spirits despite some disillusion about the commissariat, they stepped ashore into a world of misery. The country round Varna was pleasant enough—rolling downland enfolding shady, wooded valleys—although the town itself was primitive and dirty. Some of the regiments camped on the shore of the bay close to the town; others moved some miles inland on to the higher ground, ostensibly as outposts against attack by the Russians—who were at least sixty miles away anyway and were being held in effective check by the Turks at Silistria. The temperature was usually in the nineties, which made the standard issue of salt pork a little unappetizing. Almost at once the dreadful sickness swept through the army and at one stage there were seven thousand British soldiers lying helpless in the suffocating heat of their bell tents under the burning sun. There was no medical attention, and the only measure taken by the authorities in the interests of health was to increase the salt pork ration by another half, so that the sick men were forced to expend more of their sparse energy in burying the pork, which they were too ill to face, in an unsuccessful attempt to keep the flies away. Even so nature was unable to break down the plutocracy of the British Army, and while the soldiers were stricken in their thousands the officers were generally spared. There were certainly some cholera cases and a few deaths among the officers but their proportionate numbers were very considerably less than those of the rank and file—a telling commentary on the relative conditions of living.

When the British army landed at Varna the allied fleets made their base at Balchick Bay, some fifteen miles up the coast to the north. To avoid the scourge the fleets put to sea but in fact they had taken it with them. In the confined spaces of the ships, once the contagion struck it spread like fire. Imagining the germs to be brought by the winds, fit men took every opportunity to keep below decks among the infectious cases. On some ships burials at sea went on round the clock—just as, ashore, the playing of the Dead March had had to be abandoned as funerals were overlapping and the rival bands were producing unfortunate discords. H.M.S. *Britannia* had a hundred and nine deaths in two days; another three hundred men were lying below, desperately ill. If ever ships were worked by skeleton crews, almost in the literal sense, it was the British and French men-of-war in the Black Sea in July and August 1854. And yet even at sea the British officers enjoyed their comparative, and apparently divine immunity.

In July, before the cholera had really broken out seriously, St. Arnaud had heard that the siege of Silistria had been lifted and that the Russians were safely in retreat. In actual fact, Prince Gortchakoff had withdrawn all his men across the Danube, but St. Arnaud heard, from some unreliable source, that there were still ten thousand Russian stragglers in the Dobruja. This was too good an opportunity to be missed, and without telling the Turks, or even Lord Raglan whose headquarters were in the camp next to his own, he led off thirty thousand Zouaves on a hectic scramble for easy military glory. They forced-marched nearly a hundred miles into the low-lying marshy plains of the Dobruja, where there were no Russians to be found. Inevitably the unhealthy, damp conditions brought to life the lurking cholera germs. The sortie from Varna had been made in a tremendous hurry and without any preparation, so there were no supplies and the troops were shockingly ill-nourished. The cholera burst out among them like a bomb and in a few days three thousand Zouaves were dead. In the British army and navy the casualties had been serious enough; in the French army they were appalling, and so far not a shot had been fired against the Russians.

But the privilege of sending an ill-prepared force to scour the country for Russians after the Turks had driven them from the field was not to be enjoyed exclusively by the French. As soon as it had been reported that the enemy had withdrawn to the other side of the river, Raglan sent out a squadron of two hundred British cavalry under Brigadier-General Lord Cardigan—the man who was destined later to write an astonishing page of history by leading the Light Brigade in its suicidal charge at Balaclava—to make sure that the report was true. It was a simple enough reconnaissance to undertake and the information could have been obtained and reported back to the commander-in-chief in a few days. However, the flamboyant Cardigan had other ideas, and although his squadron was inadequately equipped and ill-provided with food and forage he rushed his men and horses up and down the banks of the Danube for days on end, and went out of his way to ride bombastically through Silistria and Shumla to impress the Turkish garrisons, who after all had done the fighting. He was away for more than two weeks, and thanks to the scandalous way he drove the squadron through the intense July heat the Light Brigade lost a hundred of its horses and came back to Varna in a shockingly distressed condition and with no information about the enemy at all. A few days later another reconnaissance troop, consisting merely of an officer and twelve men, rode out and obtained without any fuss or difficulty all the information which Cardigan had failed to gather. Not that the comparison between the effectiveness of the two reconnaissances was to cast any odium on Lord Cardigan who was promptly promoted major-general.

Nevertheless, in whatever way it may have been obtained, the information was specific enough. The Russian army had withdrawn entirely from the field; the threat to Turkey's independence, initiated after Menshikov's mission to Constantinople when the Tsar had sent his two army corps across the Prut, no longer existed.

There remained no justification for Britain or France to continue the war. In fact there was no war left to continue.

6

I N Richmond Park stands Pembroke Lodge, a lordly old
house which has found its level in the modern democratic
world by partial conversion to a popular tea room. A hundred
years ago it was a house in the gift of the Queen and for many
years it was occupied by the illustrious Russell family. Lord John
Russell, who was a champion of parliamentary reform in the early
part of the nineteenth century and was England's Prime Minister
for six years until 1852, lived and died there; his grandson
Bertrand Russell—whose involvement in the problems of the
nuclear age has emphasized the frightening acceleration of human
destiny in but three generations—was born there.

In 1854, at the time of the Crimean War, Lord John Russell was
President of the Council in Lord Aberdeen's cabinet. On the
evening of June 29th the cabinet repaired to Pembroke Lodge to
combine enjoyment with business by dining with Lord John and
considering, after dinner, a despatch to Lord Raglan which had
been drafted by the Duke of Newcastle, the Secretary of State for
War. This was a post which had only been created that month
and few people fully understood its distinction from that of
Secretary at War—which latter, being a peacetime appointment,
was a characteristic misnomer. The Secretary at War did not hold
cabinet rank. Responsibility to the cabinet for the direction of war
when it came, had, up to June 1854, been that of the Secretary of
State for the Colonies, and as the incumbent of this office was
not necessarily chosen for any ability to understand military
problems he had been apt to have little effect on the autocracy
at the Horse Guards. Improbably enough, the government of
the day had recognized this as a drawback, and had appointed the
Duke of Newcastle Secretary of State for War with a seat in the
cabinet. The Duke was an intelligent minister whose great delight

was to write despatches. It would have been natural for him to have felt some disappointment if, almost immediately after he had assumed office, the war had been found to be over before it had started, and opportunities for his somewhat breathless compositions had been curtailed. But he never even contemplated such a disappointment because neither he nor the people of Britain had any intention of allowing the glories of war to slip so easily from their grasp, and he, the Duke of Newcastle, was determined to see that they did not.

The ministers who assembled that evening at Pembroke Lodge were still led in theory by the pacific Lord Aberdeen, who though bowed down with sorrow at the realization that he was the leader of a cabinet which had brought the country into war showed no apparent inclination to relinquish the burden. The strongest influence in the cabinet was that of Lord Palmerston, now the Home Secretary, who, more than six months before, after the attack on Sinop, had stirred the warlike ambitions of the country by demanding in Parliament that Britain should retaliate by attacking Sebastopol. At the time Britain was not even at war with Russia, and wise counsels might have suggested that in her own interests she should keep out of it, but the demand had been heartily endorsed by a public hungry for military glory. A little later Palmerston had resigned from the cabinet on an entirely separate issue. But when the Government, almost immediately afterwards, had agreed to send the British fleet to the Black Sea—Britain was then still not within three months of declaring war—he was ready enough to reconsider his position and was soon back in office urging the cabinet on to hostilities. Now, the whole country's ambition was to attack Sebastopol, and even the liberal Mr. Gladstone publicly congratulated Lord Palmerston on having been the first to propose it.

It does not seem to have crossed the mind of any member of the cabinet that now that the threat of Russian domination of Turkey had been removed Britain might be spared the ordeal of pursuing the war. Russia had had unmistakable evidence of two deterrents to her ambitions: first, the unexpected fighting qualities of the Turks; and second, the readiness of Britain and France to give Turkey practical military support, even though it had taken some time to muster and had lurked in the background more as a threat than as an immediate menace. Yet for all its practical ineffectiveness the British and French gesture had been salutary enough, and it should not have been beyond the powers of the allied diplomats, leading from a hand which at any rate appeared to hold the winning cards, to negotiate a settlement with Russia which could achieve a guarantee of Turkish independence and at the same time avoid the miseries of war. But in England, even in the cabinet, war which would be waged at such a safe distance was the last thing people wanted to avoid. In fact what worried them most was the danger that there would be no fighting. Such an unrewarding prospect had to be resisted with determination. The enemy had disappeared from the expected field of battle in Bulgaria, so another battleground must be found quickly. There was no need to give any thoughtful consideration to where the other field should be because that decision had been made in the public mind months before. When the Russian ships had battered the Turks at Sinop they had withdrawn to Sebastopol in the Crimea, and it was on the capture and destruction of this port that public hopes had long ago been fastened.

Apart from the dubious principle of pursuing hostilities when the situation might well have been handled by peaceful negotiation, there might also have been some strategic or even local tactical objection to invading the Crimea, as the capture of Sebastopol necessarily implied. Small-scale maps of the theatre of war were certainly available but tactical information was non-existent and in England the knowledge of local conditions was lamentably vague. In fact before a landing on the Crimean peninsula was ultimately made allied ships had been sailing up and down the coast for weeks trying to find out even the elementary topography of the shore line, and when at last the invaders did choose a landing place they were to be faced with some awkward surprises. Yet even if the allied commanders in the field were a little short on local intelligence, which cannot be denied, they must at least have been able to acquire some first-hand knowledge of the main strategic implications, and their knowledge could possibly have been some help when deciding what operation, if any, was to be undertaken. But the Duke of Newcastle had no intention of being deflected from his conviction that the British and French must invade the Crimea, so he was certainly unlikely to ask for an opinion from the men on the spot who might well dismiss the idea as impracticable; and before he arrived at Pembroke Lodge on that sultry June evening he had spent some happy hours drafting a despatch which would give Lord Raglan positive instructions to comply with the public demand.

The despatch started by reminding Lord Raglan that on April 10th the Government had instructed him to "make careful enquiry into the amount and condition of the Russian force in the Crimea, and the strategic fortress of Sebastopol." Although two and a half months had since passed nothing had come of this hopeful request, for the simple reason that Raglan had no means of obtaining the information anyway; and neither in Britain nor at the two allied headquarters was anyone any the wiser about the strength of the enemy with whom they had gone to war. The Duke went on to describe how the events which had taken place in Bulgaria had "given a new character to the war," and he admitted that the whole objective of removing the Russian threat to Constantinople had been achieved without the British and French armies having been called on to meet the enemy in action. He stated categorically that "any further advance of the allied armies should on no account be contemplated." Then, with a magnificent inconsistency, he went on to give Raglan specific instructions "to concert measures for the siege of Sebastopol," allowing him discretion to refrain only if he should consider that the British and French armies were not yet ready for the undertaking. But the Duke made it clear that the exercise of Raglan's discretion would merely imply a temporary postponement of the splendid scheme, for he said, "Her Majesty's Government will learn with regret that an attack from which such important consequences are anticipated must be any longer delayed." Lest there should be any doubt of what the Government wanted, the despatch went on, "Nothing but insuperable impediments should be allowed to prevent the early decision to undertake these operations." To a general in the field, to whom must be delegated at least the minimum use of his discretion to enter into a projected operation, there could hardly have been a more positive indication of what the Government expected him to do.

In fairness to the Duke of Newcastle it must be recorded that he did submit the draft of his despatch to his cabinet colleagues before sending it to Lord Raglan as the considered instructions of the Government, and it was for the purpose of giving it that careful consideration which such an important document merited that the ministers had assembled for their dinner party at Pembroke Lodge. The dinner was everything that could be expected of it. The wines, and particularly the port, had circulated without any restriction and the members of the cabinet repaired to the drawing-room after dinner in a state of contented somnolence.

It has been the tradition, faithfully upheld, throughout the history of English politics, that the actual deliberations of a cabinet shall remain undisclosed, although historians have often made shrewd attempts to record what they have believed to have been said. But it probably can be claimed with some assurance that individual ministers have seldom broken this tradition of secrecy. The historian Kinglake has been at pains to assert that the information about what transpired at this particular meeting, which was passed to him by a member of the cabinet who was present, was no betrayal of confidence in the sense that the cabinet's deliberations were being repeated to him, for, as he maintains, there were no deliberations as such because most of the cabinet went to sleep. It was a warm summer evening and the ministers had dined well in the satiating custom of the day. The Duke of Newcastle, having waited for his fourteen colleagues to settle themselves comfortably, read out the draft of his despatch in a monotone—whether deliberately to induce torpor it would be unwise to assert. At one stage the clatter of a body actually lurching out of its chair, and the chair falling after it, caused some annoyance to those ministers who were averse to being disturbed. And it was reported to Kinglake—again without risk of disclosing utterances in cabinet because nobody uttered anything—that the Duke completed his tedious reading of the draft without any comment from his colleagues, who woke with scarcely concealed starts when the soothing drone of his voice stopped at last. Next morning the despatch was sent off to Lord Raglan without any alteration, having received the silent assent of the cabinet.

So the will of the country was conveyed to the British general. Not a little of the influence which dictated it had sprung from the redoubtable John Delane, editor of *The Times*, who had taken it upon himself to pronounce that "the broad policy of the war consists in striking at the very heart of the Russian power in the East, and that heart is Sebastopol." Later, when statements of Russian strength in Sebastopol showed an extravagant margin between a wishful guess by St. Arnaud of seventy thousand and an apprehensive estimate by Admiral Dundas of a hundred and twenty thousand, Delane was to dismiss any hesitation on that account by declaring, on behalf of England, "If our army were to perish before Sebastopol, the first thought of the nation at home would be to raise another, and go on." Lord Raglan was to be left with little doubt of what was expected of him, and lest he should be discouraged by the alarmist estimates of the enemy strength made by his colleagues, the Duke of Newcastle took care to inform him, without any authority on which to base the intelligence, that the Russian forces in the Crimea only numbered forty-five thousand. This guess, and it was nothing more, happened to be almost exactly right at the time, although of course it took no account of the troops which Russia could move with little difficulty from the principalities. But Raglan never accepted this sanguine estimate and when he did invade the Crimea he was convinced he was facing overwhelmingly superior forces, at least in number.

Raglan received the Duke of Newcastle's despatch on July 16th. He discussed its import with Admiral Dundas—whose command of the fleet was independent of Raglan and was answerable directly to the Government—and with General Sir George Brown, the commander of his Light Division. Dundas bluntly disapproved of the idea of the invasion, not from any naval considerations but because he was convinced it would turn out to be a death trap for the army. He gave his opinion to Raglan in the plain language of the sea. He said he could take the army to the Crimea and land it there but that he certainly could not undertake to supply it, nor bring it back again should it be forced to withdraw. Sir George Brown at sixty-six was a crony of Raglan and had shared with him throughout the Peninsula War the pervading influence of the Duke of Wellington. "You and I," he said to Raglan, "are accustomed to ask what the Duke would have done." In the circumstances he was sure that the Duke, without more certain information about the enemy, would never have undertaken to invade the Crimea. But Sir George's memory of the Duke, and the way he had been apt to handle Secretaries of State as mercilessly as he had handled the French, had apparently grown a little dim with age, for despite the ducal prompting he told Raglan it was clear enough that the Government was determined on the invasion and that if he, Raglan, was not prepared to undertake it he would merely be replaced by some other general who was—which was hardly the Wellingtonian approach.

Raglan, who had no doubt in his mind how hazardous the operation would be, decided to undertake it nevertheless, for he felt that he had no option and that he had received nothing less than a direct order to do so. He was not used to making strategic decisions; these had always been made by the Duke. But his was now the decision not of a weak man, submitting to pressure against his better judgement, rather was it that of a soldier steeped in a tradition of unquestioning obedience. There was certainly no suggestion of the sycophant in his reply to the Secretary of State on July 19th when he said that his decision had been made "more in deference to the views of the Government, and the known acquiescence of the Emperor Louis Napoleon in those views, than to any information in the possession of the authorities about the enemy." But not even the general's scepticism was likely to deflect the Duke of Newcastle from his purpose, although the Duke did have the grace to send him a personal reply saying, "I cannot help seeing that your decision has been taken to meet the desires of the Government, and not in entire accordance with your own opinions! God grant that success may award you, and justify us!" The Queen, he added, had been "filled with mixed feelings of satisfaction and anxiety," and he concluded his letter with a crescendo of exhortations to victory and a profusion of excla-mation marks.

On the day before Raglan had sent his reply to the Secretary of State's despatch, on July 18th, the allied commanders had met at St. Arnaud's headquarters at Varna. It was a high-powered meeting—St. Arnaud himself, Raglan, the French Admiral Hamelin and his second-in-command Admiral Bruat, Admiral Dundas and his second-in-command Vice-Admiral Sir Edmund Lyons. Lyons had at one time given up active service in the Navy to enter the diplomatic corps. He had been until recently the British Minister at Athens, but had resumed his service at sea with enthusiasm, throwing aside with some relief the frustrations of a diplomatic life. Of the six leaders who now met to plan the invasion of the Crimea, Lyons the one-time diplomat—whose experience might well have inclined him towards tranquillity—was the only confirmed champion of the idea, although all the others, including the outspoken Dundas, who knew what their respective governments required of them if they wanted to retain their commands, now gave it their dutiful support. But when it came to suggesting how or where the invasion should be launched there was less unanimity. They talked for four hours but no semblance of a plan emerged because it was evident that they knew little of the geography of the peninsula on which they were to land, and nothing about a suitable beachhead. The meeting adjourned for a reconnaissance to be made of the Crimean coast, and while a strong section of the fleet demonstrated off Sebastopol harbour itself to hold the attention of the enemy the little paddle steamer H.M.S. *Fury* took a reconnaissance party well inshore up the coast searching for a landing place for the allied armies. The party, which included neither Raglan nor St. Arnaud, consisted of five British and four French staff officers. Admiral Lyons who took over the navigation of the *Fury* for the day brought her alarmingly close inshore, and at one time the reconnaissance party was so near that a group of Russian officers, standing on the shore watching them a little incredulously, felt constrained to salute them, and not to be outdone in punctiliousness the British and French officers took off their hats and bowed. The party decided on a landing place at the mouth of the River Katcha, a decision based on no strategic consideration of what was to be the next move when the army had landed, but solely on the apparent attractions of the shore line. However, the reconnaissance was to prove quite redundant because Lord Raglan was later to disregard their choice and order the landing at an entirely different point.

The British soldiers at Varna welcomed the plan to invade the Crimea if only because nothing could have been more dispiriting than the miserable depression which the cholera had left behind. Not that the troops generally were in any condition to go into battle, as nearly every man among them had suffered dysentery, if not actual cholera even in a mild form. When the Coldstream Guards were marched five miles from their camp to the harbour for embarkation they had to have their knapsacks carried on pack-horses and not a few men fell out on the march. They were but ghosts of the splendid battalions who had marched across Waterloo Bridge but six months before although in the meantime they had not even been in contact with the enemy. The medical authorities, in their confident wisdom, welcomed the prospects of violent action for the men as the most effective cure for debility. They were confident, too, that once the troops had left behind the poisoned Bulgarian air, convinced as they were that it carried germs on every breeze, the scourge would be shaken off. That their theories were patently correct was proved at least to their own satisfaction because for some providential reason the British and French armies left the worst of the cholera behind at Varna; and, likewise, among the Turks the imams of their fleet, rowing around the ships chanting supplications to deliver the faithful from the scourge, just at the time when the epidemic was conveniently abating, were able to claim no small credit for having restored the survivors to health.

The risks of invading the Crimea may have worried the commanders, but the project held nothing but attraction for the troops, dispirited though they might be by the aftermath of sickness. No matter how slow the mail service from England, it was regular enough nevertheless, and the soldiers were left in no doubt of what the people at home were expecting of them. They had been acclaimed as heroes even before leaving Britain, so they could hardly show their faces again without a few victories to their credit. And it was clear from what was said in the letters that the people in England expected the soldiers to feel as belligerent towards the Russians as they felt themselves. Consequently while the frustrations and miseries of Varna might otherwise have induced the troops to want to return home as quickly as they could, particularly when so far as they could see there remained no likelihood of an encounter with the enemy, they were spurred on to renewed bellicosity by their loved ones who were determined not to be cheated of any chance of vicarious glory.

The sea-borne invasion of the Crimea, when it came, was not undertaken with any marked degree of strategic finesse. There was no pretence of any secrecy about what the allies intended to do, and when it was suggested to Lord Raglan that he should stage a feint on Odessa, or even that he should have it noised abroad that an attack on Odessa was the purpose of the large-scale embarkation that had been started, he dismissed the suggestion as dishonourable and unworthy of consideration by an Englishman. But although it was generally known that the Crimea and Sebastopol were the objectives, nobody had any idea about where the armies were to land because the generals themselves had not yet made this cardinal decision even by the time the invasion force actually put to sea.

The allied armada which sailed from Balchick Bay early in September 1854 was formidable enough in its numbers. In all, more than six hundred ships had been collected to take part in the invasion, either as transports or escort, and considering the besetting indecision of the authorities during the preceding months about any purposeful plan of campaign, the accomplishment of collecting them had been remarkable. Most of the credit for the scale on which, when it came, the initial invasion was launched belonged to Admiral Lyons, the only one among the commanders with his heart truly in the project. He shuttled back and forth between Varna and Constantinople chartering merchantmen, scouring the city for timber for gun platforms, and generally overcoming the twin resistances of Turkish inertia and British official obstruction. At Balchick Bay jetties were run out from the beach, and on August 24th embarkation started. In the event, the process was to take ten days, so that those troops who were unfortunate enough to be the first aboard were in for an uncomfortable experience.

Admiral Lyons, by almost miraculous endeavours, had managed to collect enough merchant ships to accommodate twenty-four thousand infantrymen, a thousand cavalrymen and their horses, sixty guns and their limbers, these with six horses each. Inevitably the accommodation for the horses was even less satisfactory than for the men, and although when the voyage started there was no bad weather comparable with what had been experienced in the Bay of Biscay when the army had first left England, the sea at times was choppy enough to cause chaos in the holds and not a few horses were destroyed. But at least the whole of the British force was accommodated in transports and none had to be taken aboard men-of-war, which were thereby left free to perform their proper role. Nevertheless, there was an impressive catalogue of what the army did leave behind at Varna: all its land transport, including six thousand pack horses laboriously collected in Bulgaria during the previous months; all the tents except of course those of the officers; the heavy cavalry brigade; a division of infantry and the whole siege train. No medical supplies were brought because the provision of these had never even been considered.

The French army, although slightly stronger in numbers, was not so fortunate and most of the troops had to be accommodated in their men-of-war—a double disadvantage, particularly in the days of lingering sail, for the troops were even more uncomfortable, and, forced to repose on whatever space was available, above and below decks, they were a hindrance to the working of the ships to say nothing of a menace to naval discipline. A few of the even less fortunate Frenchmen were taken aboard small sailing craft. In all, the French embarked more than thirty thousand infantrymen with seventy guns; there was only room for four horses for each gun, and no cavalrymen were taken at all. At the same time six thousand Turks embarked in their own line-of-battle ships, so that the whole armada carried nearly sixty thousand troops—to say nothing of some fifty English wives who were crowded at the last moment into one of the transports, mainly because they were creating an undignified disturbance on the beach in protest at being left behind in Bulgaria without any apparent means of support.

The original intention was for the armada to sail on September 2nd but the expectation that all would be aboard by then was over-optimistic and there were still many British soldiers and horses on the beach. The French embarkation, with so few horses to be put on board, had gone quickly and smoothly enough, except for twenty unhappy Zouaves who had stepped too purposefully on a pontoon which had capsized under them, and encumbered by their packs and voluminous breeches they had all been drowned. They were to be the only human casualties in the whole exercise of transporting nearly sixty thousand men and landing them on an enemy coast, which was a considerable accomplishment for those days. But the British, who had more than a thousand horses to embark, found the operation less straightforward, for although the weather was calm enough the ground swell on some days lifted and dropped the ships so violently that they were forced to wait until it had abated. So it was not until the evening of September 6th that the British embarkation was complete.

However, Marshal St. Arnaud maintained that the sailing date had been set for the 2nd and as all his troops had been embarked by then he saw no reason for further delay. He went aboard the *Ville de Paris* and ordered Admiral Hamelin to take the French fleet to sea. It was only the next morning, when he found himself uncomfortably separated from his allies, that he appeared to remember that it had not yet been decided where the invasion was to take place. To make the situation more discouraging the weather at sea had deteriorated. On the evening of the sixth he wisely decided to return to Balchick Bay.

It was on that evening, when embarkation of the British troops had now been completed, that the skippers of the merchantmen were assembled on one of the transports and briefed in the ambitious exercise which was to begin next morning. They were airily given an assurance, the value of which fortunately never had to be tested, that if the Russians came out to attack the convoy their widows would be adequately provided for. Early next morning, in perfect weather and bright moonlight preceding the dawn, the hundreds of ships lying in the bay, and waiting in the roads outside, acknowledged the admiral's signal to weigh anchor and there was set in motion a remarkable naval evolution. There could have been no better manifestation at the time of how Britain, although she had sadly neglected her military affairs, was a militant maritime nation at heart and had quietly preserved her naval competency; and moreover that the seamanship of her merchantmen was as practised as that of her fighting sailors. In a series of impeccable manœuvres each of the steamers wheeled round to take a sailing vessel in tow, and then wheeled again with its tow to attach a second. The sea was certainly calm enough and conditions could not have been better, but in an era of official indecision and incompetence the exercise of marshalling and despatching this great convoy of hundreds of ships stood out as an unfamiliar example of efficient organization. The heart of the convoy consisted of five columns of merchantmen with thirty ships in each column, and surrounding them the unattached steamers and escort ships took up their appointed places.

Once again the credit went to Sir Edmund Lyons who took over the fatherly direction of the convoy. His senior, Admiral Dundas, was engaged in patrolling off the Crimean coast in readiness for a sortie by the enemy. Not that Dundas had too strong a force for his duty. Thirty-seven of his line-of-battle ships were with Admiral Lyons as escorts for the convoy and he was left with a mere ten sail of the line, a couple of fifty-gun frigates and a dozen small men-of-war. In Sebastopol harbour lay fifteen Russian sail of the line, twelve war steamers and a number of frigates. The ships of the French and Turkish fleets were all acting as transports. Cluttered up with troops out of their element they would have been at a loss even to defend themselves. In the event the Russians remained in the harbour because despite lack of secrecy on the part of the allies they knew nothing of what was going on outside, and even if they had known a mere sortie into the midst of Dundas's waiting squadron would not have taken them very far.

The planned speed of the convoy was four and a half knots, but the French fleet mostly under sail tended to frustrate this ambitious aim and speed had to be reduced to three. So the convoy took four days and nights to sail three hundred miles; fortunately the weather was generally good and although most of the troops were uncomfortably crowded they were beginning to feel better now that Bulgaria was behind them, and the spirit of light-hearted adventure in which they had left England began to revive.

The convoy maintained its formation in creditable order, but the French and Turkish ships were sailing independently and a rendezvous was arranged forty miles west of Cape Tarkan, the westernmost promontory of the Crimean peninsula. When the rendezvous was made on the tenth of September, Lord Raglan who was in the steamer *Caradoc* received a peremptory request to visit Marshal St. Arnaud in the *Ville de Paris* where the Marshal was stated to be too ill to move. A heavy swell was running and the senior British naval officers decided that Raglan, with only one arm, could never negotiate the rope ladder up which he would have to climb on to the *Ville de Paris*. So the two generals were held mutually incommunicado. However, Raglan sent his military secretary, and at the meeting which followed it transpired that a number of French officers, naval and military, had drawn up a memorandum dissenting strongly from any plan to land the allied armies anywhere near Sebastopol itself. If a landing was to be attempted at all, and even of the wisdom of this they had some doubts, it should be made at Kaffa away on the east coast, nearly fifty miles from the town. The memorandum was supported by voluble Gallic argument. St. Arnaud, although present at the conference, was genuinely ill and in pain and he contributed nothing to the discussion. Consequently later, when the armies had been landed safely on the west coast and were for the time being in the ascendant, he was able to accept the congratulations of his Emperor on having overruled "les avis timides" of his officers when actually it had been Raglan who had been the one to disregard their protests and St. Arnaud had done nothing to silence them.

But it was clear enough now that with sixty thousand troops gathered a few miles from the enemy coast some decision had to be made about where they were to land. Not that it appeared to cause much concern to anybody that the objective of the whole expedition, the investment and capture of Sebastopol after the armies had been landed, had never even been considered in detail. The only problem before the staff at present was to get the troops off the ships and on to the land, and although Sir Edmund Lyons had already made a reconnaissance of the coast and had chosen a landing place, Lord Raglan decided to do it all over again.

7

CRIM TARTARY, the Crimean peninsula, juts out from the Ukrainian coast into the Black Sea, similar in shape to an inflated Isle of Wight but with the isthmus of Perekop, five miles wide, joining it to the mainland like an umbilical cord. Cape Tarkan, off which the allied fleets now lay, corresponds to the Needles, and Karkinitsky Bay is a Solent only curtailed by the Perekop isthmus; in place of the Spithead shores two ragged coastlines almost intertwine but never meet, like intricate pieces of a jigsaw puzzle which refuse to be fitted together. The shapes of the southern portions of the Isle of Wight and the Crimea, although on differing scales, are extraordinarily alike; Freshwater is where Eupatoria would be, and St. Catherine's Point might well be Cape Kherson, overlooking Sebastopol, at the tip of the Upland where the British and French armies were to endure their notorious agony. Like the Isle of Wight, too, the ground on the peninsula rises steadily from the northern shore to drop abruptly down to the sea along the southern coast.

But there the resemblance ends, for the Crimea is eight times the area of the Isle of Wight and lies not in the shelter of a temperate island but exposed to the savage winds that sweep down from the north across the bleak steppes of the Ukraine. The rising plateau of the peninsula, sloping gently upwards from the north, is virtually a steppe itself, although it is dotted with little villages where, in the eighteen-fifties, the Tartar inhabitants in their picturesque if unhygienic robes lazily watched their sheep and goats and their ill-nurtured cattle. They were Moslems now, these descendants of Ghengis Khan. Their ancestors had come to the Crimea as conquerors six hundred years before, but they in their turn had been conquered at last when Catherine was Empress of Russia and for a hundred years they had lived under the

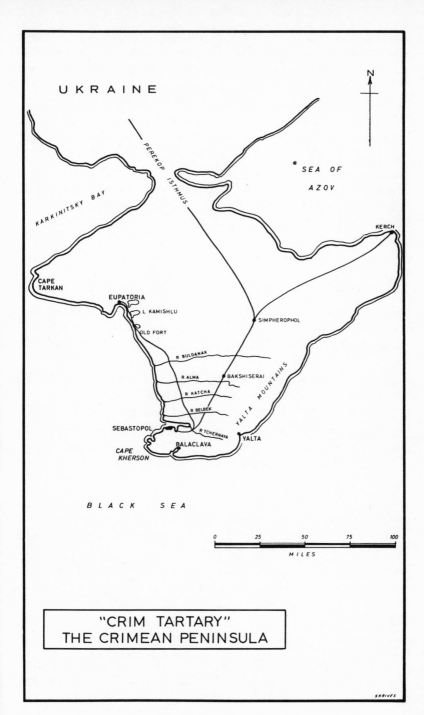

N

UKRAINE

PEREKOP ISTHMUS

KARKINITSKY BAY

SEA OF AZOV

KERCH

CAPE TARKAN

EUPATORIA

L KAMISHLU

SIMPHEROPHOL

OLD FORT

R BULGANAK

R ALMA

BAKSHISERAI

R KATCHA

YALTA MOUNTAINS

R BELBEK

SEBASTOPOL

R TCHERNAYA

YALTA

BALACLAVA

CAPE KHERSON

BLACK SEA

| 0 | 25 | 50 | 75 | 100 |

MILES

"CRIM TARTARY"
THE CRIMEAN PENINSULA

SHRIVES

Tsars, although they remained happily indifferent to Russian influences. The northern steppe is but a treeless wilderness and there is little vegetation other than coarse, tall grass and a pungent herb with a reminder of lavender in its scent—open country with nothing to break the bitter winds which bring the snow from the north. And then along the south-east coast of the peninsula the risen land falls away abruptly over the Yalta Mountains, and under their protection, along a narrow littoral, fertile slopes and nestling valleys lie sheltered from the northern blasts, where wild flowers grow in profusion; and pines and oaks, vineyards and orchards; grapes, oranges, figs, olives, pomegranates; an oasis of luxuriant beauty almost unique in the wide, unlovely wilderness that is Russia.

Indented into the west coast of the peninsula, six miles along the cliffs from Cape Kherson, is a splendid natural harbour, a long creek of deep water stretching four miles inland and nearly a mile wide throughout its length, narrowing slightly at its mouth but open to the sea nevertheless.* The Tchernaya River runs down from the Yalta Mountains into the head of the creek and a smaller creek branches off to the south to form an inner harbour. The large creek can shelter many big ships with plenty of room to manœuvre, and the Russians had established the harbour as the base of their Black Sea fleet. They had built Sebastopol, a noble town, on its southern shore, and in and around Sebastopol had grown a naval dockyard and arsenal. Along each shore of the creek bare hills rise to the high ground of the peninsula, not steeply, but high enough to give a useful view to anyone looking down on the harbour. To the east, up the narrow, winding, stony valley of the Tchernaya rise the ill-famed heights of Inkerman.

Round the corner of Cape Kherson, almost on the southern tip of the peninsula there is another, smaller and narrower creek indenting the coast. This creek stretches less than a mile inland, twisting through two right-angled turns so that its inner reach is hidden from the sea outside; and at its widest it is less than a quarter of a mile across. Here the hills, stony and bare—at the entrance, even rugged and unwelcoming—fall down more steeply to the waterside and imprison this little harbour in a circle of

* See map, p. 268

desolation. In 1854 there was on one hillside overlooking the inner reach a cluster of primitive buildings known collectively as Balaclava although they could hardly be dignified as a town, and in a straight line running over the high promontory which closed off the mouth of the harbour from the sea was a series of broken ruins dominated by the long-deserted shell of an old Genoese fort.

It was off the entrances to these two harbours that Lord Raglan cruised in the *Caradoc* on Sunday morning September 10th. He had left the invasion force, anchored off Cape Tarkan, at four o'clock accompanied by a bevy of military and naval talent consisting of the French general Canrobert, Sir Edmund Lyons, Sir George Brown and Sir John Burgoyne. The *Caradoc* sailed down the coast and stood innocently enough off Fort Constantine at the entrance to Sebastopol harbour. Fort Constantine mounted a hundred and four guns, but the presence of an unidentified vessel which happened to carry the commanders of an army intending to assault what the fort was there to guard caused no alarm or apparent interest. It was Sunday, Sebastopol was about to go to church, and the bells under the glistening cupolas were ringing out their messages of peace. To Raglan and his fellow soldiers the sight of the Russian fleet at anchor inside the harbour was of some interest although the sailors had seen it often enough in the last few months. However, they had not come to spy on the enemy but to find a landing place for sixty thousand men, so they moved down the coast full of expectant hope. They had no idea yet whether they would land their forces north or south of Sebastopol, nor had they any preference so long as they could get them ashore somewhere, for no consideration at all had been given to the manner in which the long-anticipated assault on the town was eventually to be launched.

They sailed round Cape Kherson to find the coast buttressed by steep cliffs and virtually unassailable, and although they peered into the entrance to Balaclava harbour it was obvious that, attractive as the sheltered anchorage might be, it would be a death-trap for a force making an initial landing. So they put about and rounded Cape Kherson again to return northward up the coast, passing once more under the still somnolent guns of Fort Constantine.

North of Sebastopol four rivers run westward down from

the Crimean highlands into the sea. They are the Bulganak—the northernmost—next the Alma, then the Katcha and last the Belbek, which flows into the sea not five miles north of Fort Constantine. As waterways they are inconsiderable and at most points can be forded readily; but their courses to the sea have gouged ̄steep-sided valleys through the high steppe. Consequently if any army were to land on the west coast of the Crimea, intending to march south to Sebastopol, the farther north it landed the more river valleys it would have to cross and the more opportunities would be given the Russians to take advantage of these natural lines of defence. From the sea the landing conditions naturally looked most attractive at the mouths of the rivers, for generally along the coast the hills come down to the shore line, while at the river mouths these same hills sweep back along the valleys leaving a beachhead on one or both of the banks. But of course any such beachhead would be dominated by the adjacent hills, and although Raglan examined the possibilities at each river mouth—a little cursorily perhaps—he was unhappy about them all. Lyons, on his previous reconnaissance, had chosen the mouth of the Katcha; he was a sailor and his approach to the problem had been merely to get the men ashore—what they would have to do after that was not his concern. But as the hills overlooking the beach at the mouth of the Katcha were less than ten miles from Sebastopol a landing there might have invited disaster and Raglan very properly rejected the idea. And so, a little dispirited at such lack of success in finding their heaven-sent landing place, and realizing that the farther north they went the greater the number of lines of defence they were offering the Russians, they cruised back up the coast. And there, miraculously, they found what they were looking for and their failure to plan ahead was vindicated in an instant. Ten miles north of the Bulganak they saw how the face of the hills swept back from the shore and how north of this face the land rose but gently from the level of the sea. If the armies could be landed on that stretch of coast they would be in no danger from any dominating hills. The generals examined the shore-line carefully through their glasses and for the first time since war had been declared some tactical attention was given to the actual terrain on which the troops were to operate.

The *Caradoc* was now in the sweep of a wide bay, corresponding to the Freshwater Bay of the Isle of Wight, and marked on the maps as Calamita Bay—a name with an unhappy implication. On the shore-line swinging round to the north stood the old town of Eupatoria whose history went back two thousand years to the days of Mithradites the Great. Like many an Ottoman town it abounded in churches, and to enhance the profusion one of its mosques boasted fourteen cupolas. The town stands on the edge of a salt-water lake which is only separated from the sea by a narrow spit of land across the seven miles of its width. Down the coast are two more, smaller lakes, each of them similarly cut off from the sea by a strip of land along which runs the road south from Eupatoria to Sebastopol. Raglan decided to land the allied armies on the strip enclosing the southernmost and smallest lake. Here they would be protected from direct attack on their front; they would be covered by the fleets at their rear; and the narrow approaches to their flanks could be safely guarded. How they would have moved from this comfortable little perch under enemy pressure is a matter of some conjecture. First, however, it would be necessary to make sure that no opposition to the landing would be made by any Russian force that happened to be in Eupatoria—for Raglan, of course, had no shred of information about the dispositions of the enemy—and he determined that the town must be taken and any such threat neutralized.

It was evening now, and the *Caradoc* swung out to sea and returned to the fleets off Cape Tarkan. When Raglan reported to St. Arnaud what he had decided the Marshal concurred with an unusual docility. He had been far too ill during the last few days to pursue his accustomed policy of obstruction—he was, in fact, mortally ill and had but two more weeks to live—and events had now developed so that Raglan, quite spontaneously, had begun to assume that overall control which he, St. Arnaud, had once so blatantly coveted.

On Tuesday, September 12th, the armada weighed anchor and moved slowly south-east into Calamita Bay and for the first time the English and French soldiers were to set eyes on the land of their unhappy destiny. There was nothing very remarkable about what they saw, and in the soft September sunlight the land rising to the rolling steppe evinced a misleading innocence, as if it were no more sinister than a gentle sweep of English downland. The ships anchored in the bay and the possibly formidable task of neutralizing whatever enemy force might be assembled in Eupatoria, and taking possession of the town, was entrusted to a landing party of two—Raglan's military secretary, Colonel Steel, and Colonel Trochu, who were sent ashore with an interpreter and a summons to the town to surrender. It was not a particularly hazardous undertaking for with a few hundred presumably hostile ships standing out in the bay the likelihood of a repetition of the Odessa incident seemed comfortably remote.

It happened, although quite fortuitously, that the only Russian soldiers in Eupatoria were invalids, having been sent to convalesce in the ecclesiastical atmosphere of the town; consequently there was nobody who seemed disposed to offer even a token resistance. The town's governor received the delegation with a magnificent nonchalance, and on being handed the summons he instructed his subordinates to fumigate it in accordance with the port's health regulations. Having attended to this imperative formality he read the summons carefully, and without any hesitation he agreed to surrender the town. But he insisted that any troops who landed must comply with the quarantine regulations by presenting themselves at the lazaretto for medical examination and suffering any detention there which their condition might require. When a small body of English troops landed the next morning without any apparent intention of observing the regulations the governor felt his continued presence in the town a little redundant, so he withdrew. All the other Russians withdrew with him, including the convalescent soldiers, leaving only the Tartar population.

With an enemy town now in allied hands and the campaign assuming such a character of success, representatives of the British commissariat hurried ashore to establish supplies of food for their twenty-five thousand soldiers, for which no arrangements had so far been made. The Tartar merchants seemed gratifyingly indifferent as to whether they were dealing with Russia or Russia's enemies and they showed more than a willingness to trade provided they were paid in cash. Surprisingly enough the commissariat people had expected this and had even prepared themselves for such an eventuality and they produced their bags of English sovereigns. But the Tartars showed little respect for sterling, having never seen or heard of it before. The situation would have reached deadlock had it not been for two English civilians, both gentlemen of some rank, who were discovered comfortably accommodated on the flagship, having accepted the offer of a lift to enable them to reach Russian territory where they had some private business to transact. Fortunately these gentlemen, having no apparent scruples about trading with the enemy, had provided themselves with a lavish supply of golden half-imperials, and in consideration of adequate security in English sovereigns they graciously agreed to advance the Russian currency to the commissariat pending reimbursement from some other source at a later date, so that happily trade between the allies and the Eupatoria natives was able to be started on a modest scale. Meanwhile, urgent messages were sent to Constantinople for more Russian currency.

As soon as arrangements at Eupatoria had been concluded the armada moved on again, on the afternoon of September 13th, and later that evening the fleets of the invading forces had anchored close inshore to the landing beach which Lord Raglan had chosen, some twenty miles south of Eupatoria. The ships drew up in an impressive line as if they were on review, the Turkish ships on the right of the line when facing inshore, the French to their left and the British on the French left. Thanks again to the directing hand of Admiral Lyons the deployment was a display of perfect organization; the only shortcoming of this splendid manœuvre was that it took no tactical consideration of the relative positions in which the various forces were to be landed. It is fair to assume that, even at this stage, although the commanders had discussed no actual plan, their intention to march direct on Sebastopol was certain enough, so that once the armies were ashore they would require to move off to the south—that is, to their right. Consequently the first deployment from the beachhead would be a wheeling movement, and it was inevitable that if the French and Turks landed on the right of the British they would stay there in the process of wheeling, and in the subsequent advance southward they would form the right of the column, advancing along the coast, while the British would be inland on the left. The British would march with an exposed flank while the French would enjoy cover by the British on their left and the comforting protection of the seashore on their right. Thus, in the event of meeting the enemy in battle, which after all was not unlikely, the disposition of their various army formations was pre-ordained, not by any process of generalship—Raglan and St. Arnaud had not discussed the matter, nor had they even met since Raglan had chosen the landing place—but by the exigencies of a neat exhibition of seamanship.

There was one unfortunate blunder that tended to mar the perfection of this manœuvre which had brought the fleets so skilfully into position for the landing. The stretch of beach on which the boats carrying the troops inshore were to converge from the wide array of ships was but a mile long, being the length of the strip lying between the small salt lake and the sea. Admiral Lyons had delegated to a French ship the task of dropping a buoy exactly half-way along that strip to mark the division between the French and British fleets; the French would anchor to the south of the buoy, the British to the north, and the two armies would land each on its own half of the beach. The Turks would land to the south of the French. Whoever was responsible overlooked this important duty, although it must be acknowledged that the omission had no noticeable effect on the way the skippers of both fleets took up their appointed stations without any fuss in the late afternoon. In fact the fleets anchored just where they had been intended to stand, the conjunction of the British and French nicely positioned off the very central point of the landing beach where the buoy to guide them should already have been placed. However, the French officer who had been responsible for placing it, not wishing to risk the displeasure of the British admiral next day, felt it imperative to remedy his lapse under the kindly cover of darkness, and with the first light of dawn next morning a provocative looking buoy was to be seen swinging gently with the sea at the extreme northern end of the landing strip, half a mile north of the conjunction of the two fleets. There was inevitably some confusion because clear instructions had been given that the British and French armies were to land north and south of the buoy respectively, and not a few of the British ships now found themselves lying off what was apparently the French section of the landing beach; and inter-allied relations even suffered some danger of rupture because it was immediately suspected by the British staff that the buoy had been placed deliberately at the north end of the strip of beach so that the French troops, landing south of it, would have the exclusive benefit of the lake to protect them from any direct landward attack, while the British north of the buoy would be denied that advantage. The British staff also recognized, on seeing the strip of beach at last—one mile long only, and but a couple of hundred yards broad—that although the protection offered by the inshore lake would be a distinct advantage, the crowding on to this narrow beach of fifty or sixty thousand troops might well be a little uncomfortable; and inevitably the suspicion arose that the French had artfully placed the buoy farther north to prevent overcrowding on their part of the beach.

Whatever may have been the motive—and it was probably nothing worse than sheer inadvertence—the misplacement of the buoy decided Lord Raglan hurriedly to alter his plan and to land the British troops on yet a different beach. As we have seen, there were three lakes just inshore of the coast-line south of Eupatoria, and Raglan had chosen the southernmost and the smallest. The second lake, known as Lake Kamishlu, was three miles farther north and it also was separated from the sea by a narrow strip of beach. Immediately the anomalous position of the buoy was reported to him, with its awkward implication of Anglo-French dissension, he decided to land the British army on the strip enclosing this northern lake—where the troops would have more room than the French anyway because the strip was a mile and a half long—and he ordered the boats from the British ships to be directed to it. On the maps of the Crimea that were available at the time there was marked an "Old Fort" at the point where Raglan had first intended to land. Not that there was any building or the remains of a fort to be seen. But most records state that the British army landed at the Old Fort whereas in fact it landed some miles farther up the coast beside Lake Kamishlu.

Fortunately for the allied armies their landing was entirely unopposed. The credit for this must undoubtedly go to Lord Raglan, no matter how adventitious his decisions may have been. He was certainly very lucky to find a beach that was not dominated by hills from which the enemy could overlook the landing— but anyway he found it; and he was able to put the armies ashore under cover of the commanding guns of the fleet. It would have been madness for the Russians to have opposed the landings on the flat ground round the lakes, even if they ever considered it. They would have been driven back decisively by the ships' guns which enjoyed greater range than any field artillery of those days. So long as the landing was affected within the area of a naval umbrella the troops were safe enough, but it would have been a different story farther south where the enemy would have found in the hills plenty of protection from bombardment by the fleet.

The French ships started to land their troops at half-past eight in the morning, and the British, despite their change of beach, were not far behind. The weather was still delightful and a dead calm sea lapped the pebbles and golden sand of the landing beaches so that the occasion had all the elements of a seaside excursion. The process of landing was so simple that it was found unnecessary for the soldiers even to get their feet wet, and if a boat beached before reaching the edge of the water and the men were not able to jump from it on to the dry beach the sailors quite spontaneously carried them ashore. The British soldier of those days was not dressed for paddling. He was in exactly the same uniform he would have worn at a ceremonial parade on the Horse Guards, if only because he had no other, and it was hardly suited to beach wear. The officers were dressed just as formally, in tight-fitting swallow-tailed coatees, sprinkled lavishly with buttons and gold lace, trailing their long swords over the pebbles. Some of the regiments wore hard, shining helmets with little glossy peaks fore and aft, quite inadequate for protection against the Crimean sun; others balanced shakos on the tops of their heads, while the Guards of course buried their ears in bearskins; and they all, officers and men, suffered those choking tight collars, buttoned up or tied like a stock securely under their jaws, which hardly allowed them even to turn their heads.

The authorities were still doubtful of the stamina of the British troops after their experiences at Varna, and in an unwonted gesture of fatherly consideration they decreed that the men's knapsacks should be left behind on the ships. This did not mean that the contents of the knapsacks would not have to be carried, for without these the troops could not have existed at all. The idea was to save the unnecessary weight of the pack itself, although actually this was almost negligible; the result was that the men had to wrap up their boots, their shirts and their socks, and anything else that was theirs, in a clumsy bundle encased by their blankets and greatcoats. It was not a particularly convenient way of going to war. But whatever their uniform or their equipment, when they fell in rank upon rank, as they instinctively did as soon as they had jumped on to the beach, their turnout was impeccable.

The allied landing was not entirely unnoticed by the Russians. Inland, on a low crest of gently rising ground, a few Cossacks were to be seen, their officer—who was being watched excitedly by the invaders through field-glasses as the first live specimen of the enemy—obviously making notes of what was going on on the beaches. Nobody disturbed him, and not unnaturally neither he nor his half-dozen companions felt disposed to challenge the landing of sixty thousand men, and by midday he had apparently obtained enough information to satisfy his superiors, for he and his little posse trotted off to the south. There were more Cossacks moving about the country, and on one early occasion an unexpected encounter was to send Sir George Brown galloping back to the bridgehead somewhat precipitately after he had ridden inland on a reconnaissance of his own.

A succession of wagons were seen to be moving south on the main road from Eupatoria to Sebastopol which ran right along the strips of beach where the armies had landed. The stolid Tartar drivers, with more pressing matters to think about, took no interest in an armada discharging hordes of invaders on their native shore, and continued plodding along the road quite impassively until the invaders descended roughly upon their persons and requisitioned the wagons and their contents. Whether or not they received any payment from the commissariats of allied armies for the summary removal of their possessions ever remain in doubt; the English chroniclers of the Crimea unanimously assert that the British army traditionally paid for whatever it seized from its enemies, but they are inclined to be less charitable about the French whom they accuse of persistent plunder. They maintain, in fact, that from the moment the French troops had stepped ashore in Turkey the habits of Napoleon's armies in Europe had reasserted themselves. However, some allowance must probably be made for national bias, and it has to be remembered that at this stage the British commissariat was suffering an embarrassing shortage of Russian currency; but whether they were paid for or not, the British army acquired three hundred and fifty wagons—primitive as they were—within a couple of days of landing, and a thousand or more head of cattle and sheep. The wagons were particularly acceptable because the British had brought with them no transport at all. They were not all captured on the main road, for reconnaissance parties more adequately escorted than Sir George Brown were soon moving a few miles inland, and the country was quickly denuded of its meagre supplies to make up for the shortcomings of the allied commissariats. But even so the traffic down the main road, carrying even more acceptable supplies intended for the Russian forces at Sebastopol, still moved unsuspecting into the beachhead, there to be requisitioned by one or other of the allies —either honourably or not.

The happy seaside-holiday atmosphere on the first day of the landing was to be rudely effaced during the night by heavy rain, and as the British troops had no shelter whatsoever the experience was not encouraging—not even for the officers who for once ~und themselves sharing the privations of their men. By night-
ot a single tent had been landed from the British ships. Of
o tents had been brought yet for the rank and file and
he officers had been stowed away inaccessibly in the
vhen some were brought ashore next day it was
enuine surprise, that no pack horses had been
hem so they had to be taken back on board.
itish troops had been put ashore on the
them spent the night, if he lay down at
er, under sodden blankets. There were

120

no bivouac fires, no cooking and nothing hot to drink. The soldiers suffered through the night hungry and wet, and next morning hundreds of men who had only just recovered from the drastic ills of Bulgaria were in a state of serious relapse. Within a few hours after dawn the sun was blazing in the sky and a new problem arose because the country was found to be almost waterless. Feverish men drank dangerously from the muddy pools and within a couple of days a thousand British soldiers, now desperately ill, had to be carried painfully back to the ships— there were no stretchers to ease their carrying—and in due course they were transported back to the Bosporus to be deposited, and left to die, in what were to become the infamous hospitals of Scutari.

The French soldiers, inheriting the thoughtful methods of conducting a war which Napoleon Bonaparte had bequeathed to them, were in a much happier state. Each man carried in his pack what was known as a dog-tent, just large enough for him to crawl under, which protected him from the worst of the rain if he could find ground which was not actually a hollow. The despised Turks were better off still; they were fully equipped with proper tents and within a few hours of landing they had set up a neat camp and put their superior western allies to no little shame.

The landings were completed in five days, and the armies ready to move, which was a creditable, almost miraculous performance bearing in mind the complete absence of any planning staff, at any rate in the British army, every detail of the operation being left to the happy inspiration of the moment. There was certainly the same difficulty in landing the horses as there had been in embarking them, and for periods of hours at a time rising surf held up the proceedings. At one stage it was found that the generals had been put on shore without their chargers, and the direction of the war was for a time seriously handicapped. But the troops had now been properly brigaded, and the brigades made up into divisional formations, and by September 19th the allies were ashore on the Crimean peninsula and reasonably sorted out. It was clear to everybody that after such a successful operation, unopposed though it had been, the whole campaign would be concluded just as comfortably, and a young engineer officer—

whose opinion was not to be lightly discredited, for he was later to become a general—wrote to his sister, "This is likely to prove a glorious expedition. There seems little doubt that we shall drive all before us, and that Sebastopol itself must soon yield before the well-directed assaults of such men as ours. We have calculated that the Russian prodigy Sebastopol shall be ours before the first week of October is out."

Somehow, an error must have crept into the young engineer's calculations, unless it was that he was misled by the hope of "well-directed assaults."

8

THE allied armies in the Crimea, when at last they were ready, marched south from the Old Fort with the straightforward intention of capturing the fortress of Sebastopol. There were no subtleties about their strategy and their tactical plan for the operation was unbelievably vague. They carried with them only three days' rations, although even the most sanguine among them admitted that these would have to be replenished before hostilities were actually completed and the war won. But the popular belief was that the next supplies would be landed by the fleets in the comfortable haven of Sebastopol harbour and that by then all the troubles of the commissariat would be over. Evelyn Wood—who took part in the Crimean War as a midshipman of the Royal Navy and later was to crown his career, a shade unconventionally, as a field-marshal in the British Army—said, "We all thought the army would take Sebastopol within a week or ten days." Sir John Burgoyne, whose inhibiting memories of Corunna had apparently been dispelled at last by the glorious success of the unopposed landing on the Crimea, gave it as his professional opinion that Sebastopol could be stormed and captured within two days from the time the armies started marching south. The operation was obviously so straightforward that nobody believed there was any need for involved planning. It was just a matter of marching southward and attacking the town. Sebastopol, approached from the north, was certainly on the other side of the long reach of harbour that stretched four miles inland, but north of the harbour the ground rose to a commanding level and the ships and the forts could be bombarded effectively from the heights, or so it was confidently expected. Alternatively there was a road that swung inland to pass round the head of the harbour. The allies could, if they chose, follow that road and then turn west to march comfortably into Sebastopol by the back door where the opposition would be negligible. The great thing, in the view of both Raglan and St. Arnaud, was to get the armies moving. Providence had landed them safely on the peninsula without any unnecessary planning, and providence would dictate the plan for the next operation when it arose.

The advance on Sebastopol started brilliantly enough; as a brave military spectacle it would have won the vociferous approval of the English crowds—even though their approval would have had to embrace their old enemies the French—for this was a scene from the great pageant of war set off by all the trappings of showmanship. Unfortunately the spectacle was quite lost on the few Tartar tribesmen who witnessed it with their usual stolid unconcern. Here were two armies of sixty thousand men in all, splendid in their ordered ranks, brilliant in their blue and green, their red and scarlet; their gold and silver lace; their bearskins, shakos, cocked-hats, plumes and pelisses; their polished brass, and white pipe-clayed cross-belts; the Hussars in their "cherry coloured pants" which had won some recent notoriety; regimental colours waving aloft adding more blues and greens and reds and golds; bayonets and sabres, lances and swords, glinting in myriads of little flashes; bands playing; men singing and striding purposefully in step, their boots swishing in unison through the ankle-deep grass, the sound of their steps merging into one long hiss like the continuous sigh of a breaking sea; their heavy tread crushing beneath their feet the pungent-smelling Crimean herb with its tantalizing scent of lavender.

It was September 19th, five days after the landings had been started. The armies had been due to move at six o'clock in the morning but somehow the British organization had not achieved that pitch of efficiency necessary for a prompt early-morning start—a shortcoming that was to affect events on more than one occasion—and it was nine o'clock before the columns were ready to move. Even so, half a division had to be left behind to clear up the beach, which for want of any advanced planning had assumed over the five days a state of unbelievable confusion. The French, either because they were more efficient or were less concerned with the disorder they left behind them, had been ready for some hours and had not hesitated to advertise their impatience by importunate rolls of drums and calls on the bugle. Marshal St. Arnaud, who was making a brave effort although in great pain, sent more than one provocative enquiry to Lord Raglan asking when he would be ready to start.

The armies assembled in their columns on the upland, high on the Crimean steppe, whither the divisions climbed the hill from the landing beaches independently. There, all the fuss and confusion inseparable from the marshalling of an army added to the delay, but it was a lovely morning with a fresh breeze blowing in from the sea and the prospects of an easy march were encouraging once a start could be made. The advance was to be made majestically, not in columns winding along roads or through broken country, but in a great mass of soldiery spread out over the plain. The French army, on the right with its flank on the shore-line, disposed itself in its traditional diamond formation, one division leading, two more to the left and right rear, and the fourth behind. In the hollow, in the centre of the diamond, St. Arnaud put the guns and the Turks, where any usefulness they might have had in an emergency would surely have been minimized. The British army, on the French left, formed up in what were known as "grand divisions", an impressive term which meant nothing more intricate than a square formation with a front and depth of two divisions, each division in two columns, so that it could face the enemy either ahead or on the left flank. It was a simple arrangement of his forces, without any subtleties, which appealed to Lord Raglan, and if it had actually been brought to battle on the march it probably would have been as effective as the more fancy formation adopted by the French. The French marched solidly in their divisions, but Raglan deployed an advance and rear guard of Lancers and Dragoons round the British army, and he posted lines of riflemen, extended in skirmishing order, along his exposed flank and to his front and rear.

And so the whole invading strength of the allies, which was not an inconsiderable force, was marched off in one great unit to be cut off entirely from any form of support, and if during the march the combined armies were to be attacked and driven on to the defensive they had not a man to draw on as a reserve, and any line of retreat could easily have been denied to them. The section of the British Fourth Division which had been left behind at the beach had not been left there as a reserve but was ordered to follow the main army as soon as it had finished tidying up, and there was to be no line of communication, however slender, with the beachhead. The fleets would certainly be cruising off the shore, moving south with the armies as they marched, but the ships might just as well not have been there for all the support they could have given, except perhaps for some not very effectual covering fire. For while their guns would have been invaluable if they had had to be used against an attack on the beachhead at sea level, their effectiveness would have been considerably impaired against an enemy high up on the steppe, out of sight behind the sheltering line of cliffs that ran all the way along the coast. In fact it was the cliffs which served effectually to cut off the armies from the fleets. As Raglan himself had seen so clearly—although apparently he was now quite happy to overlook it—the only possible landing places were at the mouths of the rivers and even these were dangerously dominated by the hills which swept back from the cliffs along the rivers' banks. When the armies reached the rivers—the Bulganak, the Alma, the Katcha and the Belbek—if they were not too strenuously beset there by the enemy, they might well join hands with the fleets and obtain some of the necessaries of life. But on the marches between the rivers they would be cut off entirely, and if, with only three days' supplies and an acute shortage of water, they were put to battle by the enemy—of whose strength in arms and numbers they had not the faintest idea—their plight could be unfortunate. The Duke of Wellington and Napoleon Bonaparte, watching from their respective vantage points on the Elysian Fields, must have had some bad moments.

At nine o'clock on that lovely September day these splendid looking armies moved off together and for the next hour the bands kept playing and the troops kept singing and calling cheerfully, striding comfortably in the freshness of the morning. But the hour had hardly passed before the sickly condition of the British army began to tell, the heat of the sun and lack of water added their contribution, and the first protracted halt had to be called. The supply of fresh water on the beaches had been quite inadequate and most of the men had set off to march across the arid steppe, where they might possibly be cut off for days, with empty water-bottles. By the time the sun had climbed well into the sky even the fittest were to be distressed by thirst, and soon the lurking cholera germs which had never been properly exterminated began their work. When the armies started off again men fell out of the ranks by the hundred and another halt had to be called in less than thirty minutes. Others, just able to struggle on, discarded their heavier possessions one by one—overcoats, shakos, mess-tins, cross-belts—so that the British army on its first march towards battle, although still miraculously unbeset by the enemy, left behind a trail of dying men and abandoned equipment through which the rear guard had to pick its way with some delicacy. By midday the bands and the singing, and even the quietest talking, had died away, and all that could be heard from the packed mass of sixty thousand men was the swish of their boots through the grass as they stumbled on in the blazing heat stirring up a dry haze of dust even from the thickly matted turf, and the rattle of their horses' harness and the thumping of guns and limbers over the tufted steppe.

The advance guard was made up of two squadrons of Hussars—Lord Cardigan's men in their cherry-coloured pantaloons, with Cardigan himself riding at their head confident in his ability to carry any enemy he might encounter. In fact it had long been the unanimous opinion of the cavalry officers, held in all seriousness, that any other arm of the force was a sheer redundancy, and that it would merely be necessary to loose the British cavalry against the Russians and the enemy would be routed, whatever formation they might be in. That such a puerile opinion could be held seriously, as it was, by grown up men who were at the same time professional soldiers, merely reflected the extraordinary stupidity of the officers who prided themselves on the aristocracy of the families from which they came. As a later commander-in-chief was to write of them—the cavalry officers of the Crimean war—"had they been private soldiers I don't think any colonel would have made them corporals." As we have seen, Cardigan had been promoted major-general after his inept exhibition on the Danube although he still only commanded a brigade. The Cavalry Division—which comprised the Light Brigade under Cardigan and the Heavy Brigade under a Colonel Scarlett—was commanded by the Earl of Lucan who had left England as a mere major-general but had recently been promoted lieutenant-general for no apparent reason other than to ensure his seniority over Cardigan. Lucan and Cardigan were brothers-in-law and they shared a mutual enmity which had already embarrassed Lord Raglan and had completely subverted their own relations as between a superior officer and his subordinate.

On the march from the Old Fort, Lucan rode with two squadrons of Lancers on the left flank while Cardigan led his two squadrons of Hussars in the advance guard. Behind the advance guard rode Raglan and his staff, and in the afternoon they came over a ridge and looked down into the valley of their first river obstacle, the Bulganak. The advance guard and Lucan's two squadrons had already forded the river and had trotted up the first slope on the other side, to find that the ground fell away again in a gentle dip only to rise once more to another ridge. Here, for the first time since war had been declared fully six months before, the allies were to be confronted by the enemy. Two thousand Russian cavalrymen stood ranged in a line across the ridge, and as soon as the squadrons of Hussars and Lancers saw them they halted and formed a line too. Britain and Russia were at last face to face, separated by but a few hundred yards. The French army was still to the rear, plodding along over the steppe in its diamond formation.

The range between the two lines was inconsiderable but when the Russians fired off a few shots from their carbines these were quite ineffective. Lucan galloped over from the left to join his brother-in-law. This annoyed Cardigan because it indicated that Lucan as the senior now intended to take overall command of the four cavalry squadrons and Cardigan would have to do what he was told. Not that Cardigan had any marked respect for Lucan's authority, as a number of previous incidents had shown, and he had long been in the habit of openly disputing his commanding officer's orders. And so, at the moment of an impending clash

He had shared with Raglan throughout the Peninsular War the pervading influence of the Duke of Wellington; Lieutenant-General Sir George Brown and his staff.

He decided that, intrusive or not, he would come and join the battle; General Bosquet and his staff.

between the two great powers, at the first culminating crisis of the war, the brothers-in-law sat on their horses out in front of the armies and started an argument. Cardigan wanted to charge the enemy, up hill and against obviously overwhelming numbers. Lucan, who had never before been on active service and had in fact spent the last seventeen years retired on half-pay, had no notions about tactics at all but was ready to disagree with Cardigan on principle. The Russian cavalry, perplexed by the spectacle of an entirely motionless enemy sitting quietly on their horses while their commanders argued, obligingly sat still themselves to await the outcome of the dispute.

Meanwhile Raglan could see from the high ground on the north side of the river what neither Lucan nor Cardigan could see from where they were, that behind the Russian cavalrymen on the ridge on the south bank waited a heavy concentration of infantry and artillery which in actual fact numbered six thousand men. Of course there had been no prior discussion of how the advance guard would act in any particular eventuality and Raglan had no idea what Lucan intended to do. The main allied columns were approaching the northern ridge now and Raglan called the first two of the British "grand divisions" to hurry forward on to the ridge in full view of the enemy, and to extend into line as a show of supporting strength to cover Lucan's meagre force. At the same time he sent General Airey, the Quartermaster-General, whose job it was to see that the commander-in-chief's wishes were put into effect, galloping across the river to suggest to Lucan that now his squadrons were adequately covered they should retire; for it was clear that by making such a precipitate crossing, quite out of touch with the main body of the armies, the advance guard had got itself into an embarrassing position. Raglan was not keen on dictating to his cavalry commanders, particularly to two such combustible characters as the brothers-in-law, but he was short of cavalry and he had no wish to see nearly half of what he had thrown away in an obviously suicidal attack. Of course when Airey came up to the front of the war where the argument was going on, and put Raglan's message as a suggestion, Cardigan flatly disagreed with it; so the Quartermaster-General made it an order although it had not been intended as such by Raglan who, now actually exercising a fighting command for the first time in his long military career, was not disposed to commit himself too positively in his tactical instructions. Airey, who on more than one previous occasion had had to smooth out differences between the brothers-in-law, was the most forceful character on Raglan's staff and was soon to get into the habit of making up the commander-in-chief's mind for him. He now instructed Lucan to ride back to Lord Raglan, thus leaving Cardigan with no option but to carry out the order, and the advance guard withdrew by alternate squadrons, steadily and in perfect formation, two squadrons standing while the other two retired part of the distance, and then alternating their roles, much to the chagrin and mortification of the troopers who were cheered ironically by the enemy—although the Russians, impressed by the force now extended on the opposite ridge, made no move to challenge their retirement. Meanwhile both sides had unlimbered some guns and had started shooting off at each other. As neither produced any effect they both desisted very soon, and the first encounter between the mighty forces of Britain and Russia ended quite bloodlessly. But the incident had planted, in the contumacious minds of Cardigan's cavalrymen, a mood of resentment which was to grow even stronger during the next few weeks and was to drive them to make history at Balaclava in a blaze of quite redundant glory. They resented Lord Raglan's determination to "keep the cavalry in a band-box" as he himself had unfortunately expressed it even before he left Varna, and they showed their opinion of their divisional commander's temerity by referring to him henceforth as Lord Look-on.

The Russian cavalry, and the strong body of infantry supporting them, had been sent forward from their main army to make a reconnaissance in some force. Faced clearly with an allied force so much stronger than themselves they sagaciously withdrew, and so the allied soldiers were at last able to get down to the river and to the welcome water. On this occasion the discipline of some of the British regiments gave way to disorder and thousands of desperately thirsty men broke their ranks. When order had been restored the commanders moved their armies across the river— which was really but an inconsiderable stream and by the time sixty thousand men had passed through it, had been trampled into an untidy quagmire—and they climbed up the south bank on to the high steppe again.

Raglan had now received messages from the ships down the coast that the main Russian army from Sebastopol had at last moved north to meet the invaders, and that night, goaded for the first time during the war into readiness for attack, he bivouacked his troops in order of battle disposing them, not in "grand divisions", but in an arc which covered his front and left flank, with the valley of the Bulganak conveniently covering his rear. But the night was quiet and no attack was made.

It was now certain that if the allied armies continued their march south they would meet the Russians in a major battle, and that probably next morning. At last the fleets had been able to provide some reliable intelligence, although it was information which they could hardly have failed to gather, for there before their eyes, spread out on the heights overlooking the south bank of the next river, the Alma, was apparently the whole Russian army. When St. Arnaud heard this he knew that the time had come when the pre-eminence of the French army over the British must at last be established if he was to play the part in this war that he still believed to be his right, and ill as he was he made up his mind to assert himself.

He quickly sketched a plan for the impending battle on a piece of rough paper, and with Colonel Trochu he hurried over to present it to Lord Raglan in the naïve belief that Raglan would be likely to concur. Of course St. Arnaud had no knowledge of, nor was he concerned with any tactical details which might have to be considered if the plan were put into practice, because like Raglan himself he knew nothing whatever about the ground on which the battle was likely to be fought. All he knew was that there was a river running from east to west across the allies' line of advance and that the enemy's army was drawn up on the far side of the river to dispute their passage. At what points the river could be crossed, or where the enemy strongpoints were likely to be placed, were matters of apparent unimportance.

The plan, which has been preserved for posterity, looked impressive enough although as a tactical proposition it lacked any detail at all. It was labelled "Projet pour la bataille de l'Alma", and a little rashly it carried the legend, "préparé le 19 au soir et éxecuté le 20 Sept. 1854". The French army was to abandon its diamond formation and was to be drawn up in a brave long line parallel with the river full in the face of the imagined centre of the Russian position. Two divisions were to be extended across its front, and on the plan a single arrow at its head pointed squarely and confidently at the heart of the enemy. No details were shown of how the attack was to be made, in fact it seemed that there were to be no unnecessary subtleties. The leading divisions were, presumably, simply to move forward, cross the river and rout the enemy; it was as easy as that. The rest of the French army was to be drawn up in serried battalions behind the front divisions to support the direct attack, except for one division under General Bosquet—the wretched division which, in Turkey, had had to march a hundred and fifty unnecessary miles through Adrianople —which was shown as slinking off with the Turks at half-past five in the morning along the shore-line, on the right of the main army. There was no arrow on the plan to show where this inspired diversion was expected to be headed. The British army had not been omitted altogether from the plan, although the way its part was shown did seem to have been scribbled in as an after-thought. Like Bosquet's division it was to be given a diversionary task, this time on the left. Its intended progress was shown by five dotted, rather uncertain lines, each headed by a small arrow —much less brave and confident than the bold symbol of the French attack—pointing to the Russian flank with the simple explanation, which disposed of any unnecessary detail, "Armée Anglaise tournant la droite ennemie". The plan stated, a little optimistically, that the British would also move at half-past five. No hour was laid down for the main French attack; experience had probably already suggested that it would be unwise to rely too much on British punctuality. But it was clear from the plan, which showed the French army as dominating the whole situa-tion, that the battle as a whole would have to be directed by the French Marshal.

On the evening of the nineteenth St. Arnaud and Trochu rode down to the little post house by the bridge over the Bulganak

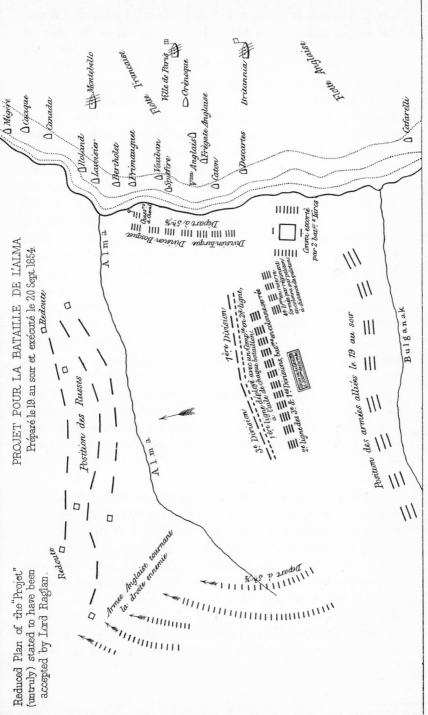

As a tactical proposition it lacked any detail at all; the plan sketched by Marshal St. Arnaud before the Battle of the Alma.

where Raglan had made his headquarters for the night, confident that they could impose their plan on the British general. St. Arnaud's pain had miraculously left him for the time being and he was unusually buoyant. He expounded his plan, with some of his old vehemence, to Raglan who, disappointedly, made no comment. It was not that he necessarily disagreed with the Marshal but he objected to advance planning in principle. He would prefer to decide how the battle should be fought when he was actually faced with the enemy—that way he saved himself the need for any concentrated thinking. But following his well-tried custom he avoided any discussion, and when St. Arnaud and Trochu left later in the evening they had no idea at all whether or not Raglan had agreed with the plan, so the course of action to be followed by the armies next day was left somewhat in the air. The only executive decision that had been taken had been that Bosquet's division, when it moved off in the quiet of the early morning, would not advertise its intention to the Russians —who were now less than five miles away—by the usual French exuberance of drums and bugles. Nothing was said about the possibility of any British troops moving off at the same time; and although Raglan vaguely promised his co-operation, St. Arnaud had no idea what the British intended to do next day. Nor, for that matter, had Raglan. Colonel Trochu, apparently quite irrelevantly, had asked Raglan at what stage of the battle he considered that the French soldiers should discard their packs; Raglan could see no point in the question and dismissed it as unimportant. But next day this seemingly trivial detail was to have an appreciable effect on the events after the battle.

When morning came General Bosquet's division moved off at half-past five; the rest of the French army was on the march at seven and by nine o'clock it had covered three miles and was getting dangerously near the enemy, so it halted and brewed coffee. The British had not yet been able to get under way; Raglan had had to reshuffle his army from the order of battle in which it had bivouacked for the night to re-form into "grand divisions", and such an evolution was quite beyond the senior officers who might have been able to deploy companies and platoons with some confidence on the parade ground but had no experience of handling brigades and divisions in the field. But at last, after much marching and counter-marching, and after the bullock wagons which had been captured from the Tartars and were carrying the all-important reserve ammunition had been disentangled from the infantry, and had been dragged at their own inhibiting speed to their positions in the line of march, the British army stepped off once again in a little more orderly condition than that in which it had struggled to the Bulganak the afternoon before. During the night contact had been made with the fleet at the river mouth and hundreds of sick men had been taken off to start their unhappy journey to Scutari. Now the freshness of the morning was back again and once more it held the promise of a lovely English summer day; water-bottles were encouragingly full, buttons and cross-belts had been cleaned dutifully and shone once again in the sunshine, and when the troops fell in they measured up again almost to what the British public would expect of them.

At last at half-past eleven, when the British army had been on the march for a couple of hours and had caught up with the French, the allies—still in their majestic formations spread across the plain—looked down a long slope where the high ground fell gently away before them and they could see, contrasting with the sun-bleached grass of the open steppe, a line of deep refreshing green marking the trees and vineyards along the banks of the River Alma. Beyond the river the ground rose again sharply, in some places in steep cliffs, and up on the heights the grass too was dry and light-coloured so that the big dark squares that marked the Russian formations, still two miles away, stood out clear and ominous.

The allies halted as their sixty thousand soldiers looked for the first time on the enemy, and up on the Crimean steppe there fell a complete, unnatural silence, until a horse neighed and was answered by another. With a touch of breathless drama, Lord Raglan and Marshal St. Arnaud rode forward down the slope, watched by their whole armies, and alone together they climbed a little mound and sat there on their horses scanning through their field-glasses the line of the river and the hills beyond. After a few minutes General Airey rode up to join them and he heard St.

Arnaud ask a little testily, as if he were determined at last to get some decision from Raglan, "Will you turn the position or will you attack on the front?" and Raglan replied, "With such a body of enemy cavalry I will not attempt to turn them." So the French plan was to be rejected, and St. Arnaud rode back to his troops across the British front a trifle dashed and without any idea of what Raglan intended to do. The truth was that the British general still had no idea himself. The only understanding between the two generals was that the French should make an attack on the right first and thereby tend to draw the enemy's attention westward. While the British army waited, Sir Colin Campbell, commanding the Highland Brigade, said quietly, "This will be a good time for the men to get loose half their cartridges." The thought had not so far occurred to anyone that they might be as near to a battle as that, and when the Highlanders started opening their pouches the whole army followed suit and a flurry of fidgety motion flowed over the ranks like a choppy little wave until the cartridges had been shaken loose and everybody was quiet again.

The commander-in-chief of the Russian armies in the Crimea was the elderly Prince Menshikov, resurrected from his thirty years' retirement from soldiering to carry to a proper conclusion this irritating consequence of his mission to Constantinople. He had chosen the valley of the Alma as the line on which to stop the advance of the allied armies on Sebastopol and he could not have chosen a better natural line of defence. The allies, approaching from the north on a front three miles wide, would be denied any cover at all as they came down the long slope to the river. Along the river bank there was plenty of cover behind the stone walls of the gardens and vineyards, whence Russian skirmishers lurking there could pour musket fire into any troops advancing across the open—and whence they could readily withdraw to the safety of their own lines if pressed—and from the heights on the south bank the Russian artillery could pick their targets with delightful ease. Menshikov had spread his formations along the hills overlooking the river on a front stretching from a western-most position two miles inland from the river mouth, to a most eastward position five and a half miles from the sea. Along this three-and-a-half mile front the ground rose sharply from the river up on to the high steppe to the south, but these slopes were not entirely inaccessible to troops or even guns, although the climb could be difficult at some points; but, nearer the sea, along the other two miles inland from the mouth of the river, steep cliffs formed the south bank, and it was clear to Menshikov—who, being fairly old, had not felt it necessary to examine the ground itself—that that part of the line needed no defending. And by keeping well inland the Russians were less likely to be bothered by the guns of the allied fleets.

The allies waited in their columns on the open slope, their strength and formations openly revealed to the enemy, while their generals and staffs made the first serious attempt to plan what they intended to do. What had been the purpose or effect of Bosquet's secret move at dawn is a little obscure because now, at midday, his division was waiting patiently with the rest, on the right of the French line at the top of the cliffs. The weather, unlike that of the previous day, was fresh and pleasant, and the British troops with their full water-bottles were in happier circumstances; the morning's march had been quite short and the really sick men had been weeded out the day before. Menshikov, by delaying to bring the allies to battle until the second day of the march, had done the British army an inestimable favour. Now, at high noon, the troops took out their unappetizing ration of salt pork and biscuits and made every appearance of enjoying it.

Shortly after St. Arnaud had returned to his own army he ordered Bosquet's division, with whom were the Turks, to move forward along the cliff. This had been part of his plan of the previous evening although now that the plan as a whole had fallen away Bosquet's purpose was even more indefinite. The division split into two brigades, advancing in narrow close columns, and one brigade under General Bouat made for the very mouth of the river where, so reports from the fleet had told them, there was a sand bar which made a crossing on foot quite feasible. On the other side there appeared to be a path up what had looked from the distance to be an unscalable cliff. The cliff was certainly formidable and rose three hundred and fifty feet from water level, but what the sailors had seen through their spy-glasses proved to be right. The climb was steep but the path was good, although it was quite inaccessible to guns—which could hardly have been taken across the sand bar anyway—so Bouat left his artillery behind on the north bank, and all his men left their packs there too. At that stage in the history of the French army the soldiers always divested themselves of their packs before a battle —a procedure which was apt to have considerable influence on subsequent events because naturally, at some time or other, they had to come back to fetch them. Even relieved of the weight of their packs, General Bouat's men found the climb to be heavy, but there were no Russians within two miles and the brigade, still in column, emerged at last on to the top of the cliff.

A mile upstream from the river mouth on the north bank was a Tartar village, known as Alma Tamack, and from here upwards vineyards and gardens lined the river. Another mile upstream stood a conspicuous white farmhouse, and both here and at Alma Tamack a road crossed the river by a ford. Apparently these roads had escaped Menshikov's notice entirely. But although the French were able to take their guns over both fords they found it impossible to take them up the cliff road on the other side. However, the two roads wound their way through gullies right up on to the high steppe and Menshikov was to receive an unpleasant shock when it was reported to him that the first French troops had made their way to the top, one brigade at the cliff edge and a second up the road from Alma Tamack.

Across the next ford by the farmhouse General Canrobert took a complete division. Canrobert was a surprisingly young general, only forty-five; he had made a popular reputation in Algeria— that paradise of opportunity for French soldiers in the first half of the nineteenth century—and he had deftly consolidated his professional prospects by playing the chief part in the massacre of Parisians on the day after Louis Napoleon had declared himself Emperor. As a fitting reward he now held the "dormant commission" in the Crimea, which meant that if St. Arnaud were to be killed or incapacitated he would assume the command. But he was an impressionable character despite his ruthless record, and the way his division had been decimated by cholera in Bulgaria had disheartened him and most of his old fire had gone. Now, he had led his division over the ford and part of the way up the

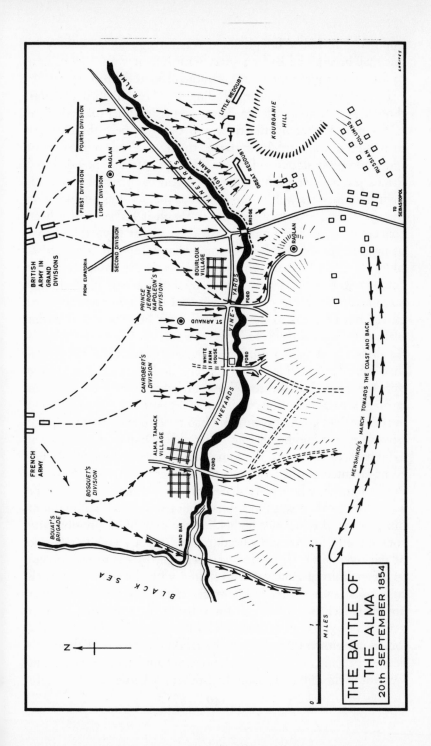

THE BATTLE OF
THE ALMA
20th SEPTEMBER 1854

opposite hill, but although there was no sign of the enemy he felt that because he had no guns with him it would be unwise to follow Bosquet's men out on to the plain at the top.

Prince Jerome Napoleon, leading the French third division, showed even more prudence. There was yet another road and ford half a mile farther up the river and opposite here the cliff-like formation of the south bank started to recede a little and to present more accessible slopes and ridges. Here St. Arnaud intended that Prince Jerome's division should cross, and the Marshal placed his own headquarters well in the centre of the division's columns so that he would cross with them, although if he had really been concerned with directing the battle he might have found that being thus surrounded he was somewhat hampered and inaccessible. However, he had avoided quite neatly the complication of having to frame any detailed orders by declaiming to his divisional commanders, "With men such as you I have no orders to give! I have but to point to the enemy!"—just like the arrow on his plan. But the hint seems to have been lost on Prince Jerome and his division, of which only one brigade crossed the river; and that brigade was able to stay safely under the shelter of the opposite bank because somehow or other a brigade from an entirely separate division, which was supposed to have been held in reserve, had got across first and had tried to take its guns up the narrow road winding up the other side. Despite this untypical exhibition of enterprise the guns and limbers had inevitably become jammed on the road so that no other troops could pass. To Prince Jerome, who hardly shared his late brother's eagerness for battle, the incident was unfortunate but irremediable and without much show of reluctance he held all the men of his division, and consequently St. Arnaud's headquarters, quietly on the safe side of the river until the battle was over—all, that is to say, except two battalions of Zouaves who shared with the ordinary French conscripts neither their indifference to the outcome of the war nor their lack of enthusiasm for a battle. Disappointed at their general's inaction they marched off quite spontaneously and joined up with another Zouave battalion on the left of Bosquet's nearest brigade, although this somewhat unorthodox behaviour was not in the end to assuage their thirst for battle.

9

THE great advance by the French army, which St. Arnaud had indicated so confidently in his plan as striking at the very centre of the enemy line, had spent itself and come to a halt without encountering the enemy at all. But it had some effect on the fortunes of the Russians that day, however indirectly, because when Menshikov heard that French troops had appeared on the top of the cliff on his side of the river he became almost apoplectic. At first he angrily refused to listen to the reports, but when he was at last persuaded that they had some substance he withdrew seven battalions of infantry, two batteries of guns and a squadron of cavalry from his defence and rode off himself at their head, in a state of irritable frenzy, towards the sea five long miles away. On the immediate front of the Russian positions the British army was now showing signs of aggressive intent and it was clear to anybody that an attack was about to develop, but Menshikov took himself off and left the conduct of the coming battle entirely to his subordinates without giving them any coherent instructions.

When the French formations had moved forward, the British "grand divisions" had been extended into line and the men were ordered to lie down because Raglan intended that they should wait until the enemy had been duly distracted by the French attack. The line which the British army would cover was to extend eastward from the left flank of Prince Jerome's division for nearly two miles up the river. Prince Jerome's left rested on the edge of another Tartar village on the north bank, named Bourlouk. A quarter of a mile above Bourlouk the road from Eupatoria to Sebastopol—astride which the British had been marching—crossed the river over a bridge. The Russians were apparently so confident that the allies would never be able to cross the river by any means that they left the bridge intact, although just after the French started to move forward they set fire, dramatically enough, to all the houses in Bourlouk village simultaneously. Above the bridge the gardens and vineyards extended along the verdant alluvial edge of the north bank, and on the other side, gouged out too by flood waters after heavy rains, stretches of level sand were buttressed by sheer banks, generally eight to ten feet high, which had to be scaled almost perpendicularly to gain access to the ground above. From these banks the ground rose steeply but more accessibly to the heights three hundred feet above, broken constantly by folds and dips and gullies, except for one wide, smooth slope—on which the bloody heart of the Battle of the Alma was destined to be fought —which started rising three hundred yards from the river and at the top of which the Russians had posted fourteen heavy guns and had thrown up an earthwork to protect them.

In later wars this earthwork would have gone down to history with a map reference or a rude name, but in keeping with the times it earned the impressive label of the Great Redoubt; and half a mile to the east the Russians had thrown up another, the Lesser Redoubt, with eight guns. Not that these represented the full strength of the Russian artillery, for posted round the slopes of the main hill feature, the Kourganie Hill, were sixteen batteries of light field guns. But these two gun emplacements were the only earthworks, such as they were, that Menshikov had taken the trouble to construct anywhere along his line of defence, although he confidently expected that here on the banks of the Alma he would hold the allied armies, perhaps for weeks, until they had been worn down by attrition and the war had been won.

The British troops, looking down the slope where they lay flat on their faces, lifted their eyes to see the ground before them which they now knew they were about to attack, and it looked formidable enough. In theory each "grand division" on deployment should have been extended into a long line two files deep, the Light and Second Divisions forming the front line, with the Third and First and half the Fourth Division behind. The deployment from column to line was quite a straightforward parade-ground movement and presented no difficulty on the score of practice, but as nobody had studied the ground previously and no calculations had been made of how long a line each division would be when extended, it was found that the lines inevitably overlapped and there was some confusion on the flanks of each company. However, the effect was not so serious and in the event—more on account of providence than efficient staff work— the lines fell into an impressive echelon formation, the Second Division in front covering Prince Jerome's left flank, the Light Division falling behind and overlapping the Second and extending farther east, and the First and Fourth behind the Light and also extending to its left.

Here the British troops lay in their long, thin red and blue lines in the sunshine—each line three thousand men, or more than a mile long—inviting the Russian batteries to open fire on them, which they did at half-past one. The lines certainly offered more difficult targets than columns would have done, but the technique of artillery in those days was not so much to rely on the plunging shell as to pitch cannon balls in front of the enemy in a low trajectory and to watch them go bouncing onwards through the ranks at an alarmingly lethal pace. The danger at the receiving end was to find oneself in the path of an oncoming ball, so even the thin red line had its measure of vulnerability. The officers remained mounted in front of their men and invited even more persistent attention from the gunners; for though their intelligence may have been limited they lacked nothing in courage. Lord Raglan, with his staff of twenty horsemen, conspicuous in their cocked hats and plumes, rode up and down the lines as a target of special attraction, Raglan himself particularly obvious in his blue frock-coat with its empty sleeve. From down the river came sounds of musket fire, and one of Raglan's young aides said excitedly, "The French, my lord, are warmly engaged." But Raglan had a little more experience of battle and he answered drily, "Are they? I cannot catch any return fire." Nor was there any musket fire from the enemy to be heard, for there was no enemy there—although that did not prevent the French skirmishers who were leading their divisions down to the river bank from indulging in some boisterous shooting.

The British soldiers lay patiently and still in their lines for an hour and a half, men mutilated by cannon balls lying where they were struck because this was a battle and no wounded would be attended to until the fighting was entirely over. Sir Colin Campbell rode up and down the lines of the Highland regiments reminding them, "Whoever is wounded must lie where he is until a bandsman comes to attend to him—I don't care what his rank is. No soldiers must go carrying off wounded men. If any soldier does such a thing his name shall be stuck up in his parish church," which in Scotland would be enough to discourage anybody.

Raglan was waiting for the French to gain the top of the cliffs, when they would swing round to engage the Russians on the flank. Then he would attack with the British army on the front. Thus without any unnecessary discussion he had completely reversed the roles of the two armies which St. Arnaud had planned. But in the event it did not even work out that way because the French never engaged the enemy at all except in some skirmishes along the river bank.

However, at about three o'clock an excited young Frenchman came hurrying to Raglan with a message from St. Arnaud saying that unless Bosquet were relieved immediately he would be "compromised"—or so the message was translated to Raglan. Raglan looked dubious and asked for the word to be repeated. The Frenchman, amazed that the British general could be so obtuse as to fail to understand a plain inference, volunteered that Bosquet was about to retreat; which may or may not have been what St. Arnaud had meant, although as the whole battle ground was visible from the north bank and it was abundantly clear that Bosquet was still nowhere near the enemy Raglan found it difficult to believe. Nevertheless, he welcomed the message as the cue he had been waiting for and he turned to an aide-de-camp to take the order—the only order he was to give during the whole battle—to his divisional generals to start the advance. The aide-de-camp nearest to him happened to be Captain Nolan, a volatile cavalryman of some notoriety, and Raglan, who disliked excitability and always believed in maintaining an impression of calm, said, "Go quietly. Don't gallop," and much against his inclination Nolan trotted off calmly to General de Lacy Evans at

144

Canrobert managed to put off the bombardment for three months; a quiet day in a French mortar battery.

Witness of unbelievable heroism by the conscripts of the Tsar; the interior of the Redan

the head of the Second Division. If, on a subsequent notorious occasion, Captain Nolan had been as calm when delivering another of Raglan's orders history might have been robbed of one of its most popular epics.

The British army rose literally from the ground and it rose at the same time to the heights that the people at home expected of it. Entirely untrained in the subtleties of war it was nevertheless disciplined in unquestioning and undeviating observance of the rules of the drill book as no British army had been disciplined before or was perhaps ever to be disciplined again. The army's magnificent discipline largely stemmed, paradoxically enough, from the stupidity of its officers who had made no study of their profession at all but blindly followed those entrenched customs that brought them such delightful privileges, and saved them the need to do any thinking. The rank and file were but a background to reflect their own splendour, a background which for this very purpose had to be kept trained and disciplined in a state of virtual automation, so that in peacetime at any rate no officer would be diverted from his own personal affairs by having to concern himself with what his men were doing.

When the soldiers rose in their lines across the Crimean steppe, cannon balls bowling towards them, wounded men groaning pitifully beside them, they automatically dressed their ranks— shining button to shining button in perfect alignment—and they marched down the uneven slope in unfaltering step. Any deviation from step or alignment, made even to dodge a cannon ball or to step over a body, would receive a reproof as a matter of habit. So they marched down to the river with parade-ground precision in the most difficult of all formations, in extended line, and the major-generals rode at their head. The English crowds would have been delighted.

Down at the river bank the stone walls round the vineyards and gardens, and the burning shacks in Bourlouk village, tended to prejudice the maintenance of a straight line, and here too the first skirmishes with the Russians took place. But impeded as they were the lines moved forward, dressed again on the river edge and marched on still in formation through the water. Some were lucky enough to wade through shallows; others stepped into pools up to their necks, struggling to hold their muskets and ammunition pouches above their heads; some had to swim; some, not a few, were shot and drowned, others just drowned; but the lines were maintained. Down the slope, through the gardens and the river, as the lines had moved forward the casualties had inevitably been heavy; one brigade lost a quarter of its strength.

The sixty-six-year-old Peninsula veteran, Sir George Brown, at the head of the Light Division—the infantry division, not to be confused with the Light Brigade of cavalry—found himself across the river and under the eight-foot bank. The bank was crumbling in parts so he put his horse at it and scrambled to the top. With white plumes hanging from a cocked hat his identity was fairly obvious. Straight ahead he could see the open slope running up to the Great Redoubt, although he was notoriously shortsighted and he could probably make out very little detail. An embarrassing selection of cannon balls, grape shot and canister was bowling down the slope towards him. Sir George Brown was clearly a brave man—if his presence up on the bank in front of his troops, whom he was apparently content to leave sheltering below, was not to be put down to sheer stupidity. But he had spent the last forty years in the Adjutant-General's office and was quite unused to making up his mind quickly so he had some difficulty in deciding what to order his division to do next. The brigade at the right of his division, after crossing the river in its immaculate line, had been forced by the narrowness of the south bank to converge and assemble in a crowd—a situation which the drill book had not envisaged—and a battery of Russian guns on its right flank (which should have been occupied with dealing with Prince Jerome if the French had been a little more aggressive) was able to pour in a devastating enfilading fire.

In command of this right brigade was Brigadier-General Codrington who had not really been intended by the authorities to come to the Crimea at all. However, as a soldier and, at the time, a colonel he had felt that if there was a war on it definitely concerned him and he had made his way out to Varna on his own initiative. He was known as an obstinate man; he had a narrow, tight little mouth, and perhaps Raglan found that the easiest way to deal with such an unorthodox situation was to take him on the strength and not to argue, for he had promoted him brigadier-general and had given him a brigade. Codrington had never been in battle before which possibly made it easier for him to make a bold, soldierly decision; for when he found his brigade in danger of becoming decimated by Russian fire from the flank—which he had no means of countering—without any hesitation he ordered his men up the steep bank to their front, up into the open field of even fiercer fire from the Great Redoubt. Like Sir George Brown—who was some hundreds of yards up the river from him—Codrington scrambled up the bank on his horse. Because of the unofficial way he had come into the war he sported no cocked hat and plumes, but the white Arab pony which he rode more than made up for his inconspicuous head-dress. While Sir George Brown's climb to the top of the bank, without any set purpose, had perhaps been a shade foolhardy, Codrington's was an act of brave leadership. The men of his brigade came swarming up after him—no longer in any lines now—and they surged forward up the slope towards the Great Redoubt in the face of a tremendous fire.

On the right of this right brigade—on the extreme right of the entire British attack, in fact—were the 7th Fusiliers under Colonel Lacy Yea, who had been brought up in the hunting field and characteristically pronounced his name "Yaw". Yea shouted to his men to extend in line and the inexorable habit of discipline had some effect. But by now there was too much noise for any proper parade-ground control. High up on the slope two Russian columns, one emerging from each side of the Great Redoubt, came marching down towards the river, and for the first time the British soldiers could see clearly the men they had come to fight—tall men, made to look taller by their ankle-length grey coats, trudging towards them in ponderous column; well-drilled enough, but even at that first instant of view obviously lacking the absolute precision of the British infantryman. They marched down the slope, a dumb mass of soldiery, their leaders clearly at a loss about what they should be doing, and by now Codrington's men, happily released for once from the discipline of the line, were anything but dumb and suffered no doubts of their own intentions. Against all the contemporary rules of war—which provided only for the perennially controversial alternatives of attack in column or advance in line, either column or line in precise formation—the British soldiers drove forward as an amorphous mob, cheering and singing, with Brigadier-General Codrington riding at their head on his white pony and Yea at the flank view-halloing them onward. They blazed away with their muskets, they stabbed at the grey-coated figures with their bayonets and they broke the Russian columns and swarmed in over the Great Redoubt. But when they came there they found that even in the short period of their attack the Russians had found time to remove all but one of the guns, for to the Tsar the loss of his guns was one of his pet aversions, and he had given portentous orders that they were never to be abandoned because he had read somewhere that the Duke of Wellington—whom he was convinced he resembled—had never lost a gun, which was blatantly untrue.

Two thousand men of the Light Division, quite spontaneously and without any advanced planning, had stormed the most formidable point in the Russian line and had captured it, although at some cost; now at least ten thousand Russians waited round them in a close semi-circle and the heavy guns which had been pulled out were being remounted in threatening positions. But the rest of the British army had halted in the shelter of the river bank. Sir George Brown had rejoined his troops below, not because he was feeling any less brave but being short-sighted he was a little bewildered; and the commander-in-chief and his staff were nowhere to be seen.

Although, in the wars fought before the twentieth century, the means of communicating orders were still primitive, the more leisurely movement of the armies gave the commanders a direct control of the battle such as the modern general can hardly hope to exert over the fast moving units of to-day, even with all his radio-communications. In the old days the generals sat on their horses at the highest vantage point watching what was going on in front of them, and they sent aides scurrying with orders to move their formations in and out of the fight. The British position before the Alma, on the slopes down to the river from which the whole battle arena could be seen, was an ideal vantage point for a commanding general. He could see how the French had failed to engage the enemy's flank; he could see quite clearly the force with which Menshikov was hurrying westward, although its purpose was not so obvious; he could see the British lines advancing towards and crossing the river, and Codrington's brigade storming and capturing the Great Redoubt. And from this live battle plan unfolded in front of him he could decide whom to order to Codrington's support and what formations to move to consolidate his unexpected success.

But that was not Lord Raglan's idea of his part in a battle. Whatever may have been his aversion to making decisions there was no disputing his personal courage and almost by instinct he sought to place himself as close as he could to the enemy. Here, on the Alma, instead of holding the threads of the battle in his hand from the commanding vantage point of the north bank, he established a somewhat unique headquarters by riding forward with his staff and making a little salient of his own protruding into the enemy's lines. He probably had no actual intention of preceding his army—nothing he did was ever planned—but when the troops started crossing the river he rode with them over the ford opposite Bourlouk village, at the right of the British line, and his staff came trotting dutifully behind him. It was here that the flanks of the British and French armies made contact, and the French skirmishers out in front of their formations, shooting doggedly at the empty bank on the other side of the river, showed some surprise at seeing a general and his headquarters staff making this unorthodox move into the enemy lines. The French themselves were taking no risks in attempting a crossing. To the left the British had started to cross, but for the time being they were waiting under the shelter of the south bank.

Raglan rode his brown bay Shadrach—who was hopeful they would soon put up a fox and was consequently taking some holding in—and he led his staff across the ford and made his way up a path to the right, no more concerned that the ground had not been reconnoitred than he would have been had he been sending a brigade there. One of his staff following him found an easier path and called, "This seems a better way, my lord," and Raglan swung Shadrach round and they all took a steep but well-marked path up the hill, bearing more to the left, and incidentally towards the Russians. At the top, as if the position had been prepared for them, they came out on to an open shelf on the side of the hill, looking towards the east. They were half a mile from the river, forward of their own lines and well inside the Russian positions. Below them to the left ran the line of the river, and along it they could see the British files crossing. Happily the hills behind them shut off their view to the west so that they could see nothing of the French inaction. But to the front and spread round them in a wide arc were the enemy troops and guns, even on the slopes which rose above them on their right. Raglan was certainly in a commanding position, although he was hardly in a position to command, for if he really had wanted to send an order to anyone in the British lines it would have taken twenty minutes or more to deliver—down the hill, across the ford, through Bourlouk village and along the river bank.

But Raglan looked round at the Russian formations below and above him, and although his horse was champing and restless for the chase he said quietly, "Our presence here will have the best effect." He made all his staff come forward to the lip of the knoll so that the cocked hats and plumes could be seen clearly by the enemy, as if he realized that their part in directing the battle might be negligible but that their presence inside the Russian lines, suggesting an almost miraculous advance by the British, might have a useful moral effect. He added, "If only we had a couple of guns up here," and an aide who was a colonel of artillery went off to fetch them.

Before Raglan was to see Codrington's brigade advance to capture the Great Redoubt another excited young Frenchman had sought him out. Almost incoherent, his cap missing, the officer gasped out a message from Canrobert—who had learnt with some relief of Raglan's proximity—"My lord, my lord, we have before us eight battalions." Raglan could but assume that he was talking about Russian battalions, although he seemed particularly concerned about the youngster's cap. After some thought he said, "I can spare you one battalion." This seemed to satisfy the Frenchman who hurried off, although Raglan took no action at all to give effect to the offer. His attention was concentrated on Shadrach's restless behaviour, and he was having difficulty in controlling the horse and at the same time holding up his field-glasses with his only hand.

Not that Raglan's failure—or it may have been his inability—to order a battalion to the assistance of the French really mattered because the alleged eight battalions which had so frightened Canrobert were merely the troops which Menshikov had hurried across the French front to meet Bosquet's division near the coast. Now they were hurrying back again. Menshikov had reached the coast, and the allied ships had started firing at him, and four of his personal escort had been killed. So he had turned and marched his troops back all the five miles whence he had brought them, an exercise that took him in all a couple of hours to complete. The only effect of this inspired manœuvre had been to reduce the Russian strength by a considerable force when the actual battle came to be fought.

Of Menshikov's three subordinate generals one was Prince Gortchakoff. Thanks to the Austrian Emperor's timely move which had protected him from the vengeance of the Turks in Bulgaria, Gortchakoff had been able to hurry his army across to Sebastopol before the allies had landed on the Crimea. Now he commanded the centre of the Russian line. On Gortchakoff's left was General Kiriakoff and on his right General Kvetzinski. There had been little co-ordination of planning between the three generals and their commander-in-chief had now left them with no particular idea of how the defence as a whole was to be conducted.

Nevertheless, the two thousand British infantrymen of Codrington's brigade who had somewhat outpaced the rest of their army were having an uncomfortable time in the Great Redoubt, beset as they were by musket and artillery fire from all sides. All they were now able to do with any profit was to lie waiting behind the parapets hoping to defend themselves from the inevitable counter-attack. This was launched soon enough by a Russian column consisting of four battalions of the Vladimir regiment, three thousand strong in all, and both Prince Gortchakoff and General Kvetzinski were subsequently to claim that they had inspired and led this attack in person. Surprisingly neither remembered having seen the other. But whoever may have been at its head, the column appeared before the British in the redoubt a little unexpectedly, coming round a fold in the hill, moving silently and bovinely but trudging over the ground without any apparently aggressive intent. The column looked so innocent that someone in the British ranks shouted, "For God's sake don't fire! Here come the French!" and when one of the buglers heard this he obligingly sounded the cease-fire.

This unexpected reception temporarily unnerved the Russians so that they halted and for some minutes there was a surprising quiet on the battlefield. Then the grey-coated men in the front ranks of the column started firing volleys into the ground, while those in the centre preferred to shoot wildly into the air. The only casualties among the British at this stage appear to have been the regimental colours which were riddled. Then another Russian column appeared on the British left flank and the position looked so menacing that an order to retire came from some untraced source and this was taken up with alacrity by the buglers. The regimental officers in the redoubt felt some reluctance to comply with the order and they held a meeting on the parapet to consider what they should do. They could well have found some shelter behind which to conduct their discussions but that would have been unworthy of the occasion, so they stood up in the open in full view of the enemy and inevitably all of them were shot down. After that there was no one left—except among the 7th Fusiliers—to dispute the order, although there now appeared among the rank and file a considerable reluctance to retire not so much on a point of honour but because the wild men in the centre of the Russian column who were directing their musket fire in a general skyward trajectory were, quite unwittingly, putting down an effective barrage between the redoubt and the river which would have to be passed through during the process of withdrawal.

However, the menace of the Russian columns was real enough and all Codrington's men began to fall back towards the river— all, that is, except Lacy Yea's 7th Fusiliers who were still on the right of the line and held their colonel in much greater awe than they held the enemy. Inevitably a handful of waverers had stayed hopefully unobserved in the shelter of the river bank. At the height of the battle Yea had had them ferreted out from their fox-holes and brought before him in the Great Redoubt where, during a convenient lull in the fighting while waiting for the counter-attack, he had meted out summary judgement. When the buglers sounded the retire, Yea forced his men to remain facing the oncoming Russian column which was now not fifty yards away, and the 7th Fusiliers did in fact hold their ground throughout the battle. One of Yea's officers was so inspired by his leadership that he rushed forward to assault the column single-handed, running his sword through a man in the front rank and hitting the next man, somewhat irregularly, with his bare fist. Inevitably he was shot dead. Then a Russian stepped out of the column and aimed his musket directly at Yea. Not to be outdone in enterprise a corporal of the Fusiliers stepped forward and shot him down, and Yea said magnanimously, "Thank you, my man. If I live through this you shall be a sergeant to-night."

By now the rearmost echelon of the British line, the First Division, which comprised the Guards Brigade and the Highland Brigade, had crossed the river. The division was commanded by Lieutenant-General His Royal Highness the Duke of Cambridge; the Guards Brigade by Brigadier-General Sir Henry Bentinck, and the Highlanders by Brigadier-General Sir Colin Campbell. The Duke of Cambridge we have seen; General Bentinck was a regimental officer of no particular prominence. Sir Colin's inferiority in rank to the major-generals and lieutenant-generals who surrounded him was owed not to any lack of seniority—he had been in the Army many years longer than most of them—but to the fact that for forty-four years he had been away from England on amazingly active service, which was not the usual qualification for promotion. Advancement to the really senior ranks could be better assured by constancy at the Horse Guards. Campbell had fought at Corunna, and had subsequently returned to the Peninsula with Wellington; he had fought in the American war, and in the West Indies; he had fought in the Chinese war of 1842; he had fought throughout the Sikh war and had even commanded divisions at Chilianwalla and Gujerat; and he had been the commander who had forced the Kohat Pass. All this was so unconventional for a British officer that by 1854—forty-six years after he had joined the Army as an ensign, during which he had been fighting with conspicuous success for forty-four—he was still but a colonel. Now at last he had been grudgingly promoted brigadier-general and given the Highland Brigade. Three years later, relegated once more to the unorthodoxy of active service, after the present war ended, he was to find his ultimate place in history by directing the Relief of Lucknow.

The Highlanders were on the left of the First Division line; to their right were the Coldstream, the Scots Fusiliers and then the Grenadiers. As the Guards battalions emerged wetly from the river the company markers were called forward and the lines were re-dressed with precision. Then the division moved forward, as they had moved so often before the public in Hyde Park, conscious that they were the "Guards" with whom were not to be confused the regiments of the "Line". In fact at a later stage in the battle, when there was a gap in the Guards' ranks, Codrington offered to fill it with some of his infantrymen but the offer was very properly refused.

The Guards and Highlanders moved up the slope towards the Great Redoubt just too late to come to the rescue of Codrington's infantrymen. These were now retiring in some haste, running the gantlet of the random fire which rained down on the long slope, and their withdrawal was to have an undignified effect on the Scots Fusiliers who had the misfortune to take the brunt of it. Many of the guardsmen were actually bowled over—all the Scots Fusiliers were driven into disarray—and one wretched sergeant had all his ribs broken. The Grenadiers on the right also faced part of the onslaught but they managed the situation more deftly, opening their ranks to let the retreating infantrymen through without so much as breaking step.

The First Division line—badly mauled in the centre where the ranks of the Scots Fusiliers had been so indecorously broken— stretched two deep for a mile and a half, tartans and highland bonnets on the left, bearskins and blue and red pantaloons on the right. At its head rode the Duke of Cambridge, and in front of each brigade rode its brigadier-general. The Russian infantry were deploying fast now—there were eight separate columns moving forward down the Kourganie Hill—and the classic trial of fighting system, line versus column, was once more to be tested. The columns perforce moved obliquely across the lines, and the lines—held for a moment in their forward movement—were able to pour fire into the masses of the columns with discouraging effect. If the columns had been handled aggressively and led to charge the lines with the bayonet, although the cost in Russian casualties would have been heavy, the lines—merely two files deep—might well have been broken and the outcome of the battle could have been very different. Gortchakoff did, on two separate occasions during this part of the battle, place himself at the head of a column and suggest that it should charge, but on both occasions the suggestion failed to find any supporters and in any case it had been left too late as the columns were already being decimated by the British fire.

At last the Duke of Cambridge gave the order, "The line will advance on the centre"—dressing must never be overlooked—"the line will advance firing." The Guards and the Highland Brigade, in a last magnificent movement of precision, marched forward, and Yea's Fusiliers on the right had the temerity to march with them; the Russian columns broke into retreat and the Battle of the Alma had been won. It was won as the result of no tactical planning; no effective attempt had been made to turn the enemy's flank; no thought had been given to where the enemy's weakness might be. The assault had been made without any subtlety, by bludgeoning straight ahead towards no defined objectives, and it had been made quite by chance against the enemy's strongest point. The generals commanding the assaulting armies had both cut themselves off from their commands, and neither of them had played any part in the battle whatsoever. It had been left to the British soldier to carry the day, not by military competence, but by sheer disciplined courage.

The victory had cost the British two thousand casualties, nearly four hundred of whom had been killed, and most of whom had fallen on the slopes below and round the Great Redoubt. Now that the battle was over the wounded still lay there, disciplined and uncomplaining as ever. Despite careful avoidance of close contact with the enemy the French had suffered over five hundred casualties, mainly from artillery fire, of whom sixty were killed.

St. Arnaud made a bold attempt to reduce the disparity between the sufferings of the two armies by officially reporting thirteen hundred French casualties, but subsequent careful research relegated this claim to the same category of imaginative fancy as the story, given prominent currency in France, of a heroic struggle at the climax of the battle between Canrobert's Zouaves and an entirely unidentifiable Russian formation. The official French account, commissioned some months later by the Minister of Public Instruction, is highly circumstantial. "The struggle was short," it says, "but it was one of those bloody, terrible struggles in which man fights body to body with his enemy, in which the looks devour each other"—which must be an alarming phenomenon to behold—"in which the hands grapple each other, in which arms dashed against arms are made to yield sparks of fire." As Kinglake remarks, "I have observed this phenomenon in fights on the stage." The epic goes on, "Dead and dying are heaped together, and the combatants trample on them and smother them." Unfortunately after the battle nobody could be found who had witnessed this exhilarating episode.

The news of the victory on the Alma reached Europe ten days after the battle, by courier to Vienna and thence by the new telegraph which had just been established between that city and Paris. In London it was first announced at one of the theatres; for at the time it was the custom of the Government thus to disseminate its more welcome items of information. The audience's reaction could certainly be described as enthusiastic although it was not quite so immoderate as the reception which was to be given in similar circumstances half a century later to the news of the relief of Mafeking. But the theatregoers of the eighteen-fifties were drawn from a less demonstrative class.

The news came on a Saturday and there were no newspapers published the next morning. When the War Office had received it during the afternoon the person responsible, in defiance of a well-ordained custom, had failed to pass it to the Horse Guards across the road. So, officially, the Horse Guards, the headquarters of the Army, knew nothing about it, and when it became public on Saturday night the soldiers considered themselves grossly affronted. Next morning, on the Sunday, an officer at the Horse

Guards felt constrained to give effect to the Army's displeasure at a slight administered by a mere civilian department by firing a series of guns. When the good people of London awoke to this cannonade they not unreasonably imagined that the fall of Sebastopol was being celebrated; for everybody was convinced that it was imminent, and of course the people who had heard the report about the Battle of the Alma which had been read out in the theatre the night before were soon able to convince themselves that they had heard something quite different. And on the Monday this wishful thinking was happily confirmed by no less an authority than *The Times* which indulged in a headline that verged for those days on the sensational, quite apart from its falsity. In type that would be regarded as modest to-day, but was positively blatant at the time, the great oracle reported "THE FALL OF SEBASTOPOL" and qualified its claim to veracity by the sub-heading "DECISIVE INTELLIGENCE".

The report that followed was as circumstantial as the French story about Canrobert's Zouaves. "It may now be confidently stated that the forts of Sebastopol fell successively before the combined forces of the assailants; that at least half the Russian fleet perished; that the flags of the allies were waving on the Church of St. Vladimir; and that, on the 26th at the latest, Prince Menshikov surrendered the place. The battles are over, and the victory is won." And although Sebastopol was a thousand miles from St. Petersburg, *The Times* went on confidently to predict that the Tsar would be compelled to leave his capital and retire to the depths of Siberia, apparently the only safe refuge from the irresistible allied armies. When the truth was at last known the people of England condemned, not *The Times*, but the military leaders who had failed to achieve this imaginative success.

In France, Louis Napoleon reserved to himself the privilege of announcing the victory to his people—he had long been waiting for some such outcome of the war to help to consolidate his still insecure position. He was at Boulogne at the time and he made the happy announcement to the troops in camp there. He authorized *Le Moniteur* in Paris to publish the news together with the plan which St. Arnaud had drawn up before the battle and which the Marshal had sent proudly to his Emperor even before the first shot had been fired. *Le Moniteur* had also received a sketch of the battle made by an officer on one of the French ships, which showed the French armies gallantly assaulting the heights along the river near to the shore, but from which any possible view of the British had been conveniently obliterated by intervening hills.

Consequently France was treated to a version of the Battle of the Alma which discounted any participation by the British at all. On top of this, the Paris press published St. Arnaud's official despatch which did little to discourage the impression that the battle had been fought and won by the French on their own, and that it had been brilliantly directed by St. Arnaud himself. He said, "I had engaged the English"—the word he used was "engagé" and, as Kinglake says, it is difficult to translate the nuance of the meaning exactly; it imported something between "I requested" and "I ordered", but it unquestionably suggested that the British had submitted to St. Arnaud's overall command. "I had engaged the English," he wrote, "to prolong themselves on their left in order to menace the right of the Russians at the time when I should be giving them occupation at the centre; but their troops did not get into line until half-past ten." He was generous enough to add that later they bravely made up for their delay, but it was clear from his account that they had played a secondary and almost obstructive part in the battle, that St. Arnaud himself had carried the heavy responsibility of command, and that the day had been carried by the French Army.

The French papers certainly never got so far as reducing Sebastopol, but when their imaginative accounts of the Alma and St. Arnaud's official despatch came to be read in England, as inevitably they did, the spirit of alliance between the two countries suffered a severe strain. However the British public, paradoxical as ever, which one day was bringing down curses on St. Arnaud's head and consigning him vociferously to perdition, the very next day was standing silenced and even converted to rendering him honour when it learnt that in actual fact he had died. For, nine days after the Battle of the Alma, the Marshal of France had joined the drafts of sick soldiers who were being constantly carried down to the ships, and a few hours later, taken aboard a French ship of the line, he died.

In St. Petersburg the Tsar waited confidently for news of a victorious battle which he was sure must already have been fought. He had given considerate orders that the allied armies, when captured, were to be treated kindly. But Menshikov, after he had been driven back from the Alma, disdained to write a despatch and merely sent a courier with a verbal message, and this wretched man had the unenviable duty of breaking the news to the Tsar. He explained the absence of a despatch by saying that Menshikov had been "much hurried" and the Tsar asked, "What do you mean? Do you mean to say he was running?"

The news of the defeat was such a shock to Nicholas that he collapsed and for days he lay on his bed refusing food, castigating his advisers for having led him on to war with Britain by their repeated assertions that the English were more interested in trading than fighting.

10

THE Russians retreated from the Alma in a state of considerable disorder and they left more than five thousand casualties on the field, most of them where they had been mown down by the British line in their packed, indefensible columns. The next river behind them was the Katcha, and Menshikov's hope was that he could prevail on them to re-form and make a stand there. But for the time being he had lost control even over the regimented hordes of his own soldiery. He had arrived back from his excursion to the coast just in time to meet the first columns withdrawing in some haste along the main road. He had hurried past them angrily, intent to find Gortchakoff and to demand an explanation. And he had found Gortchakoff, not at the headquarters where he had expected him, but trudging too, along the road, following the columns, alone, and inexplicably on foot. Menshikov demanded a report on the situation and Gortchakoff replied, "My horse was killed near the river. All my officers have been killed or wounded, and I myself have received six shots," and he exhibited to his commander-in-chief the embarrassing effect of the enemy's bullets on certain important areas of his uniform as if they were of far more consequence than the tatters into which the Russian army had been torn.

Menshikov turned away even more angrily and rode back in a vain attempt to restrain the retreating columns, and to the first officer he rode up to he shouted, "It is a disgrace for a Russian soldier to retreat." Despite all that the Tsar had done to discipline his people into unquestioning subservience to authority, the officer replied bluntly that if he, Prince Menshikov, had been there to order his men to stand they would have stood—which was not so self-evident. Even the awesome Menshikov had no immediate answer, and the columns continued on their hurried way.

The only attempt made at any stand at all once the columns had been broken by the British First Division had been by General Kiriakoff who had actually rallied some cavalry and guns and had spread them across a prominent ridge so that they might suggest that the Russian army had re-formed. In effect it was only a token stand but it had been enough to discourage Raglan from sending forward any cavalry in immediate pursuit of the retreating Russians, and if other circumstances had not conspired to do the job for him Kiriakoff might well have been the instrument of halting the allies, for they were certainly not disposed to attack any more strong points that afternoon.

But in actual fact the Russian masses, forty thousand or more, were in precipitate retreat and none of them had any intention of stopping even at the Katcha and risking a repetition of what they had experienced that day at the Alma. Dropping down to the Katcha, over which there was only one ford of any reasonable capacity, the road narrowed into a deep constricted gorge where the disordered throng, which pressed through it perforce, could have been virtually annihilated by opposition of any sort. Here the British cavalry could have vindicated their claim to omnipotence. As it was, the whole Russian army—disordered, helpless, caught in the darkness of the night so that thousands of leaderless men were left wandering and lost in the emptiness of the steppe, and tumbrils and carts filled with stores and wounded were jammed in confusion in the narrow defiles—stampeded its way over the fourteen miles back to Sebastopol. There, twenty-four hours later, when at last all the stragglers had come in, it started to assume its homogeneity again and suffered itself to submit once more to the harsh discipline of its generals.

Raglan himself could see well enough the need for following up the battle with an immediate advance, not only by the cavalry—who might strike some wounding blows but would hardly be able to consolidate the victory to the full, and were too few anyway to be of any great effect—but also by some strong infantry formations. His own Third Division, which had formed the third line in echelon following the Guards, had hardly been engaged throughout the day and the troops were still comparatively fresh; and it was not unreasonable to assume that some of the French divisions might be in the same happy condition. But now that the battle was over St. Arnaud was busy once more exercising the authority of his command, and to Raglan's request that some of the French troops should join in the pursuit he replied that that would be impossible as they had all left their packs on the north side of the river and would now have to go back to fetch them.

Other than the Third Division, the British army had spent a fairly exhausting day—it had, incidentally, won a battle which would go down in history, deservedly, as a classic victory. To send the Third Division on its own was, to Raglan, unacceptable; and in any case it was now half-past four and in less than a couple of hours it would be dark. So thanks mainly to the complications caused by the French packs the whole idea of the pursuit was abandoned, although perhaps not too regretfully, and having once abandoned it the allies found themselves committed to a halt that in the event was to last for two days and nights and was to afford the Russians an encouraging opportunity to pull themselves together in Sebastopol.

The main cause of this protracted halt, apart from a besetting indifference to haste, was that the allies found themselves with a problem which they had signally failed to anticipate. Their own wounded numbered more than two thousand, and because the armies had taken on the role of an entirely detached force, leaving no line of communication behind it, each of these wounded men, if he were not to be abandoned merely to die, had to be carried individually and laboriously to the mouth of the river there to be handed over to the kindly if inexpert mercies of the sailors. The French wounded numbered but a few hundred, and as the French army's positions were not far from the mouth of the river its task on the morning after the battle was over in a few hours. Most of the British had to be carried—literally carried in the arms of their comrades, for there was no other means— four or five miles, with no prior benefit of drugs of any sort to relieve their agonies; the only solace a man lying on the battle-field in excruciating pain ever received, or even expected, was a rare sip of water. In addition there were some thousands of wounded Russians—none of them, significantly, at the French end of the field—whom humanity demanded should receive the same service. The British wounded were embarked for Scutari, where actually they would be little better off than if they had been left beside the Alma; the Russians were also embarked on a British ship and the Royal Navy made yet another approach to Odessa where Count Osten-sacken received his wounded countrymen with surprisingly bad grace.

The French had disposed of all their wounded by the afternoon following the battle, September 21st, so St. Arnaud was able to show an exemplary impatience to move on. During the next twenty-four hours, while the painful journey from the British lines to the shore was being made hundreds upon hundreds of times, he offered repeated reproofs to his allies for delaying the advance. As he reported so righteously to his Emperor, "The English are not yet ready, and I am kept back, just as at Balchick, just as at Old Fort. It is true they have more wounded than I have"—which, in the circumstances, was generous—"and that they are farther from the sea. What slowness in our movements! War can hardly be carried on in this way. The weather is admirable and I am not profiting by it. I rage."

So it was not until the early morning of the twenty-third that the British were ready to move on again, and the two armies, in their now accepted array of columns, set off once more over the steppe towards the next river obstacle. That night they bivouacked on the north bank of the Katcha having achieved an unopposed advance of seven more miles towards Sebastopol. After the Katcha there was only one more river to cross, the Belbek; and from that last valley the allies would climb to the hills overlooking Sebastopol harbour. Now at last the way in which the town was to be assaulted had become more than an academic discussion. To the embarrassment of the generals some definite plan had to be evolved, and now at the climax of the campaign—which was to have been so straightforward and uncomplicated—there arose in the high command a difference of opinion on basic strategy. Raglan, as averse to planning as ever, favoured the direct approach to Sebastopol from the north which would involve no complicated manœuvring; in this he was supported by Sir Edmund Lyons, but for a different reason, because Lyons had always been enthusiastic about the invasion project and was now determined to join in the assault in the best tradition of British naval enterprise by sailing into the harbour and engaging the Russian fleet at anchor.

A direct assault on Sebastopol by the armies from the north implied gaining the north shore of the harbour and being carried, by some still unspecified means, across the water to enter the town. There was a large fort on the hill on the north side, which would tend to hold up the allied advance, although the fort, when it was built, had really only been sited to dominate the harbour entrance and had not been placed up on the crest of the hill, so that the allies, approaching from the north, would at one stage actually overlook it. This Severnaya—or Star Fort as it was called by the English because of its octagonal shape—had been built nearly forty years before, and like most Russian institutions was somewhat dilapidated. It was of earthen walls, ten feet thick and fourteen feet high and was surrounded by a deep ditch eighteen feet wide. It mounted forty-seven guns—although it must be admitted that only twelve of these faced north—but as the allies now stood it lay as a formidable obstacle in the direct path of the French army.

Consequently it was to be expected that St. Arnaud would disfavour the strategy of a direct advance, and when on the twenty-fourth it was reported to him that the Russians had forestalled Lyons by sinking a line of ships across the harbour mouth and, of more immediate concern to the French, that they had set up a battery of six guns to supplement the deficiencies of the Star Fort, he stated his positive refusal to undertake the assault, as if it were a maxim of war that any prospect of enemy resistance ruled out the feasibility of an attack. In this decision, to Raglan's chagrin, he was supported by old Sir John Burgoyne who had now very properly regained his caution and had apparently forgotten that less than a week before he had predicted that the allies would be in Sebastopol in two days. Burgoyne was now positive that, from the north, Sebastopol was unassailable and that any attack should be made from the south, and to subvert the minds of those who would not agree with him he produced a plan of the town which showed how weak were its defences on the southern side. It was apparently irrelevant that the plan had been drawn by a certain Colonel Macintosh in 1835—twenty years before—and that the Russians might possibly have made some alterations in the interval. Colonel Macintosh's information had been supplemented later by another unofficial visitor to the town, a Mr. Oliphant, who had been there as recently as five years ago and had written, "There is nothing whatever to prevent any number of troops landing a few miles south of the town in one of the six convenient bays"—all of which must have eluded Raglan when he reconnoitred the coast—"and marching down the main street, sacking the town and burning the fleet." At the time of writing, Mr. Oliphant had no reason to believe that his countrymen would ever necessarily want to attack the place. Nor is there any record of what qualifications Mr. Oliphant might have possessed which would confer any authority on his views but, because they were now so convenient, the allied staffs accepted them greedily and without question.

The picture painted by the deceased Colonel Macintosh and the aggressively minded Mr. Oliphant was so encouraging that it was obvious that the whole strategy of landing north of Sebastopol had been wrong, and at last even Raglan was persuaded that the allies must now march round the head of the harbour and approach the town from the south—a strategy that would make this simple campaign even simpler, or so it was now sanguinely asserted.

The decision was taken on the Sunday evening, the twenty-fourth, when the troops had lately arrived at the Belbek and were bivouacking for the night, now less than four miles from their objective—a gap which, in the event, they were to take a whole year to close. Raglan had gone with Sir John Burgoyne and some other staff officers to St. Arnaud's headquarters, and there the Marshal had sat forbiddingly upright in his chair, appearing deliberately to ignore much of what was said to him so that his manner suggested that he was showing a more than usually unfriendly disdain for his allies; but Raglan who had suffered more than anyone else from the Marshal's persistent obstruction and unfriendliness now felt for him nothing but pity, for he knew something of what St. Arnaud was suffering, and as they withdrew he said to Burgoyne, "Did you observe him? He is dying." Next morning Raglan rode over to see him again but by now St. Arnaud could not even speak and Raglan realized that for the time being at any rate, until some formal change had been made in the French command, he himself would have to carry the responsibility of both the armies. It was not in his nature to exult at finding himself in a position which he must long have desired, and throughout the confusing events of the next few days, until the French command was duly transferred to Canrobert, he directed the movements of the two allies with a characteristic humility.

So the flank march had been decided upon and the allies had adopted an entirely new strategy whose implications had been little considered. The march south from the Old Fort to the Belbek had been unorthodox enough, detached as it had been from any line of communication. The armies had been cut off entirely from any source of supply or succour during the march itself and had relied on an uncertain contact with the fleets at the river mouths which might well have been impracticable if even a moderately rough sea had got up. As it was the weather had been kind and contact had been maintained; but this had been merely providential. Now the armies were to sever even this slender lifeline; they were to march deliberately inland, still as one self-contained unit but with infinitely meagre supplies, so that the Russians—who would be faced with no difficulties in crossing the harbour themselves—could attack them on their right and from their front or from their rear. The Russians, if they were quick enough, could also send formations to harass them on their left; they could in fact encircle them completely and with consummate ease. It was a fantastically idiotic strategic conception, and the inevitable disaster to the allied armies—which they were to suffer during the subsequent months as a sort of deferred penalty—was only averted at the time by a comparable display of stupidity on the part of their enemies.

The Russian defeat on the Alma had implanted in Menshikov a conviction that his army could never defend Sebastopol against a direct attack from the north—that very attack from which St. Arnaud had flinched. While the allied generals were arguing whether they would dare assault the Star Fort, and deciding that it would be suicidal to try, Menshikov was persuading himself with equal conviction that he could never defend it against them and he was removing from it all the ammunition and withdrawing its garrison across the harbour to the town. To the horror of the Russian admirals—and to the men of the fleet in general, who were actual volunteers and were consequently less cowed than most of the Russian forces—he ordered that five of their proud line-of-battle ships and two frigates were to be sunk across the entrance to the harbour and that the crews of all the ships were to be landed and formed into defence battalions. Admiral Korniloff, one of the commanders of the two naval squadrons in Sebastopol, made a strong bid to dissuade Menshikov. He pleaded that rather than the ships be sunk the fleet should be allowed to go out and fight the allies—which may have been a brave idea but had little to recommend it strategically. But the commander-in-chief was adamant, and the seven ships were scuttled on the night of the twenty-second and during the next two days eight thousand sailors of the fleet were organized to take over the defence of the town with their cutlasses and marlinspikes.

Menshikov's apparent concern was not so much that the allies might capture Sebastopol but that they would cut his army off from Russia whence, even if the town were taken, he might reasonably expect reinforcements that might enable him ultimately to recapture it and, more importantly still, drive the allies from it into the sea. The main road from Sebastopol that traversed the Crimea to the mainland ran north-east through Bakshiserai and Simpheropol, the two inland Crimean towns. Menshikov knew that he must keep this road open if his troops were to survive and he conceived the astonishing notion of marching his whole army out along the road so that he could forestall any movement by the allies to deny it to him. The sailors, whose ships were now locked up helpless in the harbour, would be left to bear the brunt of the assault; and perhaps, although this was only conjecture, he would soon be suitably reinforced so that he could return and liberate them from their conquerors. For he had no doubt that the allies were about to capture Sebastopol with ease.

So on the night of the twenty-fourth when the allies resolved to turn away and skirt Sebastopol because the town was so clearly unassailable from the north, the whole Russian army was marching off in that very direction which Raglan himself had decided to march next morning. If when the morning came the British had got away on time a full-scale collision between the two armies would have been unavoidable; and probably, ill-led as the allies were, they would, in the circumstances, have routed the Russians —if the form on the Alma was anything to go by—and the war would have been finished in that one decisive battle which the whole British and French nations popularly believed was all that was necessary, but for which nobody had made any attempt to plan.

Raglan proposed that on this flank march the armies should move in column as they were no longer to advance over open plain. They would strike south-east and pass round the head of the harbour. Once the allies had climbed from the valley of the Belbek up to the heights inland the country grew unfamiliar and thickly wooded, so that the troops were compelled, if they left the road, to struggle through matted undergrowth holding their arms and equipment above their heads. As Raglan had ordered the main body of the army to strike across country on a compass bearing, the leading companies had literally to fight their way through the foliage.

The Cavalry Division, under the command of Lord Lucan, was ordered to set off early in the morning as the vanguard of the army. It was to take a road which, on the scanty maps in the staff's possession, was shown as crossing the main road out of Sebastopol to Bakshiserai at a cluster of buildings marked as Mackenzie's Farm, an incongruous label for that part of the world. The main road which it was to cross was the very road along which Menshikov was leading his whole army. The cavalry were to be accompanied by a battalion of Rifles, and as the Rifles were late at the rendezvous the start of this vanguard was considerably delayed and the first companies of the main column were not on the march until after eight o'clock. The column itself struck inland and then turned on to its compass course, so that it was not

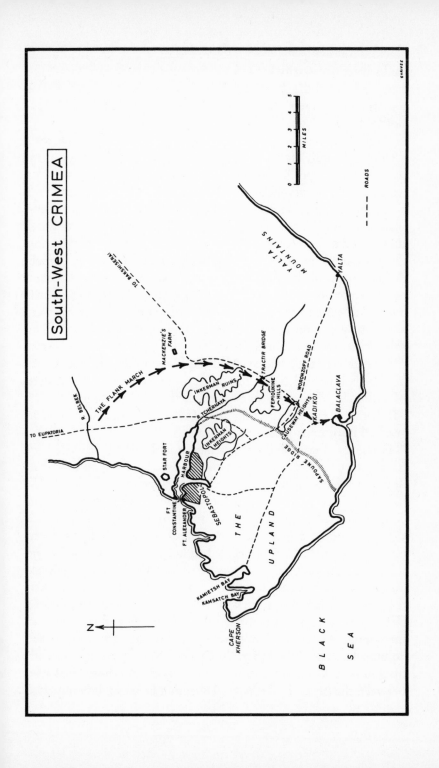

South-West CRIMEA

actually following the vanguard, and as the forest became thicker ranks were necessarily broken to allow the men to pass round the trees and round the dense and sometimes impenetrable patches of undergrowth. Soon, the usual inadequacy of the soldiers' water-bottles began inevitably to tell.

Raglan and his staff rode out away from the line of march with a troop of Light Horse as an escort, and they rode to the very head of Sebastopol harbour so that they could look down on its length to the survivors of the Russian fleet in the roadstead and to the block-ships across the harbour entrance. They had a commanding view of the whole area in and around Sebastopol and they could see no troop movements at all. In their imagination they conjured up visions of the Russian soldiers waiting at their defence posts in the various forts and strong points which they could make out round the town's perimeter—on both the north and south sides of the harbour—whereas of course these soldiers were away out on the road behind them and the strong points were virtually unmanned. They felt pleased with themselves at the clever way they had avoided the bloody combat that would have been involved in crossing the harbour and, with some degree of smugness, they rode away with their escort straight across to Mackenzie's Farm expecting that Lucan's cavalry would have reached it, or even passed it, by now.

However, Lucan and his advance guard, a little impeded by having to take their pace from the Rifles who were on foot, had deviated somewhat from the road along which they had intended to come. They had arrived at the inevitable fork in the road and equally inevitably they had made the wrong choice. The branch they had chosen degenerated into a track and finally had petered out altogether, but Lucan decided to keep on as he seemed to be following the required compass direction. But a troop of horse artillery accompanying him, led by a Colonel Maude, had taken the correct road at the fork and by one of those inexplicable chances that make the movement of military formations so intriguing, Maude had not even known that the rest of the column had taken the other. So Colonel Maude pressed on with his guns—he found some difficulty in negotiating the narrow lane between the trees—in the happy belief that he was following close behind Lucan. The main columns of the army were ranged behind this cavalry column and to the right, on a parallel compass course half a mile away. The commander-in-chief with his tiny escort was now ahead and to the left, and the three formations were entirely out of touch with each other. In the circumstances, a full collision with the Russian army might have been unfortunate.

Raglan found Mackenzie's Farm but as there was no cavalry on the road he assumed Lucan and the vanguard had already passed and was waiting somewhere ahead. Maude was there with his artillery and he reported in all good faith that he was following the cavalry. Lucan had been instructed to wait at the farm because the next move had not been decided, but the road still wound ahead through the trees, offering only a restricted view along it, and as Maude had said that the cavalry were ahead Raglan naturally believed he would find them at the turn of the road. So he and his staff trotted forward along the road believing themselves now to be safely located somewhere in the body of Lucan's force, although in fact they were actually in the van of the whole army. They came to a bend in the road and could see no cavalrymen, whereas to their front the wood came to an end and the road emerged into the open. General Airey rode forward enquiringly to look at their position.

Just before he came to the end of the trees Airey reined his horse to a stop and held up his hand in a peremptory warning to the others who were following him slowly. Across the opening ran the main road to Bakshiserai, and an alarmingly strong party of Russian troops was halted beside it. The Russians soon saw Airey and there was some mutual consternation. Raglan, when he saw Airey's hand raised in warning, very sensibly stopped his horse and remained still. Although he had no idea of the strength of the force that Airey had obviously seen, he called Maude's guns forward and he sent his escort to attack the Russians. Fortunately for the British commander-in-chief and his staff the men on the road were only the rear unit of Menshikov's army—which had passed in full force but very shortly before—and they constituted the last company escorting the wagon train, a company which had not been chosen for its military qualities.

There was an exchange of shots while the Russians scrambled for their horses and wagons, and the firing attracted Lucan who was but three-quarters of a mile away to the west. He came galloping across at the head of his cavalry and as he rode up Raglan said, with unusual severity, "Lord Lucan, you are late." The cavalry division, being in some force, rode on to deal effectively with the wagon train, and the cavalrymen enjoyed the satisfaction of cutting down their first Russians and at the same time removing a rewarding variety of booty from the wagons which had been carrying the private possessions of the Russian officers.

Now that they had come out into the open the British could see the dust of the Russian column marching away along the road to the north-east. Naturally it never occurred to Raglan that the whole Russian army was moving along that road because it is unusual for the commander of a fortress to remove from it the entire garrison just at the time when it is likely to be assaulted by the enemy. Raglan was concerned with getting the allied armies to the south of the town and he had no intention of being diverted by some incomprehensible movements of the enemy in the other direction, so he called off Lucan's cavalry from engaging the rear of the Russian column, and, quite unperturbed by the experience of having bumped with his staff into an unexpected enemy force, he rode on towards the south still in the van of the armies. The truth was that the actual direction of the armies' movement was even now a trifle uncertain, and Raglan felt the need to reconnoitre the ground himself as they advanced.

He turned right along the main road to Sebastopol and followed it where, a mile away, it swung sharply south and dropped down by a winding pass to the Tchernaya valley. The valley opens out into a square plain, like a deep box enclosed by hills, with each of its sides four to five miles long. Diagonally across the square from the south-east to the north-west flows the Tchernaya river, which, at the north-west corner, breaks through a narrow gorge into the head of Sebastopol harbour. The road along which Raglan was leading the allies followed the other diagonal, from the north-east corner where it had dropped down from Mackenzie's Farm to the south-west, and here it seemed to lose itself in the folds of the hills. Where the two diagonals met in the centre of the plain the road crossed the river by a stone bridge, known as the Tractir Bridge. Along each side of the box runs a line of hills, five hundred feet high and more. Across the north are the Inkerman heights; to the east, foothills start climbing to the Yalta Mountains; along the south runs a narrow chain of hills cutting off the plain from the sea, and to the west rises the Khersonese Upland of evil destiny, overlooking Sebastopol, where the allies were yet to suffer their long-drawn-out agony.

By the time Raglan had reached the Tractir Bridge it was getting dark and he decided that his own army should bivouack there on the plain beside the river, where at least the water-bottles could be filled. Behind the leading columns, and up the road over the pass, stretched the wagon trains which halted where they stood and made shift for the night. The head of the French column, which had followed the British on the march, only reached Mackenzie's Farm that night; in fact it was not until three in the morning that the rearguard had bivouacked there. So the allies spent the night in two knots—one at the Tractir Bridge and one at Mackenzie's Farm—with a thin string tying them together, drawn out along the road. It would not have been a major undertaking for the enemy to cut the string and surround each of the knots in detail, for a long line of bivouack fires advertised to the Russians, had they been interested, the vulnerable position of the allied armies. It is doubtful if, had Raglan tried, he could have manœuvred the armies into a more perilous position. Part of the British Fourth Division had again been left behind, this time to help in returning the sick men, of whom there was still a formidable number, from the Belbek to the Katcha. Even so the division could not be considered a line of communication as it was completely detached from the army columns which had set off on the march, and it was ordered to follow and catch up the armies on the following day. In the actual event, by midday the next day the division was still on the Katcha, almost two days' march from the rest of the British army; and the tactical purpose of its detachment was still a trifle obscure.

That night, at his headquarters in the post house beside the Tractir Bridge, Raglan decided that he would make for Balaclava, the little land-locked harbour indenting the south coast of the peninsula. It is apparent that the decision had not been made before, and that the actual destination of the armies when they set off on the flank march had not been determined, for Kinglake describes how during the night a Lieutenant Maxse of the *Agamemnon*—which was lying off the mouth of the Katcha—was sent by Admiral Lyons all the way to Raglan's headquarters to find out what the general intended. The messenger rode fifteen miles each way through the night, over the steppe between the Katcha and the Belbek, up the woodland road to Mackenzie's Farm, down the pass to the Tractir Bridge, and all the way back again. As Kinglake says, "The need for resorting to a venture like this will help perhaps to disclose the hazardous character of the Flank March." Maxse took back with him a vague report of what Raglan intended to do, and a request to Lyons to move the fleets round to the south of the peninsula to assist him in doing it.

Next morning Raglan, still riding in the van of his armies, followed the road to the south-west, and where it entered the coastal chain of hills, he came to a village called Kadikoi. In time, the British army and Kadikoi were to achieve an unhappy mutual familiarity. Here the villagers told him that he would come to Balaclava town just round the corner of the hill and that it was undefended—as it certainly was by the Russians. Raglan rode over the shallow pass, and on the other side he found a little mountain stream which opened out into a sizeable lake. The lake was enclosed by hills and stretched out lengthwise before him, three-quarters of a mile long but not more than three hundred yards across. This was Balaclava harbour, for although he could not see it, there was an inlet from the sea through the hills at the other end. During the next year, the whole of Britain's war effort was to be poured into this harbour, although at first sight it looked inadequate enough, and so in actual truth it was.

Nor, as Raglan looked down the lake, enclosed in bare, stony hills, could he have had any idea of the tragic sum in humanity that was to come and go through this little port, and of the vast materials of war that were to be carried by sweat and blood through the gap in the hills in which he was now standing. Over the next twelve months men in their tens of thousands would pass through on their way to battle and death, or would be carried back over the path, shattered by wounds or desperately ill, and certainly disillusioned. As it was, to Raglan and his staff, the harbour looked disappointing, as if it could hardly accommodate a ship of any draught.

On the hillside overlooking the water to his left he could see the cluster of shacks that made up Balaclava town, the lines of unpretentious houses stepped one above the other on the slope; and ahead, closing the harbour from any apparent outlet to the sea, rose that bleak hill which, as we have already seen, was topped by a line of ruined Genoese forts. As he looked, a burst of smoke erupted from the topmost fort and a missile of some sort splashed into the water in front of him.

So after all there was some token resistance to his coming, despite what the villagers of Kadikoi had promised. But it was nothing more than a token, for the commander of the town, who called himself Colonel Monto, had assumed that as Raglan had not sent him a summons to surrender he was in duty bound to fire off a round or two. Having satisfied honour, Colonel Monto and a dozen of Balaclava's citizens, who were all Greeks, surrendered gladly, and the British army moved in to Balaclava. At the same moment, by a miraculous and quite unplanned piece of timing, the first vessel of the British fleet edged her way cautiously in through the dog-leg of the entrance and started taking soundings.

By the time the French army at the rear of the column had crossed the plain and had begun to advance over the pass into Balaclava, the town and its environs had become a little crowded. The normal population was less than a hundred and now that twenty-five thousand British soldiers had moved in, trampling down the gardens and helping themselves to the grapes in the vineyards, any small charm the village might have possessed had become illusory, and conditions, even for massed soldiery, had become uncomfortable. As the day went on and the first ships came into the harbour it became apparent that the town's potential as a port would be somewhat limited despite the fact that the water proved deep enough for the largest British vessel, and it was clear that the British and the French could not both be accommodated in Balaclava as had been the fond intention of the generals.

That morning, St. Arnaud had been forced to accept the inevitable and to hand over his command officially to Canrobert. The Marshal had held on to the last with all the obstinate tenacity of his nature, but now he was desperately ill and they carried him back, in the Russian carriage which he had appropriated in Eupatoria, along the tortuous road to the Katcha while it was still open. Here, on the next day, the twenty-seventh, he was carried aboard the *Berthelot* and that afternoon he died at sea.

On assuming command Canrobert's first task, which he accomplished with some finesse, was to agree with Raglan what relative positions the two allied armies were to take up before Sebastopol. It was still fondly believed that the assault on Sebastopol when once launched would be successfully accomplished in a few hours, but meanwhile it was recognized that some purposeful disposition of the attacking forces would still have to be considered. There had been some understanding when the allies first landed on the Crimea that the French army, for a reason which it is difficult to fathom, was entitled to precedence and should therefore have the honour of holding the right of the line in accordance with tradition. What the grounds were on which the precedence was based is uncertain. Previous history might have suggested that the British had the honour. However, it could have been based on the superiority in numbers that the French enjoyed, but more probably it was really a reflection of Marshal St. Arnaud's preoccupation with the seniority of his rank over a mere general. So during the advance on Sebastopol from the north the French had taken the right of the line, along the coast, and had enjoyed protection on both flanks, while the British army had taken the exposed position on the left.

Now the armies were to do an about-turn, to approach Sebastopol from the south, and as any drill sergeant knows an about-turn has the disconcerting effect of reversing the flanks. If the French were to change places with the British so that they might retain the place of honour on the right they would find themselves in the now unfamiliar position of holding a flank open to possible attack, and with a long gap between themselves and their supporting fleet. It was not a position that a French general would covet and Canrobert generously conceded the place of honour to the British; however, he made it clear that he was conferring a favour and that he had been compelled to accept a position which had come about only because the British had occupied Balaclava arbitrarily and it was now too late to remedy what had been done. For, whichever army rested on Balaclava would have to take the right of a line assaulting Sebastopol from the south. But Canrobert knew that there were two good bays between Cape Kherson and Sebastopol—which Raglan had overlooked on his reconnaissance, although both Colonel Macintosh and Mr. Oliphant had been sharp enough to spot them—and he was more than content to move his army to the plain above these bays, where at the same time it would overlook Sebastopol, rather than suffer the obvious disorder which was bound to arise in the overcrowded little harbour at Balaclava.

So, without any advance planning and with no thought whatsoever about what would be called the logistics of the situation to-day, the destinies of the two armies were decided. The French army, although it was to suffer its share of the miseries of the coming winter, was established conveniently, if not comfortably, on the Khersonese Upland close to the Kamietsh and Kamsatch bays, both of which proved to be roomy, sheltered harbours from which a comparatively easy road climbed up to the plateau above. The British had marched into and appropriated Balaclava almost thankfully, and with a sense of achievement, but without any thought given to what its possession implied in terms of its strategic position in relation to Sebastopol—which was after all the object of the exercise.

II

THE only Russian soldiers now in Sebastopol were three thousand men who had lost their way and had become detached from Menshikov's column. Not even the Russians had maps of the Crimea, and this regiment, led by a General Moller, found itself back in the town after marching all day, and the general had accepted the inevitable and established an independent military command. In fact, now that the commander-in-chief had deserted, there were three separate commands in the town and no overall control: General Moller and his soldiers, Admiral Korniloff with his sailors on the north side of the harbour, and Vice-Admiral Nachimoff in the main town. The admirals with their garrisons of seamen were plainly out of their element. Nachimoff, who had commanded the squadron that had attacked Sinop so confidently, had pleaded with Menshikov to be relieved of the responsibility of commanding in Sebastopol town because he was not the sort who relished an undertaking without being sure of its success. He had even offered to serve under a junior—and thereby avoid responsibility for the defeat that he knew impended—but Menshikov had ungraciously refused to accept this well-intentioned sacrifice. Korniloff, on the north side, was equally convinced of imminent disaster, but he was less prone to despair and he faced the inevitable with commendable fortitude.

There was a fourth person of rank in the town, a Colonel de Todleben, who had been invited quite informally by Prince Gortchakoff, without any reference to Menshikov, to come and inspect the defences. Todleben was an engineer and, apparently, an exception among engineers, for as Kinglake has so amiably put it, "No one could imagine that his power of doing the right thing at the right time had been at all warped by long study of

178

the engineering art." Todleben was a mere thirty-seven but his youthful energy failed to impress the sexagenarian Menshikov, particularly as his invitation to the town by one of Menshikov's subordinates necessarily implied a lack of confidence in the great man himself. When Todleben had first come to Sebastopol four weeks earlier, in August, Menshikov had shown an understandable resentment of his presence and had declared himself to be quite satisfied that intricate land defences of Sebastopol were unnecessary as the allies would never be so foolish as to land on the Crimea. That they might attack from the sea he was prepared to concede, but Todleben was an army engineer with a fashionable predilection for saps and dynamite, which could hardly offer an effective defence against naval attack. And in any case the forts at the harbour entrance were adequately strong, for when Sebastopol had been established as the Russian naval dockyard and arsenal in the Black Sea a great deal of attention had been given to the seaward defences. However, Todleben was not easily put off and he produced grandiose plans for land fortifications round the town. Menshikov, driven on to the defensive himself, had declared that there was no money for their construction and had beseeched the Tsar to recall this intrusive sapper. However, while the recall was awaited the allies had surprised Menshikov by landing on the peninsula and he was now showing an unfamiliar eagerness to make full use of Todleben's undoubted ability. It was Todleben who had set up the battery that commanded the approach from the Belbek, which had finally scared off St. Arnaud from the northern assault even before guns had been mounted in it; but even so, after the war Todleben was honest enough to say that at the time he had believed Sebastopol to be utterly indefensible from the north despite the hurried work he had put into its fortifications.

However, whatever may have been Todleben's effect on Menshikov, it had always been far more favourable on Admiral Korniloff, and it was mainly due to the trustful partnership that grew up between these two that Sebastopol did in the end put up such a sustained defence. Korniloff was later to withdraw from the north side and to bring most of his sailors into the town itself. When he did so he took overall command of all the forces now in Sebastopol, with the full agreement of Nachimoff and Moller who were only too happy to surrender their share of the responsibility. For on September 25th an officer, looking casually out of the top window of the naval library, had seen a procession of redcoats moving across a clearing in the woodlands on the high ground to the east of the town; and as the procession continued all day, and could even be discerned as a column of shadowy figures still passing along late in the evening, it was not hard to deduce that at any rate a considerable portion of the allied armies was moving round to the south of the town. The defenders, reduced in number as they were—there were perhaps sixteen thousand men in Sebastopol now, with the embarrassing addition of nearly ten thousand civilians—took considerable heart from what had been seen from the library window as they were sure that they stood a much better chance of successfully resisting an assault from the south, and had some reason to be grateful to the allies for their accommodating move. Meanwhile nothing had been heard of Menshikov and his thirty thousand soldiers.

Under the insistent drive of Korniloff and Todleben the Russians in Sebastopol now set about strengthening the defences of the town. In the first days after the allies had been seen passing round to the south an assault was constantly expected and everybody, sailors, soldiers and civilians, worked day and night deepening ditches, raising parapets, stripping guns from the ships and carting them clumsily to the batteries. For a while the sense of having been deserted by the commander-in-chief and the army was dispelled because Korniloff was able to persuade them that Menshikov's purpose in taking the soldiers from the town was so that they could fall on the enemy's flank, although he himself was not too sanguine that the idea had even occurred to his commander-in-chief. However, this imaginative fiction was endorsed when one of Menshikov's officers arrived in Sebastopol on the night of the twenty-seventh, three days after the army had marched out and incidentally the first contact which anybody in the town had since had with it. The officer claimed with a wealth of circumstantial detail that he had just made a desperate passage through the enemy lines on the hills to the east—away from which the allies had, of course, moved south a couple of days before. He reported that Menshikov had been reinforced by ten thousand men from Bulgaria, which happened to be true, and that the Russian army was about to attack the allies on their flank in those very regions through which he, the officer, had made his way so perilously that night—which was merely fanciful. To strengthen the garrison's morale Korniloff took the officer round the defences and made him repeat in everybody's hearing Menshikov's announcement of his intention to attack the enemy, to which the Admiral added the fitting qualification, "May the Lord bless and fortify us!"

Next day, on the twenty-eighth, Menshikov's army did appear —due north of Sebastopol. During the morning he had marched out of Bakshiserai and had struck boldly across country to the valley of the Belbek, which, as any Tartar goat-herd could have told him, the allies had evacuated four days before. Surprised to find the valley so empty he had been at pains to deploy his army and advance southward to Sebastopol, convinced that he had trapped his enemy between the Belbek and the north side of the harbour. The people in the city were somewhat intrigued to see Russian troops advancing towards them cautiously over the hills, stalking an enemy who had now moved round to the other side of the town. By the time Menshikov reached the Star Fort it was becoming evident even to him that no enemy faced him, so he advanced no farther. Korniloff crossed the harbour to meet him, to find that Menshikov had apparently decided that his role was still not concerned with defending Sebastopol, for he announced that he was about to march his army off again. Korniloff's comment on this new announcement was, "Then good-bye to Sebastopol."

The allies, on their part, were hardly more resolute in their intentions and were behaving with characteristic inertia and indecision. They had sorted out their relative positions on the Upland and it was reasonable to suppose that their next undertaking would be an assault on the town which they had come so far to capture. The difficulty was, of course, that nobody had given any thought to how the final assault was to be made; the business of moving the armies round to the south side had occupied the whole attention of the commanders for some days and had provided yet one more happy opportunity to delay the need for planning the actual attack. Inevitably there now arose a new division of opinion on how this was to be done. Raglan was quite ready to send his men in to take the town at the point of the bayonet although he had not felt it necessary to work out any tactical details of how this could be accomplished. He was encouraged by the impetuosity of Sir Edmund Lyons who had brought his ship, the *Agamemnon*, right into the crowded waters of Balaclava harbour and was identifying himself far more closely with the headquarters of the army than with Admiral Dundas, his own commander-in-chief. Quite openly Lyons declared Dundas to be uninspired and wanting in initiative and he had even conveyed this opinion to Whitehall. The day after the battle on the Alma, when Lyons had still been off the west coast, Dundas had ordered him to take all the steamships to sea to follow seven Russian ships which an imaginative Turkish admiral had declared he had seen sailing off towards Odessa—this was before the entrance to Sebastopol had been blockaded. Lyons had replied, a little insubordinately, that the story was merely fanciful and that Dundas ought to know better than to rely on reports from a Turkish admiral, and had inferred, not even indirectly, that Dundas had not been watching the entrance to the harbour carefully with his own ships—which for weeks had been his self-appointed role. Lyons proved to be right about the imaginative powers of the Turkish admiral; it was clear that not a single Russian ship had left the harbour, but this revelation had not helped to restore more seemly relations between the British naval commander-in-chief and his second in command, and now Dundas was still lying with most of his fleet off the Katcha, whence the seat of war had been entirely removed, while Lyons was more actively engaged in Balaclava in conferences with the soldiers.

In the British army the opinion as to whether or not an infantry assault on Sebastopol could be successful was conspicuously divided. Sir George Cathcart, who commanded the Fourth Division and had so far missed all the actions when he had been left behind at Old Fort and later on the Katcha, had now appeared with his division on the heights above the town. He could see a convenient road running into the town through a quiet garden suburb and as the crusading spirit in his division had not yet been dulled by any fighting he declared, "I could walk into it with scarcely the loss of a man." He wanted his troops to leave behind any cumbersome equipment which they normally carried and to run into the town an hour before daybreak, where they would find the enemy in no state to oppose them, for as he explained, "We can see the people walking about the streets in great consternation." He was sure, and he was probably right, that at that stage, before the negligible garrison had been reinforced, Russian resistance to a determined attack would have been but perfunctory. When Raglan turned down his proposal for an immediate attack and explained that it had been decided that the town was first to be bombarded and that for that purpose the siege trains were to be landed from the fleets, Cathcart said, "Land the siege trains! But, my dear Lord Raglan, what the devil is there to knock down?"

For he was perfectly right. There was nothing to knock down of any consequence. Korniloff and Todleben were driving the garrison with some effect to throw up earthworks, but at that stage the vaunted defences on the south side of the great fortress of Sebastopol, with the exception of one stone tower on a hill called the Malakoff, were constructed exclusively of mud, and because the summer weather was still lingering the mud was, at the time, dry and crumbling. When the allies first stood on the Upland and looked down on to the town, before the end of September, the defences were pitiful, and Korniloff and Todleben both knew it—as also did Sir George Carthcart. By the time the allies started their great bombardment on October 17th, more than three weeks later, the defences had certainly been improved but they were still hardly formidable.

For although there were two schools of thought in the British staff, one advocating immediate assault and the other preferring to see the defences first reduced by a devastating cannonade, there was no such equivocation among the French. Canrobert and his generals were sure of what they intended to do, and that was not to attack. They wasted no time or effort in discussing the matter with Raglan, they merely informed him of their intention, and then started to unload their siege guns from their ships in the spacious waters of Kamiesk and Kazatch Bays. To the great relief of Sir John Burgoyne, whose mind had run on siege works and first parallels since the stimulating days at Torres Vedras forty-five years before, the British had now no option but to follow suit although the facilities in Balaclava harbour for unloading heavy equipment were hardly comparable with those enjoyed by the French. Lyons agreed to supplement the siege guns with guns from his ships, mainly because this would give the Navy an excuse to land a brigade to man them, for the sailors were determined to take part in any fighting that offered. So there was dragged on to the Upland at no small expenditure of manual effort a formidable array of British and French artillery to batter down the earthen ramparts of Sebastopol. Fortunately the weather was still delightful; the tail-end of the summer lingered on—it was October now, but the sun was still bright and the nights were still warm, and the promise of a pleasant campaign was still being fulfilled, and the first of the officers' ladies had landed with their horses to complete the happy holiday illusion. However, the ships' guns had to be dragged seven miles over the Balaclava pass on those little wooden wheels that may have made them mobile enough on the smooth decks of a man-o'-war but were hardly designed to trundle over stony, rutted roads, although fortunately the Crimean mud and all that it portended had not yet appeared.

On October 7th Raglan assembled his divisional generals at the headquarters he had set up at the top of the pass, where the road from Balaclava emerged on to the Upland, and announced politely that he hoped they would undertake to advance their infantry positions closer to the town. It was typical of his way of conducting war that the announcement conveyed a request and not an order. The announcement was a signal for a robust display of what Field-Marshal Montgomery has more lately termed "bellyaching"—which he has defined as commanders actively putting forward unsound reasons for not doing what they are told. Montgomery was to complain of this phenomenon in the British Army a full hundred years later. Now, Sir George Brown was the most vehement exponent of the art and he was loyally supported by his old comrade of the Peninsula War, Sir John

Burgoyne. Burgoyne had estimated that the allied casualties, if an assault were to be made before a bombardment was commenced, would be all of five hundred, and this depressing forecast had imposed a popular reluctance among the higher ranks to get any nearer to the town than could be helped—and so, instead of an immediate attack which would have stood an excellent chance of success but which was regarded as too costly in lives, the capture of the town was to be undertaken by a siege, which was to take a year, and during which the British army alone was to lose men by their tens of thousands.

So the bellyachers won and the allied commanders made the Russians a present of three whole weeks of providential respite of which Korniloff and Todleben made good use of every minute, day and night. They even persuaded Menshikov to consider the demands of the town's defence for once, and by October 6th he had graciously consented to send twenty-five thousand of his soldiers back to Sebastopol although he carefully kept the main body of his army clear of the town. At the beginning of the month Sir George Cathcart's division might well have run in before breakfast and scattered the defenders; now, an allied attack would have to face nearly forty thousand fighting men.

Nor were the allies, in reality, in any position to conduct a proper siege, which was what the use of siege trains must surely have implied. If a town is to be besieged effectively the first essential is to invest it by cutting off all access and egress, but during the so-called siege of Sebastopol which was to last for nearly a year the Russians came and went throughout at will, and brought into the town reinforcements and supplies without any hindrance by the allies; they had merely to cross the harbour to the north side and the whole country was open to them. Most convenient of all, they were free to remove the non-combatants and wounded and thereby relieve themselves of one of the most difficult problems of an invested fortress.

However, by October 17th the British and French were both satisfied that their preparations for a bombardment were complete. In yet another of his authoritative predictions Sir John Burgoyne had declared the night before that Sebastopol would fall within forty-eight hours. It must be admitted that considerable efforts had been made to achieve this desirable end and Sir John had had much to do with them. If they had achieved only the slightest degree of success he might have taken a conspicuous share of the credit.

The Khersonese Upland on which the allies had encamped, five hundred feet above the sea and the town, stretches for some eight miles east and west, and for some six miles north and south at its widest point. Along the south coast the shore-line rises sharply in steep cliffs, and these cliffs swing inland and run almost as steeply along the eastern edge of the Upland where it drops to the Tchernaya valley. Thus the Upland is a high plateau bounded on the west and south by cliffs falling to the sea, and on the east by an escarpment dropping to the river valley. To the north, towards Sebastopol, the ground first rises slightly even higher than the main plateau and then falls away in a series of rolling foothills to the town and the harbour at their feet. Indenting into the plateau, southward from the harbour, are numbers of ravines, gouged deeply into the rising hills and, at their southern ends, climbing reluctantly to the heights. Southward from the inner Sebastopol harbour—that creek which branches off from the main harbour reach—run two deep and precipitous ravines. The first, the westernmost, itself divides into two as it cuts into the hills, and one branch was called the Great Ravine while the other came to be known to the allies as the Valley of the Shadow of Death— although it was not along here that the Light Brigade made their charge despite Tennyson's near allusion. Along the trough of the second ravine rising from the inner harbour ran what was known as the Woronzoff Road, up which Menshikov had marched his army when he had deserted Sebastopol. The road climbed on to the Upland and then dropped down to cross the Tchernaya valley, meeting the road from Bakshiserai near the Tractir Bridge. Two more gorges, farther east, rose from the level of the harbour and cut their way into the Upland. Like all these features they were given names by the British—these last two were the Dock Ravine and the Careenage Ravine; and still farther to their east the gorge of the Tchernaya river cut right through the hills into the valley, separating the Upland from the heights on which stood Mackenzie's Farm.

The allies made their camps on the open plateau on the Upland —the French between the Great Ravine and the sea, and the British on their right—on the level ground south of the ridges that overlooked the town. With the summer weather still persisting, the grass dry and springy, and tents at last arriving, the conditions for encamping were ideal. But if the British moved forward on to the ridges they were restricted in their lateral movements east and west by the deep ravines. At least this had been the excuse given by the divisional commanders when they had bellyached against Raglan's suggestion that they should move their men forward from the comfortable position that they had taken up. Now, after three weeks of arduous and well-advertised preparation the French had mounted fifty-three guns across their position, which they named Mount Rodolph; while, with equal unconcern about revealing their intentions, the British had set up two tremendous batteries with seventy-three guns in all—one which stretched from the Valley of the Shadow of Death to the Woronzoff Road and was known as Chapman's Battery or the English Left Attack, and the other running from the Woronzoff Road to the Dock Ravine known as Gordon's Battery or the English Right Attack. In the accepted manner of siege warfare, the ground in front of each Attack was traversed by parallels, which in our day we would merely call trenches. Again the French had shown the wisdom of their choice when they had taken the left of the line, for their ground was soft while that across which the wretched British soldiers made praiseworthy efforts to dig their parallels was but a thin layer of soil on top of solid rock.

The French and British lines, mounting a hundred and twenty-six guns—a fantastic weight of artillery attack for those days— formed an arc of no small menace round Sebastopol. Their main targets were two apparent strongholds in the unbroken line of earthen defences which the Russians, now that they had had such a gratuitous opportunity, had thrown up all round the southern perimeter of the town; one of these targets was called the Flagstaff Bastion, and the other the Redan.* Round the Flagstaff Bastion and the Redan strong batteries had been set up, and although they had no masonry to protect them the positions had

* See map, p. 268.

been turned into creditable imitations of forts. The Russians, too, had been busy stripping their ships of many guns, and by the time the bombardment opened they had nearly as many pieces in position as the allies, a state of affairs which was apt to cancel out all the British and French preparations.

The allied plan, such as it was, was to reduce these two strongholds by a devastating bombardment of round shot and shells lasting most of the day, after which, provided that the cannonade had been effective enough, the infantry would storm the town in the late afternoon. The conception of the attack was so straightforward that, as usual, it occurred to nobody that it might be necessary to indulge in any detailed planning. It was not even thought necessary to lay down—and it was certainly never understood between the gunners and the infantry, nor was it agreed with the French—what time the barrage would cease and the troops would go in.

To a world that has been regaled with stories of the barrages on the Somme and before El Alamein, the details of the bombardment of Sebastopol on October 17th, 1854, must necessarily sound puny. At the time it was of a weight such as had never been known or even conceived before. In prospect it had suggested that little human life would be able to survive within its radius. In actual effect eleven hundred Russians were killed or wounded—among them the stout-hearted Admiral Korniloff—a heavy enough casualty list in those days, particularly as there were still as many round shot among the projectiles as explosive shells. During the first part of the nineteenth century the percussion fuse had been invented and even the British Army had begun to use it, so that shells that burst on impact were beginning to take their toll, but the radius of their blast was comparatively limited and they had little incendiary effect. Most of the casualties were caused by direct hits from cannon balls—sometimes first made red hot—which could be just as lethal as high explosive if their victims happened to be standing in their line of flight.

Other than killing eleven hundred Russians the bombardment effected nothing and brought the allies no nearer to the capture of Sebastopol. The cannonade opened at half-past six in the morning and during the day the allied batteries on the Upland were to fire nearly nine thousand projectiles and the Russians were to reply with twenty thousand; although the allied casualties amounted to less than two hundred, mainly because most of their troops were able to keep back on the plateau out of range of the Russian guns. Even so the price of two hundred casualties with no effect might well suffer by comparison with Sir John Burgoyne's estimate of five hundred and the capture of Sebastopol. The main reason for the more generous expenditure of shot by the Russians was that most of the men in the batteries were sailors who had been brought up to believe that the only effective gun practice was a broadside. They lined their guns up as if on deck and fired them all off together with true naval exuberance. At half-past ten they scored a direct hit on the magazine on Mount Rodolph and the resultant explosion killed fifty Frenchmen and tended to discourage the French gunners. Not many minutes later a small ammunition caisson blew up close by and the effect was devastating. Nobody was killed but the succession of explosions in the French battery had become so unnerving that General Canrobert, who was of a timid disposition himself as his behaviour on the Alma had proved, asked the French artillery commander if he would not care to withdraw his men and the commander, grateful for the opportunity, acted on the suggestion with some alacrity. Thus ended the French contribution to the first allied attack on Sebastopol.

The British batteries kept on firing well into the afternoon and some heroic work was done serving the guns under the tremendous enemy fire, until soon after three o'clock they too scored a lucky hit on an ammunition dump in the Redan, killing a hundred Russians and blowing up most of the battery. Unlike the French, the Russians were not in the fortunate position of being able to give up the fight at will, but with no guns to protect them the surviving defenders in that part of the line were obliged to fall back, leaving an inviting breach in the defences and a way open into the town. But it would have been expecting overmuch of the allied command to grasp such a tactical opportunity. In fact for some hours now it had been agreed between Raglan and Canrobert that, as the French batteries had been forced to cease firing comparatively early, the grand strategy of the day had been dislocated beyond recovery and that the second half of the programme, the launching of infantry attacks at an unspecified hour, must necessarily fall away. So thus, with the destruction of the Redan and its invitation to further success, the British contribution to the land attack on Sebastopol ended too.

From the sea the allied navies had made a contribution to the day's futility which was just as inept, at any rate in its conception. The original suggestion that the fleets should share in the armies' triumph had obviously come from Lyons. He proposed, on his own initiative, that the ships should start bombarding the forts at the entrance to Sebastopol harbour at the same time as the barrage was to open on land, and he said to Raglan, "We shall hear each other at half-past six in the morning and I am not without hopes of our seeing each other in the course of the day in Sebastopol." Like the armies, the fleets were expected merely to force an entry to Sebastopol by bombardment; no subtleties were considered necessary.

Dundas, of course, was the naval commander-in-chief, but he and Raglan never met to discuss this combined action which was to be of some importance in the prosecution of the war, and Dundas is on record as having agreed to participate only with a good deal of reluctance. On October 14th he did discuss the proposal with the French admiral, and Hamelin agreed that the fleets should sail along the coast, past the forts, firing as they went. There was, of course, no suggestion of entering the harbour because of the line of sunken blockships, and how Lyons expected to effect his meeting with Raglan is a little obscure. Both navies were short of ammunition so the admirals had to ask the generals to choose whether they would prefer the ships to start firing when the land bombardment opened in the morning, or as the infantry attack went in in the afternoon—because it was certain that their fire could not be sustained all day. To make such a positive decision was beyond the generals' capacity and they replied, characteristically, that they would like the fleets to fire half their ammunition during the bombardment and the other half at the time of the attack. No time, of course, was specified as to when the infantry would start the attack, but the signal for the fleet's second instalment would be the cessation of fire by the land batteries. As, in the event, the French batteries, which were those nearest to the coast, ceased fire at half-past ten when their magazine blew up, the sailors enjoyed the illusion for some hours that the soldiers were bravely storming Sebastopol. The illusion began to wear thin when it became obvious that whatever might have happened in the town it was having no effect at all on the ability of the forts to sustain an intimidating fire.

However, on the day before the bombardment Hamelin had told Dundas—with characteristic French disregard for any agreement reached with their allies—that he had no intention of starting firing before ten o'clock in the morning anyway, and Dundas who was worried about his own ammunition had concurred in this new proposal with some relief. Nobody had bothered to mention to the generals that the supporting fire which they had been promised from the fleets at half-past six, and which presumably they regarded as an integral part of their strategy, was not to materialize, but in the context of haphazard planning the omission was hardly remarkable. Dundas and Hamelin now agreed that their two fleets would sail from the Katcha, where they were still lying, at eight o'clock. They would form into line and pass across the harbour mouth, and to maintain station the sailing ships would be propelled by steamers lashed alongside their seaward beam. The weather was still obligingly calm, and although the actual object of the exercise was nebulous the prospects of a successful manœuvre were promising.

But it would have been disappointingly out of character for the French actually to play their part in what had been agreed on, and at seven o'clock on the morning of the seventeenth Hamelin came aboard the *Britannia* to announce to Dundas that he would not be taking part in the procession as planned and that he intended to anchor his ships off the harbour mouth so that they would fire at the forts only when stationary. He explained that orders for this unorthodox naval manœuvre had come from Canrobert—to whom, as commander-in-chief of all the French forces, Hamelin was answerable. Canrobert was now quite inaccessible and it was therefore useless for Dundas to start arguing with Hamelin, who announced categorically that either he anchored or he took no part in the operation at all. It was clear to Dundas that there would be little to gain by sailing his own ships across the harbour mouth in order to bring his guns to bear on the forts if a line of French ships had already anchored there; and so he had no option but to fall in with the new French plan and to order his ships to anchor also in an extension of the proposed French line, so that they would take their place, too, as invitingly fixed targets for the guns of the Russian forts. Hamelin had cunningly chosen, for the position of his ships, the southern half of the harbour entrance, across which he proposed to anchor them in a wide arc. Here the water was comparatively deep and his ships could come within attacking range of Fort Alexander without any danger of grounding. Across the northern half of the entrance the shore shoaled gradually and ships standing in close enough to bombard Fort Constantine—which Hamelin had gratuitously left for the attentions of the British—would have to operate in dangerously shallow water. But unless Dundas were to withdraw from the project altogether—and that would be more than his reputation at Whitehall could withstand, for he had already shown an unfashionable lack of enthusiasm for the whole idea of invasion—he had no alternative but to take the northern station.

The forts which the allied fleets proposed rather rashly to bombard were very different in substance from the landward defences of Sebastopol. They had been built, not altogether ineffectually, to withstand just that sort of attack which they were now to experience. Their walls, six feet thick, were of stone and their vaulted roofs were covered by beds of earth twelve feet deep. There was nothing in the ships' lockers that could hope to have any effect on them. Fort Constantine mounted ninety-seven guns and Fort Alexander, which the French had chosen as their target, only fifty-six. All the guns in these two forts were casemated, and the likelihood of their being disturbed except by lucky shots through their embrasures was comfortably remote. The French certainly had another target to deal with, the Quarantine Fort on the south side of the harbour entrance, which had a power of considerable retaliation. This fort had been built on a conveniently star-shaped promontory jutting out into the bay and it actually mounted fifty-eight guns, although only a

The valley is like a deep box enclosed by hills; looking down on Balaclava plain.

The British soldier of those days was not dressed for paddling; a private in full marching order.

sixth of these could be brought to bear on any one target. Also, all its guns were in the open, firing over the parapet on the flat top of the fort—there were no lower galleries—so that by effective fire an attacking fleet could, in this instance, well discourage the gunners.

Hamelin must have felt that something dramatic was expected of him, and although his countrymen would hardly be likely to appreciate a Nelsonian touch, it was obvious where the inspiration came from when he led his ships to their stations in the line flying the signal, "La France vous regarde". Lyons, when he brought the *Agamemnon* round from Balaclava and learnt what the role of the British fleet was expected to be, prayed that his own countrymen would certainly not be looking. But he managed to persuade Dundas to allow him to detach a small squadron of steamships and lead them as close under the guns of Fort Constantine as the shoal would allow. A few hundred yards north of the fort, round the headland of Cape Constantine, the shoal receded towards the shore and Lyons was confident that he could bring his ships along, under the protection of the cliffs, and enfilade the fort. Dundas gave the permission, probably because it had already come to his ears that the Secretary of State for War, the Duke of Newcastle, was listening to reports from Lyons of the commander-in-chief's general attitude of timidity. His first reaction had certainly been lukewarm, for although conceding to Lyons that he should take his squadron inshore, he had bade him "seek a great victory but only by a path of safety," which was a little sophistical. However, later, he was to redeem the conscience of the Navy by spontaneously signalling to Lyons, as the squadron was feeling its way, at first a little warily, between the line of anchored British ships and the shore, "Proceed and attack the batteries." There was no equivocation about this, and Lyons, the diplomat turned buccaneer, for once had full licence with which to exploit his thirst for action.

The inshore squadron made a gallant attack on the virtually impregnable Fort Constantine, but like many another gallantry on that day it was entirely wasted for all the effect it had on the war. Five steamships went in, first the *Agamemnon*, then the *Sanspareil*, the *London*, the *Arethusa*—she who had played so sportively with the batteries at Odessa—and the *Albion*. The last three named were to be badly damaged in the action, and to suffer a number of casualties. Later the great three-decker line-of-battle sailing ships, the *Queen*, the *Rodney* and the *Bellerophon*, stood in to add their weight of guns, and the *Rodney* went aground. By ten-past five in the afternoon, after nearly seven hours of action, Lyons was compelled to withdraw his squadron; Dundas ceased fire at half-past five and his fleet weighed anchor. The *Rodney* was towed off the shoal by a steamer at half-past six. The French line had been breaking up for some hours and each ship had retired independently.

The naval contribution to the day's score of projectiles hurled on Sebastopol was seven thousand. Their effect, according to Kinglake, was that a hundred and thirty eight Russians were either "killed, wounded or bruised". The effect on the stone forts was, of course, negligible. The allies suffered five hundred and twenty casualties on their ships—a comparison with the Russian losses which offered yet another commentary on the estimated cost of an assault which might have been made successfully three weeks before, but which the British generals had dared not face.

After October 17th even Sir Edmund Lyons's faith in aggressive action against the forts was shaken, and the feeling of disillusion among the allies generally was hardly softened when the mail arrived from England on the very next day with *The Times* announcement that Sebastopol had fallen.

12

OBVIOUSLY the first responsibility of the British high command was to protect the army's life-line through Balaclava harbour. The main British strength of some twenty-five thousand men was encamped on the Upland, and to guard the vital flank—that living artery that was the road through Kadikoi to the harbour—Raglan had given Sir Colin Campbell, to whom he had delegated the defence of Balaclava, five hundred Highlanders of the 93rd Regiment—to-day the Argyll and Sutherland Highlanders—a thousand or so Turks, in whom the commander-in-chief had expressed his complete lack of confidence, and a hundred invalids. The cavalry division was certainly encamped down on the plain of Balaclava, with Colonel Maude's single field battery, but despite the pretensions of the cavalry themselves it was not usually accepted that without the help of other arms fifteen hundred horsemen could make a successful stand against all possible comers. For it was obvious that the most effective move the Russians could now make would be to cut off Balaclava harbour from the British and this idea had even occurred to Prince Menshikov. That he would probably launch a full-scale attack on Balaclava was elementary, and indeed he was preparing to do just that by assembling a force of twenty-five thousand men —twenty-five battalions of infantry, thirty-four squadrons of cavalry and seventy-eight guns—among the hills on the eastern edge of the Balaclava plain.

Although the plain, to which we have referred hitherto as the valley of the Tchernaya, is like the bottom of a box with deep sides, four or five miles square, there is a considerable wide, but not very high, ridge—what the English would call a hog's back— running across it east and west, and along this ran the Woronzoff Road. The British named the ridge the Causeway Heights. The name Woronzoff Road arose because it led from Sebastopol to the estates near Yalta, in the mountains, of the Woronzoff family which had boasted two Russian imperial chancellors. At the time of the Crimean War the youngest Woronzoff, now aged seventy-two, who had been a soldier and had fought with conspicuous success against Napoleon, was living there in retirement and some of his old memories must have been sadly disturbed as he listened to the French guns bombarding Sebastopol.

North of the Causeway Heights is another cluster of low hills known as the Fedioukine Hills, so that between these and the Heights there is a depression, which the allies named the North Valley. Between the Heights and the coastal hills shutting in Balaclava harbour is another depression, the South Valley. Raglan had chosen the Causeway Heights as the first line of defence of Balaclava and along them the British dug four so-called redoubts, spread over a distance of two miles, each of which would have given little protection to a donkey. Into each they sent a hundred wretched Turkish soldiers with a couple of old naval twelve-pounders, rejected by the army for the assault on Sebastopol—these to halt the oncome of a whole Russian army. South of the ridge, that is to say on the Balaclava side, rose a round hillock, slightly higher, which was honoured by the name of Canrobert Hill, and on here a whole Turkish battalion was posted with the generous armament, in this instance, of three of the twelve-pounders. Canrobert Hill was overlooked by another, higher hill to the east, called Kamara, from which it could easily be dominated by enemy guns but which the British appeared to think unnecessary to occupy even with Turks. The rest of the Balaclava defence force, the five hundred Highlanders, some thousand more Turks and the hundred invalids, were held back near Kadikoi to dispute any attempt to approach the harbour. Sir Colin Campbell, who might have been expected to show more realism, said in his report on October 20th, "I fancy we are now very strong as well as secure."

The cavalry division—the Heavy Brigade, the Light Brigade and Maude's guns—were encamped in the South Valley, although the commander of the Light Brigade, Major-General the Earl of Cardigan, did not deign to sleep in the camp and retired

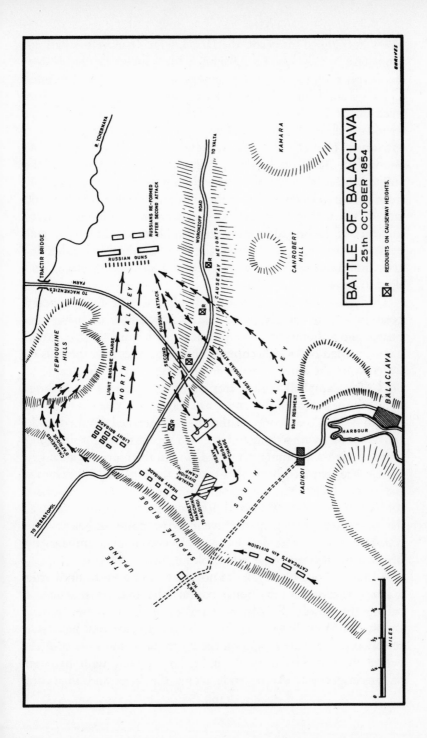

BATTLE OF BALACLAVA
25th OCTOBER 1854

⊠R REDOUBTS ON CAUSEWAY HEIGHTS.

every evening to his yacht, the *Dryad*, which had been sailed out from England for him by a friend, a Mr. Hubert de Bergh. Mr. de Bergh found it diverting to attend the war as an interested onlooker and he usually accompanied the major-general on whatever might be the occasion, official or not—although he kept prudently clear of any actual fighting—and nobody thought him intrusive. The *Dryad*, with a French cook aboard, was now moored in Balaclava harbour, taking up valuable space. As the military business of the day was seldom finished when the major-general retired to his yacht for the night, his brigade-major would ride down to the harbour every evening after dinner to have audience of the brigade commander, and later would have to ride back four miles to the divisional camp. Cardigan's brother-in-law, the divisional commander, was not so happily placed and slept in camp.

The Turks on the Causeway Heights, feeling their exposed position a little acutely, were taking no chances of being surprised, and although it was a practice which Lord Raglan would have frowned on as unbecoming, they sent spies into the hills to watch what the Russians were doing. One evening they came to Sir Colin Campbell with a story that the Russians were about to attack them that night, and when the report was passed on to Raglan he sent Sir George Cathcart—who seemed destined to do the odd jobs—with a thousand men who spent the night shivering on the Heights. Nothing happened, and in the morning an angry Sir George marched his troops back to the Upland. So when on the night of October 24th another report from the same source told of twenty-five thousand Russians preparing to attack at dawn—which proved in the event to be quite authentic—the number in itself sounded improbable and Raglan impatiently brushed the message aside and took no further interest.

Although Lord Cardigan did not stir from his yacht until after a late breakfast, the divisional commander made a practice of calling the whole division to stand-to an hour before dawn. Lucan may not have seen much active service but he was a relentless disciplinarian, and on the morning of the twenty-fifth, before the day was properly light, he was out with his staff on an inspection. As he rode along the lines and then out on to the plain towards Canrobert Hill a cannonade was heard from the east, and as the light started to grow one of Lucan's staff noticed, a little belatedly, that a signal was flying on the hill indicating that the Turkish battalion there was being attacked. After some commotion the Turks were seen to be abandoning their position. The British staff, who were perhaps expecting too much of a battalion of Turks to resist the entire Russian army, were later to impute a lack of valour on the part of these gentry, but as a hundred and seventy Turkish soldiers were killed before the remainder wisely decided to withdraw a considerable fight must have been put up. The Turks in the other redoubts along the Causeway Heights certainly saw no attraction in risking casualties on the same scale before being inevitably driven out, and before the Russians had had a chance to move along the North Valley towards them they had picked up their blankets and their more intimate possessions and had swept down the South Valley in a determined spirit of migration.

Lord Lucan ordered the cavalry to move out on to the plain, and as the Earl of Cardigan was unavailable at the time it fell to Lord George Paget, his second-in-command, to mount the Light Brigade. The divisional general made no comment, for he was fully acquainted with his brother-in-law's habits, and if the truth were to be known was privately relieved to be free of him. The Russians were now moving across the North Valley in threatening columns and Lucan started manœuvring his squadrons with a fine pretence of harassing their flanks, although to his cavalrymen— who were eager to charge anything—he seemed over-concerned that they should not become actually engaged with the enemy.

Unlike the Battle of the Alma, in the direction of which Lord Raglan had taken no part and from which the British had emerged victorious, the series of engagements that were to follow on this day—usually known collectively as the Battle of Balaclava—were, unhappily as it turned out, to be directed by the commander-in-chief himself. However, perhaps it is not altogether right to infer that events were entirely dictated by him, for every order he issued took some time to deliver to its recipient, and in some instances it was received after the situation it sought to deal with was over and forgotten. But there is no doubt that his orders did exercise a considerable influence on the fortunes of the day even though they were frequently misunderstood. He had already placed his general headquarters on the Upland, near the edge of that ridge overlooking Balaclava plain known as Sapouné Ridge, so now he was in one of those ideal positions for a commander-in-chief with the battlefield and all those engaged on it laid out before him like a plan, himself safely out of range of the enemy. Unfortunately he failed to grasp the elementary fact that the plain was not level and that anybody on one side of the Causeway Heights—or of any of the hills for that matter—was unlikely to be able to see what the enemy was doing on the other.

At half-past seven Raglan sent his first order to Lucan, saying, "Cavalry to take ground to left of second line of redoubts occupied by Turks." As there were only four redoubts all in one line and the Turks had already abandoned them the order was ambiguous. However, Lucan felt some obligation to comply with what the order appeared to mean and he withdrew his whole cavalry division towards the Sapouné Ridge, and when they reached the foot of the ridge he turned the two brigades in line to face east, looking out along the South Valley. There he was effectively cut off from any view of the Russians who were advancing west along the North Valley on the other side of the Causeway Heights. Raglan saw no reason to acquaint Lucan with the enemy's movements because he was quite unaware that Lucan could not see them himself. He did order the Duke of Cambridge and Sir George Cathcart to assemble their infantry divisions and march them down on to the plain although he had no very clear idea of what they were to do when they got there, but while the Duke complied readily enough Cathcart indulged in some effective bellyaching, reminding Raglan of the previous false alarm and refusing to believe that the Russians were actually attacking. It was not until after ten o'clock, two and a half hours since Canrobert Hill had been taken, that he was persuaded to defer to his commander-in-chief's wishes, and he did at last bring two of his brigades down on to the plain after most of the excitement was over. The Duke of Cambridge, in the event, marched his division along a ridge half-way down the slope of the hills, and his men never reached the plain where the battle was actually being fought. Canrobert, the French general, with an unusual show of alacrity, sent down two regiments of Chasseurs d'Afrique, and these horsemen were actually to play an effective part in the later engagements.

As daylight grew it became clear to those who could see them from the Upland that the Russian columns moving across the North Valley consisted entirely of cavalry, two and a half thousand grey-coated horsemen massed in two solid rectangles. Soon, a detachment of some four hundred were seen to break away from the rear column and to ride south over the Causeway Heights making for Kadikoi and the road to Balaclava. Even after they had crossed the Heights and had ridden down into the South Valley they were hidden from Lucan's cavalry because they happened, quite by chance, to ride in a shallow trough. But they were not hidden from Sir Colin Campbell and his Highlanders, nor from his thousand Turks. Realizing at last what he had been let in for, Campbell told his men, "Remember, there is no retreat from here. You must die where you stand." Unexpectedly, nobody was called on to obey the last part of the order. And perhaps the first part was not properly translated to the Turks, for as soon as they saw the Russians they retreated in some disorder to Balaclava harbour calling loudly for a ship to take them away to safety.

The 93rd Highlanders waited for the Russian horsemen behind a long mound. The Russians were advancing confidently, for they had seen what they believed to be the whole defending force withdrawing in haste to the harbour. When they came within musket range the Highlanders rose from the ground, and as was to happen so often in this war, the steady, valiant discipline of the British soldier redeemed the stupidity of his commanders. Five hundred tartan-trewed Highlanders, ready if necessary to die where they stood, faced and drove off the Russian threat to Balaclava, at least for the time being, and suffered little injury in the process.

The Russian horsemen swung away from the Highlanders in front of Kadikoi and returned to their main column, crossing the Causeway Heights again and dropping down into the North

Valley. By this time one of Raglan's orders had just reached Lucan telling him to detach eight squadrons of Heavy Dragoons—from the cavalry division still lined up at the foot of the Sapouné Ridge, at the west end of the South Valley—and to move them towards Balaclava to support the Turks "who are wavering." By this time the Turks had wavered all the way down to the harbour, clamouring to be taken off on a ship. Lucan knew nothing of what was going on, nor even that Campbell had been attacked, but he ordered Brigadier-General Scarlett, who commanded the Heavy Brigade, to take the squadrons as Raglan had instructed. Scarlett, a sensible officer, stout and phlegmatic, was only fifty-five and had never been in a fight, as the cavalry division had not even been engaged on the Alma. He led off the squadrons—5th Dragoons, Scots Greys, Inniskilling Dragoons, 4th Dragoon Guards—some in open column, others in threes, as if they were merely out to exercise their horses. He himself, with an aide-de-camp, a trumpeter and an orderly rode casually on their left, and as the whole detachment had to pass along the edge of the cavalry division's camp the troops became split up, stepping over tent ropes and making their way round lines of haltered sick horses.

Scarlett's aide-de-camp was a Lieutenant Elliott who had a brilliant record of active cavalry service, although in the prevailing tradition of the Army it had been of little avail to him in his career because it had all been served in India. Fortunately for the Heavy Brigade that morning, his experience suggested to him that in the present circumstances some degree of alert was necessary, for the brigade was passing within eight hundred yards of the ridge of Causeway Heights, so that even if an enemy formation were within a thousand yards it could still be out of sight. While Scarlett had set his face towards Kadikoi, in very proper execution of his orders, Elliott took a greater interest in the line of the Heights from which direction there was the distinct probability that the Russians would appear; and sure enough they did. The two and a half thousand Russian cavalrymen, who had been moving westward along the North Valley, finding no opposition from the redoubts, had wheeled south, still in massed columns, and were moving over the Causeway Ridge down the slope into the South Valley, their advance aimed quite by chance directly at the flank of the eight squadrons of the Heavy Brigade—who numbered eight hundred horsemen at the most.

When Elliott saw the Russians and called out to his commanding officer, Scarlett faced the surprising situation with commendable calm. He immediately ordered his heterogeneous column to wheel left into line facing the Heights—he himself, of course, being on its left was now between the two opposing lines —so that two squadrons each of the Inniskilling Dragoons and the Scots Greys became the Heavy Brigade's front line, to go down in history as "Scarlett's three hundred". The Russian masses were already coming down the hillside towards them at a trot but the British cavalry were far from ready to go into action and they declined to be hurried. The line into which they had been wheeled had to be properly dressed, and while this protracted process was going on the officers had to sit their horses out in front, facing their troops, with their backs to the oncoming enemy, until the major of each regiment ordered "eyes front" when they could at last turn unhurriedly and face their front. Scarlett, with his little entourage, also had to face the brigade until all the business of dressing was finished, and by now the Russians were but four hundred yards behind him.

On the Sapouné Ridge, where a large audience had gathered settling themselves comfortably on convenient rocks and ledges to watch the pretty battle, the excitement was considerable. This was to be one of the spectacles of the war for which the visitors had come such a long way. Captain Duberly, who was escorting Lord Raglan, had sent a horse down to Balaclava to fetch his wife, for clearly the events that were building up would be worth watching and in his message he had enjoined her to hurry and not wait for breakfast. The Earl of Cardigan was more fortunate, for he had finished his breakfast, and at the decent hour of half-past nine he had ridden calmly up from the harbour and had rejoined the Light Brigade which was still waiting where Lucan believed Raglan to have ordered it, at the foot of the ridge. From the heights above, the onlookers could see that the Heavy Brigade line, after it had been so meticulously dressed, was growing restive and its right appeared to be pressing forward to get at the enemy, but Scarlett restrained it very properly with a wave of the sword and the dressing was laboriously picked up again. For the spectators it was like watching a football match, picking out and commenting on the actions of the individual players; they saw Lucan ride across to speak to Scarlett, offering advice, like a captain to a scrum half.

Then two things happened at once. Scarlett with his aide-de-camp, his trumpeter and his orderly—who incidentally bore the intimidating name of Shegog—turned round to face the enemy, and at the same moment, for no apparent reason that history has been able to fathom, the enemy halted. Probably the spectacle of regiments dressing by the right when about to be charged had something of the same bewildering effect on the Russians as the argument between Lucan and Cardigan had had on them on the former occasion at the Bulganak. Halted or not, the sight of the enemy only four hundred yards away came as something of a shock to Scarlett. The drill book, from which he was not in the habit of departing, demanded that a charge should only be set in motion by a series of successive orders—like getting into top gear. Each of the orders must first be sounded by the brigade trumpeter and then repeated by each regimental trumpeter. The first order was "the line will advance at the walk"; then, "the line will advance at the trot"; next, "the line will advance at the gallop", and finally, "the line will charge". There was no order that provided for jumping a gear if in a hurry, although like many modern drivers some officers had got into the habit of disregarding first gear and going straight into the trot. Not that any British cavalry officer in the Crimea had, up to that moment, had occasion to order the charge anywhere but on the parade ground.

However, the shock of finding the enemy unexpectedly close was a little much for Scarlett. Until he turned round he had been calm enough, but now the injunctions of the drill book deserted him and he shouted to his trumpeter, "Sound the charge!" and at the same time he put his own horse straight into a gallop. Elliott, with the trumpeter and Shegog, felt impelled to follow suit and the four men went charging towards the Russians, leaving an ever-widening gap between themselves and the lines of the Heavy Brigade whose regimental trumpeters had no licence to depart from the prescribed sequence of orders. Lumberingly the lines moved forward, first walking, then trotting, then galloping, and then at last charging towards the stationary Russians in the wake of their brigadier-general who was now at least fifty yards ahead of them.

The charge of the first wave of the Heavy Brigade whereby, against all the canons of military practice, three hundred horsemen in two thin lines charged a solid mass of two and a half thousand stationary cavalrymen, was made uphill, and its initial impetus was not a little handicapped because the horses on the left of the brigade had to pick their way over and between the tent ropes of the cavalry division camp—some of the riders were actually thrown when their horses stumbled over the ropes—and, at any rate during the walking and trotting stages, precise dressing had to be preserved. The line taken by Scarlett and his three companions was clear of the tents and the turf was smooth and springy so that despite the uphill going they attained a fair speed before they had covered the four hundred yards to the Russian column, and when during their hectic progress over the ground Elliott shouted to his brigadier that they were leaving the troops behind, Scarlett turned in his saddle and waved his sword above his head in the traditional heroics of the cavalry charge leader, shouting ineffectually against the general din. But he made no effort to check his pace and he turned again to his front and rode on, to pass close by an officer sitting his horse in front of the Russian line into whom Elliott, passing on the other side, plunged his sword up to the hilt. Elliott could not withdraw his sword immediately so that his impetus swung the Russian round like a capstan until he could pull it clear, and then waving his blood-and-gut smeared weapon Elliott crashed into the front of the Russian column where Scarlett, the trumpeter and Shegog were now somewhat heavily engaged.

The effect of four apparently demented horsemen charging the very centre of the front of a massed column of waiting cavalrymen was less devastating to the four men themselves than might have been expected. The Heavy Brigade horses were all of sixteen hands so that their riders in every case topped the lighter mounted

Russian cavalrymen. Scarlett, after eight minutes of continuous barging and jostling, lashing about and parrying sabre thrusts with his sword, was to fight his way right through the Russian mass and, deflected a little by pressure of his opponents, to emerge at last from one flank of the column with but a few scratches; the trumpeter and Shegog, who indulged in the same violent exercise with no little relish, were apparently unscathed too, and although Elliott received some disfiguring slashes about the face and head he survived robustly enough after the later application of several stitches. The truth was that the Russians were too crowded to be able to use their weapons effectively.

Scarlett's three hundred, when they had formed their lines, had gone into the charge in classic style. In theory there were two lines of horsemen, and these were maintained rigidly enough even during the gallop. But in the final charge, when formation is allowably forgotten, the front line inevitably fanned out because the Russian column which was its target presented so wide a front, and the riders in the rear moved up into the gaps; so that when the three hundred met the enemy they were virtually in a single line. When the line of Scots Greys and Inniskilling Dragoons crashed in, each horseman wedging himself between two opponents and bludgeoning his way inwards, there arose confusion enough and many individual and bloody fights ensued. The contestants writhed together, hacking at each other as best they could, but even the thickness of the Russian overcoats afforded some effective protection against the British blows. The Heavy Brigade had been caught unprepared for close fighting and were wearing neither their shoulder-scales nor their gauntlets. The adjutant of the Greys, when he had fought his way well into the enemy ranks, forced his charger round so that he faced towards the rear. He had the proverbial stentorian voice and he shouted to his troopers, "Rally!", "Face me!", and in the middle of the seething fight the British soldier's instinct for maintaining formation took charge. The onlookers high up on the ridge could see the red and blue coats of the British cavalry forcing their individual ways through the surging throng and sorting themselves into some semblance of a line while the dark grey of the Russian masses closed behind them, and were obviously engulfing them.

The other squadrons of the Heavy Brigade, interrupted in their leisurely march towards Kadikoi, had by now been formed up in the rear in their separate regiments, the 4th Dragoons to the left, to their right rear the 1st Dragoons—the Royals—next, towards the centre, the 5th Dragoon Guards, and on their right another squadron of the Inniskillings. As their brigadier-general had galloped away fecklessly at the head of the first wave, they were left without orders but now they could plainly see the wings of the Russian column swinging round to engulf the three hundred, and once again sheer courage was to step in to redeem a succession of British blunders. The officers of each of the formations left behind acted spontaneously and decisively enough, and in the next few minutes they led their squadrons in four separate charges, two on the Russian right flank, one in the centre on the heels of the Greys, and one on the enemy's left flank. So the Russians who had swung round to encircle the Greys and the Inniskillings were now themselves attacked from the rear, and the grey coats in their turn were enfolded by more lines of red and blue until the confusion of the battle was complete.

Up to now the Russian column, by its sheer inertia, had held its ground, but the four new blows struck at it even by inferior numbers had their inevitable effect and the mass of seething horsemen, jostling and belabouring each other, began to move up the hill, first almost imperceptibly but once the movement started there was nothing to stop it. Horses in the rear files of the column, whose riders had taken no part in the fighting, began to be pressed backwards, and in no time the column, which had been such a rigid formation, had broken completely and the grey-coated riders were disengaging themselves and galloping away up the Causeway Heights. Individual British cavalrymen attempted to follow their recently made private enemies, but the whole force of the Heavy Brigade was now too disorganized for any pursuit and the instinct for formation reasserted itself, among officers as well as troopers, so that the various regiments fell to sorting themselves out rather than to risk dashing blindly over the ridge, whither the Russians had now disappeared as suddenly as they had first materialized. The whole affair had been over in less than ten minutes, and the Russian threat to Balaclava had been beaten off a second time with but seventy-eight British casualties, a reasonable enough price in the circumstances.

⟋ The Light Brigade, at whose head Lord Cardigan was sitting not five hundred yards from the battle, had made no move to come to the assistance of the Heavy Brigade. The brigadier's inaction inevitably aroused some subsequent criticism and the brothers-in-law were to blame each other for what had transpired, taking their quarrel as far as the correspondence columns of *The Times*. Cardigan protested that "Lieutenant-General the Earl of Lucan, my superior officer," had given him orders on no account to leave the position and to defend it against any attack by the Russians. Apparently a Russian column, two and a half thousand strong, five hundred yards away, surging down the hill towards Balaclava, was not to be construed as attacking. Lucan's version of what he had said included a back-handed reference to the commander-in-chief's somewhat ambiguous order. He said he had told Cardigan, "You'll remember that you are placed here by Lord Raglan himself"—inferring that he, Lucan, would never have done anything so stupid—and he went on, "My instructions to you are to attack anything and everything that shall come within reach of you, but you will be careful of columns or squares of infantry."

If, at that stage in the day's events, Cardigan's inaction suggested some discreditable traits as a cavalry leader the suggestion was to be abundantly dispelled a couple of hours later. But at the time the spectators in their comfortable seats on the Upland were naturally inclined to be critical, although the French were generous enough to believe that the Light Brigade's restraint had something to do with the rules of boxing, to which the British owed notorious reverence, and which, they understood, prohibited interference in a fight. In truth, Cardigan was as eager to join the fight as anybody, for there was one thing that never was in doubt and that was his personal courage even though its manifestation may have been prompted by sheer mental incapacity. However, he was just as eager to effect his brother-in-law's discomfiture. For months he had been asserting that Lord Raglan had promised him command of the Light Brigade independently of Lucan, the divisional commander, and

The Crimean winter of 1854-55 has become a legend of history; a group of the 47th Regiment in winter dress.

They made history at Balaclava in a blaze of redundant glory; officers and men of the 8th Hussars.

for a long time he had behaved as if this somewhat unorthodox conception of the chain of command was an established fact. At one stage Raglan had tended to endorse the illusion by dealing with Cardigan direct in the brigade's affairs, and he had made certain dispositions, particularly at Varna, which had given the impression that Cardigan was not answerable to Lucan. It was an impression that had gained a considerable hold in the army. Not unnaturally Lucan had raised some trenchant objections and Raglan had at last been obliged, despite his own inclination to avoid committing himself, to confirm officially that Major-General the Earl of Cardigan, the brigadier of the Light Brigade, was in fact responsible to his brother-in-law Lieutenant-General the Earl of Lucan, the officer commanding the cavalry division. So now, at the moment when the whole responsibility for the issue of the war had fallen on the shoulders of the cavalry, Cardigan felt disposed to register his disapproval of the commander-in-chief's shameful treatment by adopting the procedure of the modern trade unionist and working to rule. Lucan was his immediate superior so he would do what Lucan ordered and no more. When the Heavy Brigade had at last broken the Russian column and still Cardigan had made no move, the commander of one of his brigade's regiments, Captain Morris of the 17th Lancers, had ridden up to him and had said, "My lord, are you not going to charge the flying enemy?" and Cardigan had replied, "No. We have orders to remain here."

The Russians had now disappeared entirely from the view of the British cavalry. The whole cavalry division was, in fact, still in the South Valley and to the staff watching from the Upland it appeared quite content to remain there and to regard the battle as over. This continued inertia constrained Raglan to issue his third order, which was a masterpiece of imprecision and obscurity. "Cavalry to advance and take advantage of any opportunity to recover the heights. They will be supported by the infantry which have been ordered to advance on two fronts." The first part of the order certainly offered Lucan a free hand, but as he could see nothing of the enemy and as Raglan had the Russian movements in full view it might have been more helpful if the commander-in-chief had suggested in which direction the proposed advance by the cavalry could most profitably be made. As for the two fronts on which the infantry were said to be advancing, the Duke of Cambridge's First Division was plodding along a ridge, well above the level of the plain, and Cathcart's two reluctant brigades were only now starting to make their long descent down the escarpment. In fairness to Raglan, it seems quite probable that he intended that the First Division should move along the Fedioukine Hills and Cathcart's brigades along the Causeway Heights; but as neither ever reached these objectives the intention, praiseworthy as it may have been, was wasted, and the fact that Raglan failed to convey it to Lucan really made little difference.

However, it was sufficiently clear to Lucan that any advance that Raglan might have in mind, unspecified as it was, must be to somewhere other than in the South Valley which was now demonstrably free of any enemy. So he ordered Lord Cardigan to move the Light Brigade across the Woronzoff Road, at the western end of the Causeway Heights. With an unusual readiness to obey his brother-in-law without argument, Cardigan led his brigade across the road and drew it up in squadrons, still at the foot of the Sapouné Ridge, facing down the trough of the North Valley. The ground straight in front—smooth, springy turf, such as had been so agreeable for the Heavy Brigade's charge—fell away slightly, but from the saddle the men of the Light Brigade could see, at the other end of the valley a mile and a quarter away, confused dark shapes which were obviously the enemy. They could see too that whatever the enemy might be doing there he had with him a number of fair-sized guns. On the hills on each side of the valley—the Fedioukine Hills on the left and the Causeway Heights on the right—the enemy was more in evidence; in fact on the Causeway Heights he was dragging from the redoubts abandoned by the Turks the old twelve-pounders, intent that these should be despatched without delay to St. Petersburg where the Tsar was in dire need of some restorative to his morale.

Raglan and the gallery on the Upland could, of course, see exactly how the Russians had regrouped after their rout by the Heavy Brigade. Early in the morning the Russians had sent a strong force—eight battalions of infantry, four cavalry squadrons and fourteen guns—on to the Fedioukine Hills, and now a whole infantry regiment together with a field battery was moving westward along the Causeway Heights. The discomfited Russian cavalry appeared to have been rallied and were regrouping in columns ranged across the eastern end of the valley, and across their front a line of twelve field guns was being drawn up. These new dispositions were perfectly arranged to deal with any British formations that could be so monumentally stupid as to move straight down the middle of the valley where they would be assailed from the front and both flanks all at the same time. It would be flattering the Russians to call their dispositions a trap, because the setting of a trap suggests some stealth. The plan of their positions was perfectly open, at any rate to the British commander-in-chief looking down on it. It was so open, in fact, that to blunder into it would be positively insane. So it might have been of some advantage if Raglan had told his divisional commander down on the plain what he could see himself, but it never occurred to him that the overall picture of the battlefield might not be too perceptible to those actually on it, even from the saddle of a horse.

Having received Raglan's order to advance Lucan acted on it by waiting for three-quarters of an hour. He had no intention of disobeying the order but, as he explained afterwards, he was waiting for the infantry of which there was no sign, and the explanation is not unreasonable. In the course of subsequent mutual recriminations it became clear that while Raglan had said in his order that the infantry would support the cavalry, Lucan had it firmly fixed in his mind that the role of his cavalry was to support the infantry, although he had no idea of what the infantry was supposed to do. Raglan grew understandably impatient, particularly when he saw the Russians removing the guns from the redoubts without any hindrance. So he composed what, by his standards, was a more precise order and General Airey wrote it down in pencil on a rough piece of paper and signed it. It opened, "Lord Raglan wishes . . ." as if to imply that direct orders had so far had no effect so Raglan was now obliged to fall back on his more usual method of exercising command. "Lord Raglan wishes the cavalry to advance rapidly to the front, and to prevent the enemy carrying away the guns. Troop of horse artillery may accompany. French cavalry is on your left. Immediate."

This became known as Raglan's famous "fourth order" and it was handed to his aide-de-camp, Captain Nolan, the volatile cavalryman, to deliver with all haste to Lord Lucan. Nolan made a dramatic descent of the escarpment, where it dropped most steeply from the Upland to the plain. He was a skilled horseman and he disdained the easy, circuitous path. He scrambled down in minutes, whereas any other rider would have taken a quarter of an hour or more. Nolan was the known high-priest of the gospel that cavalry was the decisive arm in war, and when the word went round the onlookers who the messenger was—who was in such an obvious hurry—hope was at last revived that something worth watching might now occur, for nothing had happened for a whole hour after the Heavy Brigade charge and the spectators were beginning to despair that there would be any more play that day.

Meanwhile Lucan had come to the conclusion, which happened to be correct, that the war had deserted the South Valley and so he had moved the Heavy Brigade also across the Woronzoff Road and had stationed it behind and to the right of the Light Brigade. Nolan came galloping up with Raglan's order and delivered it to Lucan who was waiting in front of his troops as he had been waiting for the last three-quarters of an hour. It can be fairly assumed that Nolan was feeling some annoyance at the cavalry's inaction and was inclined to blame Lucan. Although Nolan was but an aide-de-camp and his influence on the present events was theoretically limited to delivering Raglan's order, he was known to hold strong and even impassioned views on the use of cavalry in war, for he had written a book on the subject. So the assumption that he was critical of Lucan is fair enough and it is certainly borne out by his behaviour to the lieutenant-general. Lucan took the little scrap of paper from Nolan and read what was on it deliberately, while Nolan overtly chafed even at the extra delay that Lucan's deliberation implied. Lucan saw Aireys' signature on the order, and because he knew too that Nolan was Airey's own aide-de-camp he jumped to the understandable conclusion that the order had been conceived by the Quarter-master-General for whose capabilities he had less respect even than he had for those of the commander-in-chief. He told Nolan that the order was impracticable for any useful purpose and that its execution would involve great risk and unnecessary losses. It was not the sort of comment a divisional commander usually makes to an aide-de-camp.

Nolan had heard the discussion between Raglan and Airey when they had framed the order and, because of his special beliefs, he was only too ready to further any proposal to launch a cavalry attack. He said—and his voice assumed an unusually peremptory tone for a captain to use to a lieutenant-general— "Lord Raglan's orders are that the cavalry should attack immediately."

But apparently Lucan saw nothing out of place in arguing about the commander-in-chief's orders with an aide-de-camp. "Attack, sir?" he asked. "Attack what? What guns, sir?"

The last vestige of Nolan's respect for this general who hesitated to launch a cavalry attack left him, and he raised his voice so that those around could hear him, and he swept his arm in the general direction of the valley to Lucan's front and declaimed, dramatically enough, "There, my lord, is your enemy! There are your guns!" As Lucan himself was later to say, the remark was addressed "in a most disrespectful but significant manner."

It has been fashionable to impute to Nolan a deliberate intention to launch the cavalry on a suicidal attack down the middle of the valley, directly at the Russian guns—as, in the event, the Light Brigade was in a few minutes to be launched. His own dogmatism about the role of cavalry has been adduced as proof of some such maniacal intent. But the imputation is absurd, for the evidence of his actions entirely contradicts it, and but for a chance question put to him by Lucan, which even he could never have anticipated, his own part in the whole affair must necessarily have been confined to delivering Raglan's written order. To suggest that, as he scrambled precipitately down from the Upland, he determined to engineer an action which had not been ordered by the commander-in-chief and which Lucan would be unlikely to undertake of his own accord, and that he accomplished this extraordinary purpose by a vague gesture of his arm, is pure sophism. It certainly was not Lord Raglan's intention that the attack should be made where the Light Brigade did in fact charge. His previous order, the third order, which Lucan admittedly had not acted on, had been specific that the objective of a cavalry advance was to "recover the heights"; this new, fourth order was characteristically vague but it did again suggest that the purpose of an advance by the cavalry was to "prevent the enemy carrying away the guns", and this the Russians were doing on the Causeway Heights, on the right of the valley, and not plumb down the centre. Nobody, reading the two orders with the slightest attention, could have mistaken what Raglan was getting at, although when the Light Brigade did charge it swept down past the redoubts, from which the guns were being taken, without giving them a glance. But an aide-de-camp entrusted with an order, no matter how frenetic his own ideas might be, would hardly be likely to betray that trust by deliberately misrepresenting what his commander-in-chief intended—which has also been imputed to the wretched Captain Nolan.

Not that Nolan's behaviour to Lucan was particularly commendable. Those who witnessed it said later that they were surprised that the general did not immediately put him under arrest. Instead, Lucan trotted off alone to the Light Brigade in front of which Cardigan sat with his sword drawn, as if to emphasize that he, Cardigan, had been waiting to go into battle all the morning. Lucan read out Raglan's order so that there was no doubt even in Cardigan's mind of what the commander-in-chief had actually said. Lucan added, "Advance steadily and keep your men well in hand." Cardigan, in an exaggerated gesture of respect, raised his sword to the recover and swept it downward in a salute, saying, "Certainly, sir, but allow me to point out to you that the Russians have a battery in the valley in our front, and batteries and riflemen on each flank." Lucan shrugged his shoulders and said, "I cannot help that. It is Lord Raglan's positive order that the Light Brigade attacks immediately."

It is usual for an attack to have a specific objective but neither Lucan nor Cardigan had mentioned one, although Cardigan, by his remark, had definitely inferred that the attack was to be made straight down the valley and Lucan had said nothing to suggest that the inference was wrong. Captain Nolan's subsequent behaviour, after the advance had started, was to suggest almost incontrovertibly that he knew Raglan's intended objective to be the guns on the heights, and that when with a vague sweep of his arm he had indicated the general direction of the valley and had said "there are your guns" that was what he had meant, although some chroniclers have preferred to believe that he was talking about the guns at the far end of the valley. From where the Light Brigade was waiting a movement either straight down the valley, or towards the redoubts, would start in almost the same direction; the difference between the bearings of the two objectives was but a few degrees. So it would be possible for a brigade actually to start moving forward, and to cover quite a distance, before it would become plain to someone imagining it to be headed for the Causeway Heights that it was, in fact, headed straight down the valley.

Although the commander-in-chief's order had merely been "to advance" there seems to have been no doubt from the moment Lucan spoke to Cardigan that the Light Brigade was committed to charge something; what or why was unspecified. No actual purpose for a charge was even mentioned, mainly because neither of the brothers-in-law gave it any thought, but for some reason Lucan considered that the brigade's front was too wide although his opinion could have been related to no particular tactical consideration. Cardigan disagreed with him for equally unsubstantial reasons. The front line, as it was now drawn up, consisted of three regiments, the 13th Light Dragoons, the 17th Lancers and the 11th Hussars—this last, Cardigan's own regiment in their cherry-coloured pants. Lucan disregarded Cardigan's protest and rode across himself to order the Hussars to fall back, and consequently they became the second line. Behind them, in the third line, were the 4th Light Dragoons and the 8th Hussars. Captain Nolan, who apparently felt that he had discharged his staff duties for the time being, rode over to place himself beside Captain Morris at the head of the 17th Lancers.

Cardigan disdained to wait while his divisional commander fussed about detaching the 11th Hussars from the front line. He rode across to Lord George Paget at the head of the 4th Light Dragoons and said, "I expect your best support; mind, Lord George, your best support," which was the only tactical instruction of any sort that he gave before committing his brigade to battle, and then he trotted back to the front of his troops. Immaculately turned out, as if on parade in Hyde Park, he sat erect on his charger and ordered, "The brigade will advance at the walk," and the Light Brigade started its move down the valley. Soon it had changed to the trot and it was then that from the left, from the front of the 17th Lancers, Captain Nolan came cantering across. He rode across right in front of the major-general, an action by a junior officer that was unforgivable. He swung round, to face the oncoming brigade, and shouted something which nobody could hear, for the brigade was coming within range of the enemy and the guns were already opening up. The first shell burst close ahead of Cardigan and a splinter struck Nolan, probably in the spine, for it apparently paralysed him. The impact of the splinter, striking some vital part, caused him to emit a piercing, almost maniacal shriek. His terrified horse charged to the rear, through the lines of the Light Brigade, Nolan still shrieking, his body still stiff in the saddle, his arm and sword still straight above his head, until, behind the last line of the brigade, his horse swerved and he pitched out of the saddle on to the grass, stone dead.

To Cardigan's limited power of comprehension Nolan's behaviour suggested insubordination—a patent attempt to usurp his own command of the brigade. It was quite beyond him even to suspect that Nolan might have some other, even remotely justifiable reason. Clearly, after the brigade had covered some hundreds of yards it had suddenly dawned on Nolan that Cardigan had misunderstood the order and was headed, not for the guns on the heights but straight down the valley, and he had taken panic action to try to deflect it from what he knew would be—and in the event was to prove—a death-trap. That such an explanation never even crossed Cardigan's mind confirms what his own interpretation of Raglan's order had been all along.

So the Light Brigade rode on straight down the valley, the trot breaking into a gallop. At its head, erect, unswerving, never so much as glancing aside, a splendid figure, rode Major-General the Earl of Cardigan, who had never been in action before, who was where he was because of his aristocratic rank and because he had been rich enough to buy his commission and his command, and who had not the haziest notion inside his shallow brain of what was implied in leading seven hundred horsemen to inevitable disaster. The troopers of the brigade—the ordinary British soldier, yet once again to be sacrificed by the stupidity of his commanders —followed unflinching, in perfect line and in perfect order. The farther down the valley they rode, the more intense became the fire from both flanks. Men and horses fell and the gaps closed up, and the lines rode on. Watching on the Upland, General Bosquet threw his arms in the air and exclaimed, "C'est magnifique, mais ce n'est pas la guerre." He would have been even more pertinent if he had said that it was not even sense. The brigade was already being decimated, and at the end of the valley, the objective of their charge, there was still a battery of twelve guns, and behind the guns thousands of Russian cavalrymen. Over the first long, long mile Cardigan kept the pace of the brigade down, against all natural inclination of cavalry under fire to increase their pace to their objective. But Lucan had said, "Advance steadily, and keep your men well in hand," and Cardigan was working strictly to rule. Once, Captain Morris, pressed forward by the urgency of his Lancers, moved up level with the major-general, suggesting by his action that the pace might well be increased, but Cardigan stretched out his sword and waved him back. It was the only occasion during the whole ride when he relaxed his strictly ceremonial bearing.

At last, within a quarter of a mile of the guns, Cardigan perforce increased the pace. At first the increase was imperceptible but a subconscious pressure, imposed mainly by the line behind, was urging him on and his own charger broke into an incipient gallop so that the troopers following him pressed even more urgently forward, and the pace grew faster and even faster. But never was the properly ordained distance between the leader and his front line abused; each man, hardly suppressing his impatience, kept his eye on the brigadier's cherry coloured pantaloons and the white stocking on the near hind leg of Cardigan's chestnut charger. Now, too, those in the front line could see quite clearly the brass muzzles of the Russian cannon shining in the sun and the gunners busily serving them, and the brigade—or at least those of it who were still alive—pressed forward even more urgently to have the whole business over and finished. And so the pace increased yet more and the charge of the Light Brigade at last broke into a gallop. Cardigan, who would never admit that the charge had not been made unhurriedly and in perfect order, later estimated that he reached the guns at seventeen miles an hour. Now, when the front line was no more than a bare hundred yards from the very mouths of the guns the whole battery fired a salvo and what was still left of the brigade suffered yet more dreadful carnage. Men were wiped off their saddles, their terrified horses crashed forward, anywhere, wedging themselves where they could between two galloping companions or swinging away in confusion from the straight line of the charge. The lines were completely broken and there remained no pretence of formation. But those who were still mounted thundered on towards the guns, which were hidden now in a dense cloud of smoke. So far the ride had taken not more than ten minutes; in the event the rest of the action was to take but another ten.

When the battery fired that final salvo—it was to be its last, for in a few seconds the Lancers were slashing away at the gun crews and the gunners were cowering under the guns or running anywhere to escape this handful of British horsemen who were so clearly demented—Cardigan was, of course, even closer than the front line. He was so close that being between the line of fire of two guns none actually bore upon him and he passed unscathed between the shots so that the flashes of flame following the discharge spat out past him on each side. He was later to say that his only feeling throughout the ride, and even when charging the guns, was of anger at Nolan's shocking insubordination—and the evidence of the scale of his intelligence endorses that what he says was probably true. He carried his anger, at the gallop, right through the smoke of the battery. He had chosen a line leading to a space between two guns when he had still been some way away, and now he crashed through this narrow gap and through more gaps between the crowded guns and limbers, gaps which the prudent rider even at a walk would carefully have avoided. His impetus took him clean through the battery so that he was still galloping after he had passed the guns and gunners, until, nearly a hundred yards beyond, still completely unscathed he found himself charging single-handed what appeared to be a whole regiment of Russian cavalry drawn up across the ground in front of him. Behind him, in the battery, his troopers had reined in their horses and were cutting down the gunners, but they were hidden in a pall of fog and smoke, and Cardigan, their brigadier, was the only man who had passed right through and now he stood alone to challenge the Russians.

There is a pretty story that a Russian officer, a certain Prince Radziwill, who had met the Earl in London before the war, was sitting his horse in front of the regiment that now faced Cardigan and that the Prince recognized him and called out to his men forbidding them to harm him. Rather, it is said, were they told to capture him alive, and two cossacks went forward to effect this. Not unwisely, Cardigan pushed them off and turned his back on the Russian cavalry. That encounter was the limit of his charge and incidentally the end of his active participation in the engagement. At the height of the Battle of Balaclava, Major-General the Earl of Cardigan rode back through the battery—he said afterwards that he saw none of his men there so he felt no obligation to remain—and without undue haste, still sitting his horse with parade-ground punctilio, completely undisturbed and miraculously untouched by the enemy's fire, calmly returned up the valley down which he had led the Light Brigade only ten minutes before.

Of the six hundred and seventy men of the Light Brigade who had moved off at Cardigan's first command only two hundred and thirty reached the guns. The rest had been shot down or their horses had been shot under them. Thirty survivors of the front line actually entered the battery. The others swung off and passed on each side of the guns, most of them still in their regimental formations but each regiment reduced to less than half a hundred riders. The fight that ensued with the Russian cavalry squadrons drawn up in rear was inevitably confused. To a lieutenant of the 11th Hussars one Russian officer actually surrendered his sword, but the taking of prisoners was obviously impracticable in the circumstances. During the fighting behind the guns the casualties to the brigade, compared with those suffered during the charge, were small. The remnants of units, under their individual officers—the names that earned the greatest lustre were Lord George Paget, Colonel Shelwell and Colonel Mayow—drove some of the Russian cavalry formations as much as a quarter of a mile to the rear, and the Russian infantry battalions, waiting at the far eastern end of the valley, formed squares in readiness to resist this terrifying charge of British cavalry.

But it was all quite hopeless and purposeless. Less than a couple of hundred light cavalry were pretending, valiantly enough, to menace an army of over twenty thousand men drawn up in formal array—and now they were to find themselves menaced in their own rear by squadrons of Russian lancers dropping down into the valley from the Fedioukine Hills and Causeway Heights. The men of the Light Brigade who were still alive and mounted, with the notable exception of their brigadier, were all behind the Russian guns now, virtually inside the Russian lines, and they had gravitated into two groups, one at each side of the valley, one being rallied by Lord George Paget and the other by Colonel Shelwell. Lord George was looking for Cardigan, remembering that Cardigan had enjoined his, Lord George's, "best support". In fact officers were constantly asking, "Where is Lord Cardigan?" —not because his apparent absence aroused any suspicions, anybody could have been lost more than legitimately in that confusion—but he was, after all, the brigadier and they were entitled to look to him for guidance and orders.

The time came when both Lord George and Colonel Shelwell were to turn and find squadrons of Russian lancers advancing on their little groups from behind. It was obvious to both that they must make good their withdrawal as best they could, and immediately. Shelwell chose to lead his party which now numbered seventy in a direct charge to break through the Russian squadrons; it was a desperate chance and it came off. The British cavalrymen charged blindly into the lines of waiting Russian horsemen and out the other side. Once again, the direct encounter with the enemy caused comparatively few casualties.

The commander of the Russian cavalry who were drawn up right across Lord George's line of retirement had seen how Shelwell, on the other side of the valley, had broken through by direct assault, so he moved his men back until their line was set at an angle. Waiting thus they menaced the retreating British riders more dangerously, for they could pounce on their flank as they passed by. But miraculously Lord George's party got by too; and so the hard-pressed survivors of the Light Brigade entered almost the worst of their ordeal that morning, and in the long uphill drag up the valley they suffered yet again the awful carnage dealt out by the Russians from the Causeway Heights. The valley was a shambles: horses with shattered limbs thrashing about unable to rise; dead horses lying on top of men still living, but trapped under them; riderless, terrified horses; wounded men dragging themselves painfully along inch by inch; and all the time more men falling as the Russian guns and riflemen on the heights kept up their fire and the Russian lancers swept across the valley to cut down the stragglers.

And so the Light Brigade returned from its charge. It had all been done, and eternal history had been made, in twenty minutes. The first to reach the western end of the valley was the man who had led the charge, still as immaculate and unruffled as ever, and still, even according to his own account, railing at Nolan's contumacy. He rode up to General Scarlett; with no reference to the fight, with no reference to the brigade that had followed him almost to annihilation, he merely complained to Scarlett of Nolan. "Imagine," he said, "the fellow screaming like a woman when he was hit!"

Then, later, came Paget and Shelwell and their men, or those who were left of them. As they came in, a small group or a lone horseman at a time, those who had been watching raised a cheer. When Paget saw Cardigan already waiting, quite composed, he said, "Hallo, Lord Cardigan! Were you not there?"—and so there was sown that little seed of disbelief, that was to grow into quite a plant, that the Earl of Cardigan had never charged with the Light Brigade, although he never ceased giving the world unblushing accounts of his own part in the affair.

Bad as they were the casualties of the Light Brigade would most certainly have been worse had not the French cavalry generals, Morris and d'Alonville, led their Chasseurs d'Afrique along the Fedioukine Hills and driven off the Russian forces there just before Paget and Shelwell started their long ride back. They had come down from the Upland at the first alarm in the early morning and it was to them that Lord Raglan had referred in his fourth order, "French cavalry is on your left"— and for once the British were to be in France's debt. By driving off the Russian gunners from the hills the French cavalry at least removed the menace to the retreating brigade from one side of the valley. Perhaps if General Cathcart had refrained from belly-aching he might have been in time to render the same service on the Causeway Heights.

But when the Light Brigade mustered, on a slope looking down towards Balaclava, it was an unusual roll-call that accompanied the muster; no snapping out of answers to names, for there were few there to answer. As one after another man was called, and at first there was silence, his few comrades who remained would take up a discussion of where or when they had seen him last, and the officers waited patiently while each tragic story was unfolded. Two hundred and forty-seven men were missing from the ranks, and four hundred and seventy-five horses had been killed— all in twenty minutes. To balance the cost nothing had been accomplished except the writing of another page of redundant glory. Cardigan, who was immensely pleased with himself, rode to the Upland to report to Lord Raglan. But the experience of watching seven hundred horsemen ride into a trap had been a nervous strain even for the equable Raglan and he was fuming with anger. "What did you mean, sir," he flung at Cardigan, "by attacking a battery in front, contrary to all the usages of warfare and the customs of the service?" But Cardigan, who had been working to rule, was not to be drawn. "My lord," he answered, "I hope you will not blame me, for I received the order to attack from my superior officer," carefully adding, in case Raglan needed any corroboration, "in front of the troops," and he rode on down to his yacht for a bath. When Raglan had resumed his normal calm he was inclined to think that Cardigan could hardly be blamed for what he had done and he wrote, shortly after, "Lord Cardigan acted throughout with the greatest steadiness and gallantry, as well as perseverance."

Lucan, right at the beginning of the affair, after he had seen Cardigan move off to the attack, had decided to support him with the Heavy Brigade and he had led it forward himself down the valley in the wake of the Light Brigade. But the Heavies were much slower in getting into their stride and soon there was a tremendous gap between the brigades. As they advanced ponderously Lucan's aide-de-camp was killed beside him; the assistant quartermaster-general lost his horse; the assistant adjutant-general lost his bonnet; and Lucan himself was hit in the leg, so he decided to call the whole thing off. "They have sacrificed the Light Brigade," he said to Scarlett—who had no doubt of who "they" were to whom Lucan was referring—"they shall not sacrifice the Heavy Brigade if I can help it." So he prudently halted the brigade and withdrew it out of range of the enemy's guns. A month later he was to be relieved of his command on account of what "they" had done.

For when Cardigan had cleared himself Raglan transferred the blame for the whole affair to Lucan. His first words, when he saw him after the battle, were, "You have lost the Light Brigade!" —which tended to upset Lucan because, as he had already said, he was convinced it was "they" who had lost it. "They", of course, were Raglan and Airey. But when it comes to a dispute between a commander-in-chief and a subordinate general about which of them has been wrong the commander-in-chief holds a strong position. The Duke of Newcastle, and Lord Hardinge, and the Queen, came to the conclusion from reading Raglan's reports that "the general discipline of the army must be greatly prejudiced by any misunderstanding between your lordship"—Lord Raglan —"as the general officer commanding Her Majesty's forces in the field and the Lieutenant-General commanding the Division of Cavalry." The misunderstanding, as it was called, had arisen because Lucan had suggested in a letter, which he had refused to withdraw—although Raglan had sent Airey three times to persuade him to do so—that had he not ordered the Light Brigade to charge he, in turn, would have been disobeying Raglan's orders; while Raglan put it that "from some misconception of the instruction to advance the Lieutenant-General considered he was bound to attack at all hazards." It was the accusation of "misconception" that upset Lucan.

Lucan returned to England and when he arrived in London he asked for a court-martial, which was refused—so the official blame for the loss of the Light Brigade remained on him, and his commander-in-chief was saved any embarrassment which a disclosure of the ambiguous orders might have occasioned. But the controversy over the Earl of Cardigan's behaviour during the Charge, and whether or not he ever took part in it, raged on for years; eight years later he was still suing a Colonel Calthorpe for libel contained in a book the colonel had published, and the case achieved the notoriety of trial by the Lord Chief Justice. Cardigan won on a technical legality, so the result was inconclusive and Colonel Calthorpe's accusation that he had retreated from the battle prematurely was never effectively refuted. But to those who sought to blacken Cardigan's name the Lord Chief Justice did remark that any reflection on the man who had led the charge of the Light Brigade "should be generous and liberal criticism."

Meanwhile the Fedioukine Hills, the Causeway Ridge and the whole plain of Balaclava had been left in Russian hands, and by losing control of the Woronzoff Road and thereby reducing their link with the port to an unmade track up the face of the escarpment, the British on the Upland had sown for themselves the seeds of unbelievable hardships during the coming winter months.

13

THE allied intention in landing on the Crimea had been to capture Sebastopol and this had implied some containment of the Russian forces in that town. After October 25th it was the allies themselves who were contained. They were surrounded, partly by the enemy and partly by the sea. Their only advantage, in fact their only salvation, was that they were on high ground. Their line, starting from the west coast where the French on Mount Rodolph looked down over the entrance to Sebastopol harbour, running eastward along the ridges of the Upland as far as the Tchernaya valley, bending backward south and even southeast along the Sapouné Ridge and finally swinging out eastward again in a little salient to enclose Balaclava harbour, was fully twenty miles long. And now that the Russians were able virtually to invest the position the line needed to be watched carefully by pickets along its whole length. Picketing a line twenty miles long, round the clock, in rough country with no proper defence works and no lateral communications, occupied a large proportion of the whole force; nor had the allies the numbers to man it in any depth.

The day following the Battle of Balaclava was a Sunday and the Russian commanders very properly went to church. Before they went they had made no plans for any operation but during the service they must have been impelled by divine inspiration to attack their enemies for whose discomfiture in no small measure the day before they were now giving thanks—for they hastened out after the blessing to arrange that a Colonel Federoff should immediately lead four thousand infantrymen out of Sebastopol up on to the heights of what was known as Mount Inkerman.

The name arose from a ruined village called Inkerman which stood on the face of the hills rising on the eastern side of the

Tchernaya valley—the significance of the ruins seems to have been lost in the jungle of history. Mount Inkerman, on the western side of the valley, is quite detached from the ruined village and forms the complex of hills that comprises this north-eastern corner of the Upland. The hill is prominent enough even among the considerable heights along the Upland's northern ridge. Its summit is a plateau more than six hundred feet above the town and runs north and south for three miles. The western edge of the plateau is formed by the Careenage Ravine and on the east it is bounded by the Tchernaya valley. Numerous deep gullies branch from the ravine and valley to indent the plateau so that its form is like a misshapen oak leaf, two and a half miles across at its widest part, narrowing at its waists to less than half a mile and at its southern end, where it slopes gently down to join the main plateau of the Upland, to a narrow neck of land but four hundred yards across.

Colonel Federoff's Sunday afternoon excursion climbed to the northern end of the plateau, at its widest part, and there the colonel spread his men out in three parallel columns and sent them to advance southward along the hill. Another Russian battalion had also been sent to advance up the Careenage Ravine. The only immediate hindrance to the advancing Russians were little groups of British pickets spread at wide intervals across the plateau who put up an adequate enough show of resistance but dropped back nevertheless. However, their musket fire attracted the attention of the British Second Division camp, pitched not a quarter of a mile south of the neck connecting Mount Inkerman to the Upland, and three field batteries rode out in dashing style, unlimbered, and started shelling the Russian columns. The widest portion of the plateau, whence the Russians were advancing, now came in for the special attention of the guns and it acquired then and there the name of Shell Hill. But the Sabbath inspiration must have been inadequate, for the Russians suffered nearly three hundred casualties and decided to withdraw. That concluded the engagement known later as the Lesser Inkerman and it was all over in time for tea.

The main effect of the skirmish was to induce, particularly in the British Second Division, a dangerous contempt for the Russians and an equally dangerous satisfaction with the British

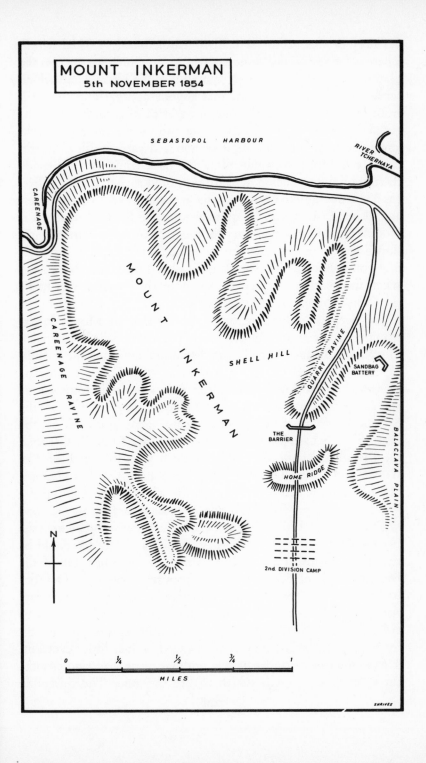

MOUNT INKERMAN
5th NOVEMBER 1854

SEBASTOPOL HARBOUR

RIVER TCHERNAYA

CAREENAGE

MOUNT INKERMAN

CAREENAGE RAVINE

SHELL HILL

QUARRY RAVINE

SANDBAG BATTERY

BALACLAVA PLAIN

THE BARRIER

HOME RIDGE

2nd. DIVISION CAMP

N

0   ¼   ½   ¾   1

MILES

SHRIVES

defences in that sector which, in truth, hardly existed at all. There is a ridge, rising some ten feet or so, which runs across the plateau just north of the neck joining it to the Upland and which serves as a sort of screen so that anyone approaching the neck must make a detour round one or other of its ends. It runs for a couple of hundred yards west to east and then it turns in a right angle and runs another couple of hundred yards south to north. Its only use for troops defending the neck could be to provide them with cover behind which they could shelter from gunfire, for it was too high to be used as a parapet and it had no embrasures, and although it would be quite an obstacle for any attackers it would really only be necessary for them to run up its conveniently sloped face to the top whence they could look down commandingly on the defenders. The British called it the Home Ridge and when the Battle of Inkerman was properly joined it was to be the focus of much fighting attention.

The deepest gully indenting into the side of Mount Inkerman on the east, branching from the Tchernaya valley, was called the Quarry Ravine. A road from Sebastopol ran along the bottom of the ravine and climbed up its head to debouch on to the plateau at the top and then to run right over the Home Ridge and along the narrow neck dropping down into and through the Second Division camp. It was a convenient approach to the camp from Sebastopol. In a sanguine attempt to block this road the British had built what was dignified with the name of The Barrier and referred to with some reverence in staff circles as a key-point in the defences, although the whole work was nothing more than a three-foot-high pile of loose stones across the road where it emerged from the ravine. On the eastern edge, where the plateau dropped to the Tchernaya valley and whence could be seen the remains of the real Inkerman on the other side of the river, a couple of British guns had been taken earlier in October to fire off a few rounds at an attractive target across the valley. An earthwork, not more than twelve feet long and some six to eight feet high, had been thrown up hastily as some protection for the gunners while they were engaged in their little diversion. This mound of earth, for it was nothing more, had two embrasures cut in it through which to fire the guns. The miserable emplacement was called the Sandbag Battery although the guns had already been taken away for use elsewhere. These—the Home Ridge, The Barrier and the Sandbag Battery—were the only defence works on the perimeter of Mount Inkerman, and when the real Battle of Inkerman came to be fought they were to receive attention out of all proportion to their almost negligible value.

After Colonel Federoff's Sunday excursion the next nine days passed quietly enough. The British and French busied themselves improving their arrangements for besieging the town, for the static siege was now the accepted strategy. The soldiers expended most of their energy labouring—digging parallels, constructing batteries, carrying shot and shells up from the harbour—and still had to provide pickets round the clock. Summer was retreating fast and the skies, so sunny since the allies had first landed, were becoming obscured by rain and mist while the nights were already abundantly chilly although the real cold of the Crimea was reserving its full impact for a later visitation. Even so there was a mood of optimism on the Upland, for the Russian masses had been held off in the Battle of Balaclava, and driven off Inkerman on the following day, and Sebastopol would soon be battered to ruins. To pursue this last sanguine purpose Raglan and Canrobert agreed on November 4th that they would meet next morning and plan the definitive bombardment of Sebastopol—a meeting which, if it had come off, might have marked an unprecedented exercise in allied joint planning.

The Russians on their part had been planning for some time. The news of the Alma may have prostrated the Tsar, but among the higher military circles in St. Petersburg it had merely confirmed what had long been believed, that success in war, at any rate for the Russians, depended on facing the enemy with a vast numerical superiority, and numbers was the one attribute with which Russia was so fortunately equipped. The allies had sixty thousand men on the Crimean peninsula—to defeat them Russia must engage them with twice that number. There would be no difficulty in arranging that, for the supply of impressed soldiery was almost inexhaustible. To arm them adequately was another matter, although it was not believed to be of much importance.

For weeks Russian troops had been pouring into the Crimea over the long roads from the Ukraine and by November 4th a hundred and twenty thousand had gathered in a semicircle of but a few miles' radius round the allies. By waiting so accommodatingly for a whole month without doing anything the allies were now faced with an enemy force that was out of all proportion to the modest garrison which they might have challenged with some hope of success at the end of September. Of course Raglan and Canrobert, who were to plan their master-stroke next morning, had no idea at all of this. In British staff circles the acquisition of furtive information about what the enemy was doing was still regarded as a little shameful.

The defeat on the Alma had not enhanced Menshikov's reputation with the Tsar, but he held an unassailable rank in the nobility and it was a little delicate to question his right to continue directing the campaign. Nevertheless, the Tsar decreed that even though Menshikov should remain the nominal commander-in-chief the great new armies that were gathering in and around Sebastopol should be commanded during the next assault on the allies by a certain General Dannenberg, who had no military success of any sort to his credit. It was a peculiar position for Menshikov and he apparently accepted it with a submissiveness that seems entirely out of character. At five o'clock on the afternoon of November 4th he issued an order—which was as lacking in detail as any allied order—to attack Mount Inkerman on the morrow, and, obedient to his imperial master, he clearly deputed command of all the troops in action to General Dannenberg. But lest his own position however nominal should be misjudged he made it clear in the order where he, the commander-in-chief, would be stationed during the battle, although in the event nobody came to consult him about anything. Two of the Tsar's younger sons, the Grand Dukes Nicholas and Michael, had come all the way from St. Petersburg to witness the great defeat of the allied armies that was impending, and next day they would be sitting on their horses with Menshikov on a convenient hillside. Fortunately for the imperial sensibilities the battleground was obscured by a kindly mist during the best part of the fighting. When Menshikov's formal order came to be acted upon at four o'clock the next morning twenty thousand Russian infantrymen would be moving towards Mount Inkerman in two massive columns, and behind them a hundred thousand more would be waiting in reserve. Like the allied commanders preceding the first bombardment of Sebastopol, the Russian generals were convinced the war would be over next day.

The dawn of November 5th was miserable and wet; a kind of Crimean weather which was now becoming familiar to the allies. A thick mist swirled over the whole of Mount Inkerman. The edges of the plateau on the top are covered with bushes and the steep sides rising from the ravines are even more thickly wooded so that the ground chosen by the Russians for the battle was quite different from that on which the previous battles had been fought, on the Alma and in the Balaclava plain. There, large formations of troops had moved and fought together; here, the battle was to be fought in dozens of separate clashes.

Old General de Lacy Evans was laid up in bed in the Second Division camp and a hitherto obscure general named Pennefather was acting for him in command of the division. Pennefather had himself been out on the crest of Shell Hill the afternoon before, and looking down over the country towards Sebastopol harbour and east across the Tchernaya valley, he had seen nothing but flocks of sheep being driven to pasture. At four o'clock on the morning of the fifth an aide-de-camp from Raglan's head-quarters had, as a matter of routine, ridden out to visit the pickets. He had heard church bells ringing in Sebastopol which was manifestly unusual for that hour of the morning and if he had been a little more imaginative he might have suspected something, but he had reported to headquarters that the night was exceptionally quiet although by then twenty thousand Russians were already on the move not three miles away, plodding patiently and silently in their columns. If the Russians were to accomplish nothing else, they were to spring a surprise on the allies on a grand scale.

By five o'clock the first Russians had come upon the British outposts on Shell Hill and as on the previous occasion the musket fire of the pickets as they withdrew attracted attention in the Second Division camp. But through the darkness and the drizzle and the thickness of the bushes there could be no indication of what was really portending, so when reports started coming to Pennefather of contact with the Russians at separate points he sent out little bodies of troops to reinforce the pickets, and from that first casual decision the whole character of the Battle of Inkerman was to develop. Throughout the whole morning, until after noon when the fighting stopped, the British troops who were involved never at any time operated as a cohesive body. The battle was to be a series of entirely unrelated engagements between British, and on one occasion French, groups—they could seldom be called proper formations—each of a few hundred soldiers, fighting Russian columns which consisted in every instance of thousands, and which were handled just as disconnectedly.

Very soon, in response to reports from pickets on both sides of the plateau, most of the Second Division had been hurried off in small detachments and the camp was virtually emptied. Lord Raglan, in a state of cheerfulness ill-suited to the weather, arrived to join Pennefather, but he scrupulously avoided any interference in the direction of events and seemed unperturbed that the whole Second Division had been committed piecemeal and that no action had been taken to arrange any support for it. Canrobert rode up too, to make the formal gesture of offering to place at Pennefather's disposal any French troops that he might need—for where St. Arnaud had been openly obstructive Canrobert sought at least to pretend co-operation—but his generosity went no farther than the offer. Somewhere to the rear General Bosquet, whose division was camped on the southern end of the Sapouné Ridge overlooking the Balaclava plain, had actually mustered his troops and was leading them in the direction of the sounds of battle. He met Sir George Brown and General Cathcart conferring together. Both the British generals were out of touch with what was happening on Mount Inkerman, but to them Bosquet's move seemed intrusive as he had not been invited into the British lines by anybody, and they told him so. Bosquet, apparently with some relief, returned with his division whence he had come.

By half-past six the Russians had brought twenty-two guns on to Shell Hill and were bombarding the Second Division camp, but as no one was left in camp there were no casualties although the shelling caused a lot of havoc. Under cover of bombardment and through the confusion of the British pickets who were all out of touch with each other, the Russian right wing, on the edge of the Careenage Ravine, was making a considerable advance and the foremost skirmishers were already round the edge of the Home Ridge screen, ready to enter the neck and so come down from Mount Inkerman on to the plateau of the Upland itself. But from the First Division camp, away to the south-west, General Buller and two hundred and fifty men of the 77th Regiment were marching quite spontaneously towards the sound of battle. They could see nothing, but the sounds were getting ominously close so they extended into line and suddenly a number of shapes loomed out of the mist. Colonel Egerton of the 77th said, "There are the Russians, general, what shall we do?" and Buller who had not thought this out before either, said unhesitatingly, "Charge them!" and the two hundred and fifty men of the 77th went in among the Russians—who incidentally numbered at least two thousand—with bayonets and rifle butts and drove them back into the mist and into the thick woods on the edge of the ravine. This was to be the pattern of a dozen or more similar encounters during the next few hours.

For the time being the 77th had successfully disposed of the enemy's right but now the columns on the Russian left were to advance up the Quarry Ravine and on to the plateau where the British, a little optimistically, were relying on the defensive qualities of The Barrier and the Sandbag Battery. Soon, seven hundred British soldiers on the eastern ridges of the plateau, in isolated groups, were fighting seven thousand Russians advancing up through the bushes in five separate columns.

Raglan still forbore to interfere, so the various divisions of his army had received no orders for concerted action and Pennefather was riding backward and forward across the plateau, striving valiantly enough to control the situation, but without any certain idea of what he was up against or what he should do. Not that he could do anything else now with the men who were already engaged, for they were all committed in close fighting and could not possibly have been withdrawn. The allies in the Crimea were now facing a major attack by an army with a potential of over a hundred thousand men, and the actual troops committed to hold them off amounted to less than four thousand, hastily thrown together in little groups with no communication between them and without any guidance or concerted plan at all. The headquarters staff had certainly joined Raglan on the heights and some attention to the tactical problem might have been expected, but the mail had just come in from England and the officers were somewhat preoccupied distributing letters.

Some of the British groups were running short of ammunition so that they were unable to face the oncoming Russians any longer and men started falling back towards the rear, walking singly and apparently aimlessly across the plateau and past the Home Ridge down to the camp. It was afterwards said that one of the strongest impressions left of the Battle of Inkerman was the number of single soldiers to be seen strolling about. The word had gone round saying where ammunition could be found if anybody wanted it, which was an unusual way of supplying troops in battle, and many men accepted this as licence to fall back as they pleased. But where ammunition was still lasting out, and where there was some control over the amorphous groups that had been thrown together without proper arrangements for command, the officers kept rallying their men and the struggle became a repeated story of bayonet charges, driving the Russians over the edge of the plateau into the wooded gullies, and the Russian columns regrouping and counter-attacking and making lodgment on the plateau again, in each instance a few score British soldiers standing up against and driving away ten times as many of the enemy.

At the Sandbag Battery ten thousand Russians were by now attacking the seven hundred British, although each of the contending forces was considerably split up. But the fate of the wretched little earthwork itself was inevitable and after heavy casualties on both sides the Russians temporarily acquired the mound of earth that was as valueless to them as it had been to the British. It was at this stage that the Duke of Cambridge brought the Guards Brigade into the battle. A really compact formation, particularly with the military qualities of the Guards, could have been used to some effect if it had been directed with even some small thought of tactical considerations. But the noble Duke, acting with masterly independence, sent his men in a counter-atttack on the Sandbag Battery where their value was to be completely dissipated in an epic of misapplied gallantry. His seven hundred men marched blindly into the still swirling mist and into the confusion of the wooded ground, to find that their muskets were so wet that the percussion caps would not ignite. So, appearing out of the fog almost like superhuman figures, towering above the bushes in their long, dark grey coats and their bearskins, they charged with their bayonets, they fought hand-to-hand, they picked up stones and hurled them at the enemy, and they recaptured the Sandbag Battery. Like so many other gallant incidents in this war it was magnificent, but the Guards had contributed nothing to the strategy of the battle except to fight their way into a position where the enemy had no difficulty in encircling them.

The Duke of Cambridge, when he saw the predicament into which he had so blithely sent his men, rode back to find Cathcart to urge him to bring the Fourth Division to the rescue of the Guards. But Cathcart was in one of his more intractable moods. When the British army had left England the Government, for some unfathomable reason, had given Cathcart the Dormant Commission, to succeed Raglan should anything happen to the commander-in-chief. Raglan had disapproved of the appointment from the start because he believed it should have been given to Sir George Brown who was not only his closest friend but happened to be the senior general. Consequently he had made it known to nobody else—except to Airey, which was unavoidable—and after the army had landed on the Crimea he had made no attempt to take Cathcart into his confidence. In fact twice during the march he had left him behind with the rearguard completely out of touch with the army so that if anything had happened to Raglan on those occasions a delicate situation could have arisen. This unsatisfactory relationship between the commander-in-chief and his chosen successor had come to the ears of the British Government, probably from Airey, and not unwisely they had at last decided to cancel the appointment although they had named no immediate alternate. Cathcart had received notification of their decision on the day after the Battle of Balaclava, and as he knew that he had not particularly distinguished himself on that occasion he had since tasted some dregs of bitterness. Now, as if to emphasize in Raglan's presence his new state of subordination he rode over to Pennefather, who at the time was talking to the commander-in-chief, and asked Pennefather where he wanted him to place the men of the Fourth Division. Pennefather, true to the tactics he had adopted for the battle, said, "Everywhere!" It was an unconstructive suggestion but it drew no comment from Raglan who was quite content not to have to make any decisions. So Cathcart's Fourth Division—or at least the comparatively small part of it which he had brought along with him—was split up into little groups and sent into the battle piecemeal, like all the other troops.

A few minutes earlier Raglan had ridden over to the Sandbag Battery where he had seen clearly what was happening. He might have come back to Pennefather advocating the withdrawal of troops from a position that was obviously developing into a trap, but instead he declared that it would break the hearts of good soldiers to tear them away from the fight—which was an odd reason to justify leaving them there to be wiped out.

Pennefather had sent Cathcart's men "everywhere", so Cathcart had been left with no troops to lead, but a little later one of his brigadiers turned up quite unexpectedly with four companies of infantry. Cathcart had already made his gesture to emphasize his subordinate position so he now fastened on to these new men determined not to offer them to Pennefather. For he had suddenly conceived the novel idea of taking four hundred men down into the Tchernaya valley and attacking the Russian army, some tens of thousands strong, on the flank. He did mention this inspired notion to the Duke of Cambridge and the Duke tried to dissuade him, not so much because he thought it would be suicidal but because he was still hoping for help for his Guards. The Duke hurried over to Raglan to inform him disapprovingly of Cathcart's intention—perhaps a little unfairly because it seemed to be everybody's battle and the generals were doing just as they pleased —and for the only time that day the commander-in-chief gave an order. Cathcart had by now taken his men to the extreme right of the British line, facing eastward over the Tchernaya valley, and he was about to move down the slope when Airey came hurrying over to tell him that Raglan ordered him to support the Guards, and not to descend the hill "nor leave the plateau anywhere." Cathcart was as argumentative as usual but Airey said explicitly, "Those are Lord Raglan's orders," and rode away.

As it was the only order given by the commander-in-chief all day it deserved a better fate, but Cathcart blatantly disobeyed it and led his four companies down the hillside. For some reason they were the only men on the field that day without greatcoats and their red uniforms stood out conspicuously even among the trees, so that their misguided move on the enemy's flank lost the element of surprise, which could have been its only vindication, and it also achieved the distinction of drawing the enemy's artillery fire from some batteries down the valley. Cathcart extended his men in a long line which lost all cohesion in the thick bushes, and before long he found that he was achieving little to threaten the Russian flank, and that his own four companies were the ones who were outflanked and that they were also now cut off from the rear. He said to his brigadier, "I fear we are in a mess," and a few minutes later he was killed.

The other divisional commander, the Duke of Cambridge, was finding himself in a mess too. Musket fire had opened up inconveniently behind him and he believed at first that his own troops were firing on him from the rear, until suddenly, in a scene wholly in keeping with the events of this unique battle, when nothing could be surprising, a British naval captain appeared out of the bushes fittingly accompanied by a midshipman on a white pony. Before disappearing as mysteriously as he had come the captain was able to convince the Duke that it was the Russians who were firing from behind, and His Grace, determined to extricate himself before it was too late, took the bold but effective course of riding right through the enemy. His horse was shot under him and his arm was grazed by a musket ball, but he came through. Now he was in a state of some distress, for he had left his precious Guards surrounded by the enemy. One of his staff said brightly, "The Guards, sir, will be sure to turn up," an observation that was meant to be consoling even though it could hardly have been based on any sound reasoning. In the end six hundred remnants of the Guards Brigade did at last turn up, but they were only half the number of men who had gone into battle.

A little earlier two French battalions from Prince Napoleon's division on the left had arrived with the usual French exuberance of drum and clarion and had drawn up in line between the Home Ridge and the Second Division camp. As the French never fought in line it should have been clear that they had no immediate intention of going into battle. By now the British were being hard-pressed so there were no complaints this time that the French were intruding. In fact the new arrivals quickly acquired some popularity and more than one harassed British general invited them to come to his assistance. But the young French officers commanding the battalions explained that they had not actually been ordered to advance and fight the enemy, and that as they were only junior officers they must wait for instructions from some higher quarter. Their popularity waned abruptly. The Duke of Cambridge argued with them pompously and was openly rude to them, but even that had no effect. The French officers were voluble, but adamant, that they had no authority to commit their battalions to battle. The Duke broke away from the unprofitable argument on a note of disgust and to show his disdain he rode his horse straight through the French ranks.

By half-past eight the mist had cleared a little and although the Russian generals could hardly pretend to have planned a climax to their assault, which had so far been merely a series of arbitrary thrusts wherever a convenient approach could be made, they now launched their strongest single attack. Six thousand men, in two broad columns one following the other, marched up the road from the bottom of the Quarry Ravine and facing them at the top were two thousand British soldiers at the most, scattered in little groups, and the hardly formidable impediment of The Barrier. By now the Russians had brought a hundred guns up on to Shell Hill and these were delivering a heavy weight of shot on to the British groups on the plateau at the head of the ravine—although in the event the damage by the guns was to prove more costly to the Russians themselves who were marched straight into their own barrage by their officers.

The Barrier was hardly noticed by the attackers despite the

squandered heroism of the little knot of British soldiers defending it, and the columns advanced up the road to the Home Ridge. They climbed the face of the ridge and looked down apparently unopposed towards the Second Division camp. The only immediate sign of their enemy were Lord Raglan and his staff and a rear view of the two French battalions which were now marching smartly away. Kinglake reports that on seeing the prompt move to the rear by the French "Raglan uttered an exclamation of astonishment and annoyance" and at the same moment one of his staff, General Strangways, was struck by a shell and killed. Raglan and the rest of his staff obligingly moved to one side. At that point Colonel Egerton with his two hundred men of the 77th—the regiment that had driven off the first Russian attack that morning and seemed destined that day to turn up at the right moment—came marching from the west directly into the flank of the retiring Frenchmen. Colonel Egerton grabbed a French officer unceremoniously by the collar and demanded in scarcely intelligible French to know why his men were marching the wrong way. The Frenchman explained, in the impeccable logic for which his race is famous—even, apparently, a little resentful that Egerton could have been so obtuse as not to have appreciated it for himself—"Mais, monsieur, voilà les Russes!"

The 77th had been marching in column from west to east and Egerton quickly formed his men into line facing the enemy by the simple expedient of a left turn, and they advanced up the ridge towards the Russians. Their example—or perhaps Egerton's rough handling of the officer had something to do with it—encouraged the Frenchmen to turn back, and apparently without any sanction from higher authority they now actually advanced towards the enemy although they showed no disposition to revert to the line formation in which they had nearly been caught. They were in column and intended to remain so; only the British were so crazy as to fight in line. So the force, eleven hundred men in all, that was now advancing to attack the Russians on the ridge, consisted of a British line on the left and a French column on the right—unorthodox perhaps but characteristic of the battle.

However, the effect of this unusual formation was never fully tested because just when the French started to advance a British officer, a Colonel Daubeney, who had with him thirty men of the 55th Regiment near the western end of the Home Ridge, decided to add his own contribution to the battle by charging with his thirty men into the flank of the leading Russian column, which was three thousand strong. The ensuing scrap, although this time between infantrymen, was like that of the Heavy Brigade at Balaclava with individuals too crowded together to swing their weapons effectively—this time it was bayonet and rifle butt—and ten men of the 55th, including Daubeney himself, emerged from the other side of the column miraculously alive. The effect of this impudent onslaught was probably far greater than would have been that of a frontal attack, and the Russian column was thrown into utter confusion—a confusion duly enhanced by the French who became so excited that they beat their drums, blew their clarions, shouted and cheered, breaking their ranks and rushing into the 77th line so that the British too, who normally fought silently, started cheering which was more than the Russians could stand. They retreated, and the allies drove them back into the Quarry Ravine; so the great enemy thrust past The Barrier had become just another of the day's many episodes of attack by the Russians and subsequent rout.

Shortly after this Raglan had one of his rare inspirations. He sent for two eighteen-pounder siege guns which had recently been landed from England and which at the time were the most formidable armament in the Crimea, although perhaps they were hardly orthodox weapons for use during an infantry battle. Seventy-five strong men were needed to drag each one painfully yard by yard and the supply of eighteen-pounder shot that they required was not carried too easily about the battlefield in those days. But their unconventional use on this occasion unquestionably saved the day, for although it was now clear that the Russian columns, no matter what their strength in numbers, were no match at all for the real fighting qualities of the British soldier, the British casualties had been shockingly heavy and if the Russians had merely kept on repeating the sequence of attack and withdrawal, undesigned as it may have been, their numbers must inevitably have told in the end. By half-past nine the mist had cleared entirely and the two guns opened fire on the Russian batteries on Shell Hill which could now be seen on the skyline, where the sudden arrival of a series of eighteen-pound iron balls obviously caused some intense embarrassment.

At ten o'clock when the two siege guns had considerably quietened the Russian cannonade, Bosquet decided that, intrusive or not, he would come and join the battle. He had spent the morning since his previous unwelcome incursion watching a Russian force under Prince Gortchakoff whose purpose was to make a feint attack on the Sapouné Ridge. The feint had been so successful that it had not even deceived the French. Now Bosquet avoided contact with any British generals and moved his division to the right of the line, where Cathcart had staged his unhappy demonstration. He made the choice mainly because a bareheaded French officer, waving a naked sword, had come galloping up to him with a panic cry for reinforcements, although at the time that sector was particularly quiet. Bosquet's division approached its position in grand style with the usual fanfare of bugles and drums, and not unnaturally the noise attracted the Russians so that they moved in to the attack and an engagement ensued in which the French were quickly driven back whence they had come. That was the sum total of Bosquet's contribution to the battle.

By now, five hours after the battle had started, some other French formations had moved across from the west and the allied forces facing the Russians on Mount Inkerman actually grew during the morning to thirteen thousand of whom two-thirds were French. So in effect the major role in directing the battle could now well fall on Canrobert. Canrobert had spent the morning amiably with Raglan. His arm had been cut by a piece of shrapnel and he had dismounted and was having the bandage adjusted. Pennefather, encouraged by the sight of all the new French battalions, rode up declaring that the fight could now be finished and victory achieved if these thousands of Frenchmen could be thrown into the battle. Naturally he had not worked out any detailed plan; the French, presumably, would go "everywhere".

Canrobert was polite enough. In fact he was effusive in his admiration of Pennefather's aggressive attitude. "Quel brave!"

he exclaimed to Raglan, "Quel bon general!" But his enthusiasm stopped short of ordering his own troops into the fight. The offensive, he declared, should now be abandoned. Raglan was fired with Pennefather's enthusiasm and he felt some disappointment at Canrobert's attitude, so he rode quietly away to avoid any argument.

Eleven o'clock came and although the Russians had been constantly driven back whenever they had approached Home Ridge they still virtually held Mount Inkerman. The two British siege guns had fired a hundred shots between them which was all the ammunition that had been brought up, and now a line of mule carts was struggling up from Balaclava with a hundred more. A pause came in the fighting. The enemy troops, who had naturally been prepared for battle that day, had brought rations with them; most of the British, except those who had been on night picket duty, had been called hastily from sleep. Those who had been on picket all night had been forced to keep on fighting. None of them had had any breakfast and there was no hope of a distribution of rations. A third of all the British soldiers who had taken any part in the battle at all were now dead or wounded; the rest were almost exhausted—some of them had been fighting continuously for nearly six hours. The Battle of Inkerman was no tactical exercise like the Alma or Balaclava, unplanned tactically as even they had been. Here on Mount Inkerman close combat had been sustained all the time and every move in the fight had depended on the individual British soldier, who had fought as always with that unquestioning discipline which may have been drilled into him relentlessly but was valiant enough nevertheless. Now there was a lull and the British soldier sat—or more universally he lay down—to take a rest, and nothing short of an immediate attack on him personally by the enemy would induce him to move either forward or back.

On the edge of a gully on the side of the plateau one of the regimental officers, Lord West, conceived the idea that it would be feasible to advance along the plateau and attack the nearest Russian battery on Shell Hill. He could muster a hundred and fifty men, and it was these hundred and fifty who, in the event, were to accomplish what Canrobert had refused to undertake with seven thousand, although it must be admitted that they were most unwilling instruments of military glory. They were weary, hungry, soaked through, and not a little disillusioned. Lord West ordered a Lieutenant Acton to muster one company—now reduced to sixty in number. The men rose—they had no option in face of a direct order—they fell in unwillingly and Acton moved them forward so that they formed the centre of a line between two other companies. He said to the officers of the other companies, "If you will attack the battery on either flank, I'll do so in front." Neither of the other officers thought much of the idea; they protested that their companies were not strong enough and that their men were tired. Acton said, "If you won't join me I'll attack with my company," and he ordered his men forward but the open dissent of the other officers encouraged them to disobey and no one moved. "All right," said Acton, "I'll go by myself." He strode forward and much to his discomfiture he found himself forty yards ahead of his company before the first man came running out of the ranks to join him. After that the resistance of the whole company inevitably collapsed, although it was some time before their example was followed by the companies on each side who had their own officers' resistance to reinforce them.

Acton's advance to the battery could hardly be described as an attack. The men were so tired that they could only toil slowly along; paradoxically this was their salvation, for it gave the Russian gunners time to limber up the guns and drag them away, and although Acton himself managed a spurt to the battery at the end the Russians had gone before he got there. And, slowly encouraged by what Acton had so bloodlessly accomplished, other officers now appeared from the surrounding bushes on the edge of the plateau cajoling their men forward, so that soon a few hundred unwilling British soldiers were dragging themselves wearily along the plateau in unavailing pursuit of the Russian artillerymen who were now obviously determined to withdraw altogether.

The day was quite clear now and the sun was even trying to shine through. Raglan could see what was happening on the plateau and he decided at last to intervene in the day's events and send one more appeal to Canrobert to pursue the Russians with the fresh French soldiers. It was clear that the sequel to the Alma was to be enacted all over again and the defeated Russians would be allowed to withdraw unmolested. Raglan hated embarrassing situations and he had no inclination to ask Canrobert himself, with the probability of a blunt refusal, so he sent the request by Pennefather. Canrobert, of course, refused and history has been unable to find any reason to justify him.

Once the Russian guns had started moving off the hill Dannenberg simply gave up. Menshikov and the Grand Dukes were still sitting where they had been all the morning, not half a mile away from Dannenberg's position on Shell Hill, but Dannenberg made no reference to his nominal commander-in-chief before he ordered all the Russian forces to withdraw. When Menshikov realized what was happening he galloped over and shouted, "It's impossible for us to fall back." Dannenberg said, "If your highness thinks otherwise have the goodness to give the orders yourself and take from me my command." But Menshikov, who knew surely enough to what place the Tsar had relegated him, was not to be provoked and he turned away and rode back to the Grand Dukes to put the best face he could on the situation.

So the Battle of Inkerman was over and the allies were still on the Upland. Mount Inkerman, and the gullies beside it, were strewn with dead and wounded. More than ten thousand Russians had fallen in a few hours where the Tsar's patient, plodding soldiers had been thrown against the British without any tactical plan, and even without any finesse. Six hundred British soldiers had been killed and nearly two thousand more had been wounded; the Guards Brigade had lost half its number in less than an hour. Many of the British dead had first fallen wounded and had then been killed by the Russians, clubbed or bayoneted, where they lay. Of this there was ample proof in the nature of their wounds. A message was sent under flag of truce to Menshikov taxing his army with these atrocities, and the Prince replied that any such action by his soldiers must have been prompted not by ruthlessness but by a sense of outraged piety. As the Tsar had said when war was first declared, Russia was not fighting for the things of this world, but for the Faith.

14

ON the morning of November 5th, the day the British
drove back the Russian attacks on Mount Inkerman,
another battle in the war was started, a battle that was
to save the British army from destruction more effectively than
all the siege guns that Lord Raglan could muster—although for
many months those taking part in it were to suffer nothing but
reverses. The battle was opened by a woman, and the troops she
had at her disposal with which to fight it were at first but thirty-
eight other women. Of these, twenty-four were nuns; the other
fourteen had no physical and few moral attractions although
they all claimed some nursing experience—which in those days
could mean very little. This little company of shock troops, led
by Miss Florence Nightingale, faced a more murderous enemy
of the British then all the armies of the Tsar.

The military exercises in the Crimea had started with the allied
march from the Old Fort which had culminated in the Battle of
the Alma; the flank march had followed and Sebastopol had been
bombarded; the allies in their turn had been attacked on the
Balaclava plain and on Mount Inkerman; and during it all a
shocking load of sick and wounded men had been mounting up.
The French had a reasonably efficient ambulance and hospital
service in the field, and, primitive as medical treatment was in
those days compared with that of the twentieth century, the
French casualties—which were comparatively few, apart from
the cholera visitation which in most cases had been fatal anyway
—had the benefit of at least some basic attention. But in the
British army there was no such organization at all. A few drunken
old pensioners had been sent out as medical orderlies but nearly
all these had themselves succumbed already, and men in the ranks
who were unwanted for any other duty—which in itself was a

reflection on their ability and intelligence—were told off to act as nurses for the wounded without any medical knowledge and with even less capacity for sympathy. A wounded or sick man, if he survived the nurses' handling, was merely dumped in a marquee, which may have boasted the designation of a field hospital but had no such advanced equipment as a bed, and he was left alone lying on the ground either to get better or die, or, if both these eventualities failed, to be moved in due course to the infamous establishments at Scutari.

This was no new state of affairs. The Army had suffered the lack of any pretence to proper medical services just as acutely in previous wars but most of these had been fought in remote parts of the world and nobody except the wretched soldiers themselves had ever known about it. The situation during the Crimean War has gone down in history as something unique only because for the first time the truth was inconveniently revealed to the British public.

The initial jolt to public complacency came on October 9th when *The Times* published the first of a series of blistering reports from William Howard Russell, its enterprising war correspondent who had made his way to the Crimea without any official sanction, although he had found no difficulty in taking a passage in a British transport and living with the troops in camp because there was no restriction on civilians mingling with the Army. The report was the first of a barrage that was to descend thenceforth day after day for months. Russell described in sordid detail what could have been written about any war. It had been written about wars in the past but only after they were all over. Never before had it been served up as live news, when it was actually happening. Russell told his readers that now, at the very moment that they were reading about it, their soldiers were lying bleeding from their wounds, dying painfully from want of attention— still wearing the only clothes they had brought with them to the Crimea weeks before, and in all probability had never taken off since, now soaked in blood and filth and crawling with lice; with no protection from the weather although winter was already coming on. He told them how the whole transport system to and from the Upland, such as it was, had broken down and how the

246

dreadfully wounded men—and there were thousands of them—had to be carried down to Balaclava on an agonizing journey that took nearly all day. He told them that when the wounded were taken aboard the transports they were no better off, for they lay out on the open deck and shattered men whose very survival depended on lying still were rolled against the ships' bulwarks in fearful, screaming agony; he told them how on the voyage from Balaclava to the Bosporus the death rate ran at ten per cent, and those who enjoyed the doubtful fortune to survive the journey were in worse condition than when they had come aboard and had now to face the horrors of the Scutari hospitals.

The term "hospital", applied at any rate to one of the establishments in Scutari, was perhaps a little imaginative. When the British army had first landed in Turkey and had settled down to an apparently indefinite stay Raglan had taken over an established hospital in Scutari which, within the limits of Turkish westernization, could make some remote claim to the title. The British called it the General Hospital. It had nine hundred beds, which seemed more than sufficient at the time when there was no immediate prospect of fighting, but it was hardly adequate for an army of twenty-five thousand men if they should happen to become involved in any battles. When the army moved to Varna the cholera epidemic taxed the General Hospital's primitive resources to their limit, and by the time the British had moved on to the Crimea and the wounded from the Battle of the Alma had started to arrive the General Hospital was overflowing.

So a second building was turned into a hospital by the simple expedient of naming it as such. No other preparation of any sort was considered necessary, nor had it any but the barest facilities for accommodating human beings, whatever their physical condition. The building was an enormous empty barracks which was so vast that it was almost like a town itself, with seemingly unending dormitories and corridors, passages and closets, all bare and empty of any furnishing. Part of the barracks had already been occupied by British soldiers when they had first come to Scutari and when they had moved out they had not left it any more habitable than they had found it. It still did service as a military depot, used indiscriminately by men and horses in transit to the Crimea, and down in its cellars all the female camp followers of the army had finally been collected—or at least the two hundred or so who had survived—and here they now existed in conditions of unbelievable squalor, accepted by those using the depot as a providential amenity. The tremendous building rose in three wings in a hollow square, with high towers at the corners, and as a lasting monument to British occupation one of the wings had been gutted by fire. This bare, dilapidated, filthy, damp, verminous building now became the Barrack Hospital and within its unpromising confines Florence Nightingale was to light her legendary lamp.

Russell's despatches stirred national sensibilities so deeply and so instantaneously that when *The Times* opened a relief fund on October 13th, thirty thousand pounds were subscribed in a few days. Naturally the authorities strenuously denied that anything could be wrong with the army or its medical services and in a vain effort to muzzle Russell they protested that the only effect of his despatches could be to help the enemy and that consequently they should be suppressed. But even though it may be possible to keep inconvenient facts from an inquisitive democracy for a time, only the smallest corner of the curtain of concealment needs to be lifted and the veil is certain to be ripped right off. Once Russell had made the first exposure of what was going on there was never any hope of again concealing the truth.

The man in the Government actually responsible for the army's medical services, such as they were, was Sydney Herbert, the Secretary at War—not to be confused with the Duke of Newcastle, the Secretary of State for War, who was more concerned with creating casualties—and by one of those coincidences that are the ingredients of history Herbert was a neighbour and a close friend of Miss Nightingale and he knew her as that rare phenomenon in the England of the day, an intelligent, educated woman who had not only taken up nursing seriously herself but even believed that it was an exclusively feminine occupation.

The public clamour became so furious, so quickly, that within a week the Government had been stampeded into conferring on Miss Nightingale, at Herbert's insistence, the inspiring title of "Superintendent of the Female Nursing Establishment of the

English General Hospitals in Turkey." Not that there was yet any female nursing establishment to superintend. However, this deficiency was hurriedly remedied by a frantic recruiting drive in London which increased the establishment from nil to thirty-eight—twice as many as Miss Nightingale wanted, for she knew the disciplinary problem involved in taking a batch of women into the heart of an army—and which attracted, apart from those enlisted from religious orders, women with little to recommend them. As one of Miss Nightingale's friends wrote, "Only one of them expressed a desire to go from a good motive. Money was the only inducement."

But the women, such as they were, were recruited quickly enough, and while it had taken the British army four months to arrive in Turkey, Miss Nightingale was there in two weeks. She left London with her unpromising band on October 21st, travelling overland to Marseilles and thence by sea, and they sailed into the Bosporus on November 3rd. Florence Nightingale had with her a pathetically weak force with which to nurse the whole British army but fortunately for the army she also carried a more formidable weapon—authority to spend *The Times* Fund. The Government, for their part, had lavishly presented her with a thousand pounds, which she used mainly to buy supplies of invalid food, and a chit to draw on the commissariat, which facility was in the event to prove quite useless. When she arrived in the Bosporus and it came to the ears of Lord Stratford de Redcliffe that she had *The Times* Fund to dispose of, he hastened to assure her that she would find nothing to spend it on in Scutari and he proposed that it be used to build a Protestant church in Constantinople. This was not because he had any particular religious leanings; but the establishment of a western church in the Ottoman capital would have marked a triumphant climax to his diplomatic career.

On the morning of November 5th, at the very time when the soldiers were beating back the Russians on Mount Inkerman, Miss Nightingale and her party were landing from a small boat at the rickety, stinking landing stage that gave the only access to Scutari from the Bosporus. Carcasses of dead horses floated in the water that lapped the beach and packs of starving dogs fought to secure what they could of the carrion. It was not an attractive landfall for a party of women, nor did it suggest an encouraging welcome to patients arriving at Scutari seeking a return to health. The track, for it was no road, that led up to Scutari from the shore did duty also as a drain. When the ladies reached the hospital they found that it shared unstintingly in the prevailing filth and slime and the whole place exuded a revolting but nevertheless readily identifiable stench.

By now the dormitories and corridors of the Barrack Hospital were no longer deserted vaults. They certainly boasted no equipment as hospital wards other than line upon line of roughly made wooden bedsteads, with a few bare tables that had never been washed, and in each ward a wooden tub that served an unceasing functional demand, all other sanitary arrangements having entirely broken down. There was no other equipment whatever. But more than a thousand wounded men from the Alma, and hundreds of soldiers who had succumbed to the lurking cholera germs during the march to the Old Fort, had survived the voyage to the Bosporus and had been taken painfully ashore at Scutari in small boats, and hauled even more painfully on to the landing stage and up the dreadful track, to be dumped in the Barrack Hospital. There they were now free to add to their ills by contracting those fevers and diseases which conditions at Scutari offered such encouraging opportunities to breed and spread. Apart from actual treatment by a doctor, which was rare, nobody gave them any attention beyond providing them with the barest minimum of food. There were a dozen male orderlies, and one clerk to issue supplies. There was one kitchen which boasted thirteen coppers and nothing else, and in the coppers meat and tea were boiled indiscriminately. There were no utensils except tin basins, which had to be used for both drinking and washing—the water supply had broken down and each patient was given a pint a day no matter what his ills—and if a patient felt inclined to eat the half-raw meat served to him cold he had to tear it from the bone with his fingers, provided the orderlies had left any meat on the bone. Mostly, men just lay on their beds in apathetic silence, still in their ragged clothes but without any further covering to protect them from the cold except the blood- and mud-soaked blanket which each man had brought with him—if it had not been stolen whilst he slept or lay unconscious. There they waited to die, which usually did not involve a long vigil.

Naturally no accommodation had been arranged for Miss Nightingale's party, and the thirty-nine women crowded into six small rooms in one of the towers—each room might comfortably have held two. The corresponding accommodation in the other tower was fully occupied by one major. There was no furniture in the rooms but they did find a corpse. Vermin were a matter of course. Miss Nightingale set her women to work scrubbing up their quarters, much against their inclination, for the cleaning operation was clearly going to be a long job and they had already caught brief glimpses of the pathetic scenes in the hospital and were impatient to rush in and get to work among the wounded with little understanding of what the horrors and the chaos really implied.

But from the start Miss Nightingale refused to allow her nurses into the wards, or anywhere else near the patients, unless they were actually requested by the doctors. The very conception of her mission was clearly a reflection on the capacity of the medical gentlemen to handle what they had been appointed to do and she was determined that none of her actions nor those of her nurses would appear to be directed at reminding them of this awkward implication. The doctors pointedly ignored her, so she kept her women cleaning and scrubbing their own cramped quarters and tearing up rags for future use, despite their reiterated complaints that it was not for this that they had come all the way from England.

On November 6th the first of the wounded from the Battle of Balaclava started to arrive but Miss Nightingale would still allow none of her nurses to go near the men. She had already made one tentative offer of invalid food, which she had brought with her, but she had been reminded sharply that the hospital was a military organization and was not authorized or even willing to accept unofficial supplies. That the supplies might help to save a few lives or even to relieve a little of the appalling suffering was irrelevant. So the women went on tearing up rags, muttering rebelliously that Miss Nightingale clearly had no compassion for suffering humanity.

251

For three days the wounded men poured in continuously and by November 9th a state of indescribable disorder had been achieved. The new arrivals suffered not merely shattered limbs and mangled bodies; they were dying of starvation, most of them had scurvy, and as soon as they had had a chance properly to inhale the very special atmosphere of the Barrack Hospital they developed an acute diarrhœa. For many there were no beds and they were carried in and put down, just as they were, on the cold stone floors. Whatever physical demands their condition made most of them were unable to move. Some were carried off the boats already dead; some died on their stretchers while being jolted over the track up to the hospital; others died almost as soon as they were laid on the floor. The scenes were so dreadful and all was such chaos that for a few days even the doctors forgot that Miss Nightingale was an unwelcome intruder and she was able to send her nurses into the wards at last. However, when the climax of the emergency had passed and conditions in the Barrack Hospital had returned to the more normal state of chaos the doctors reasserted their very proper authority so that the nursing activities of Miss Nightingale and her women were once again narrowly circumscribed, and hundreds of men who might at least have been granted even a little comfort were left to die in lonely agony.

But even if the opportunities for actual nursing were limited Miss Nightingale had her other source of relief in *The Times* Fund, and slowly she started to equip the Barrack Hospital and to provide the most elementary necessities for succouring dying men, much to the disgust of the authorities. What she was to accomplish over many months was to be a triumph of the determination of one lone woman to fight and defeat the frustrations, stupidity and criminal obstruction of hundreds of men operating a system that was no system at all. She had cabinet authority to requisition on the commissariat for anything she wanted, but the commissariat, even if they had what she required —and surprisingly enough they often had—were powerless in the bonds of officialdom to let her have it.

When war had been declared the Army had boasted a commissariat that operated for some imaginative reason in Ireland and the colonies but nowhere else, not even in England or Scotland. How the Army at home was victualled was an intriguing political mystery. But as the army proceeding to Turkey would clearly need to be fed and supplied with the necessities of existence a foreign commissariat had been hastily set up. However, when Miss Nightingale arrived at Scutari she found the rule to be that no supplies of any sort for a hospital could be drawn from the commissariat. The regulations laid down that they must be provided by the Purveyor's department, which was an entirely separate organization relying, nevertheless, on the commissariat to supply what was wanted although having no authority to demand that it should. The offices of Commissary-General and Purveyor were entirely independent with no official connecting link. Nor did the personal inclinations of the gentlemen concerned induce them to work together. When the foreign commissariat had been formed, early in the year, a Mr. Filder who was now sixty-four and on half-pay and had served in the Peninsula forty years before, had been appointed Commissary-General. The Purveyor, Mr. Ward, was seventy and he had also served the Duke of Wellington. To supply an expeditionary force of twenty-five thousand men Mr. Filder had been given three clerks, while in the Purveyor's department the veteran Mr. Ward enjoyed the services of two clerks and three messengers. Nobody had given any thought to where the Commissary-General's duties finished and the Purveyor's began, or vice versa, and Mr. Filder was later to admit publicly that he had never been able to work this out for himself.

Finding that she could get nothing from the authorities Miss Nightingale started buying medical supplies, invalid food and even hospital equipment, virtually for an army, with *The Times* Fund, and even with contributions from her own pocket, for happily she was a lady with a considerable personal fortune. When she suggested that the burnt-out wing of the Barrack Hospital should be made serviceable to receive five hundred more patients of whose arrival Lord Raglan sent a warning early in December, the hurdles of officialdom were so insuperable that she was forced to undertake the whole work herself—recruiting and supervising Turkish labourers, paying them out of her own pocket, ordering equipment, buying the bare necessities of hospital existence such as spoons and forks, knives, kettles, towels, blankets; preparing bedshirts and pillows for the patients—unheard-of luxuries for mere soldiers—of which the army authorities expressly disapproved. And when eight hundred instead of five hundred men arrived some ten days later and she was ready to receive them, many of the hardened soldiers, who would have accepted the horrors of the Barrack Hospital unmurmuringly with never a breath of complaint nor sign of emotion, broke down and cried when they found that a miracle had taken place and that they were being treated as human beings each with a pillow and a clean blanket and even if necessary the convenience of a bedpan. The story of what these men found was taken back to the Crimea so that henceforth, throughout the misery that was being endured on the Upland, Miss Nightingale's name came to be spoken almost reverently in the ranks although it gained little honour among the authorities. The doctors at Scutari were now ready enough to accept that she should purvey the whole hospital, but in their view that gave her no official standing nor any claim to their regard.

After the Battle of Inkerman, Lord Raglan at last grasped what should have been evident for months, that the allied armies would have to spend the winter on the Upland. The Russian attack had inconsiderately postponed the definitive bombardment of Sebastopol. In fact Canrobert and Raglan never even met to consider it. The British army had been severely mauled and the weather was worsening rapidly so that there were more immediate matters to engage their attention. On November 8th, three days after the battle, when signs of winter could be seen unmistakably in the sky, the inescapable truth dawned on Lord Raglan and he informed Mr. Filder that the army would be remaining on the Upland through the winter and blandly ordered him to "make provision accordingly." As, officially, Mr. Filder had not previously been so informed, the order conferred on him and his three clerks the manifestly impossible task of effecting within a few days the re-equipment of the whole army, which had landed on the Crimea in high summer. The chief interpreter, Mr. Cattley, whose job it was to carry out negotiations with local sources of supply, having no yearning to become involved in the chaos and recriminations that were certain to arise, wisely tendered his resignation, and a number of the more wealthy Army officers, who could afford to do so, equally wisely resigned their commissions and made for home. Lest their motives should be misunderstood and their personal courage questioned they explained that as the army would be in winter quarters it was unlikely that there would be any fighting. When the troops did come to experience the circumstances of their winter existence most of them would have preferred the fighting.

The Crimean winter of 1854-5, which has become a legend of history, arrived just before dawn on November 14th. The hurricane that brought it blew all day, sweeping the Upland with rain and sleet, and literally razing the allied camps to the ground. All the tents were ripped away, so were the marquees and even the blankets under which the sick and wounded lay. In Balaclava harbour every ship was torn from its moorings and many were wrecked and battered to pieces, while ships in the roadstead outside tried desperately to beat through the narrow entrance to shelter and merely piled up among the rest, and hundreds of men were drowned. On the Upland the troops sought in vain for even the slightest shelter from the ice-cold blast. In the evening the force of the wind dropped a little and snow started to fall, but not a man had any shelter during the night nor any suitable clothing to protect him from the fearful cold. The whole organization of supplying food or anything else merely collapsed. No fires could be lit and the troops shivered in helpless misery; some even froze to death.

The hurricane was not such an ill wind that it blew no good for the authorities. When the public sought later to seek out the perpetrators of this crowning blunder, which had committed the British army to a winter on the Crimea without any warm clothing, those who might have been held responsible declared, by a happy inspiration, that ample supplies had in fact been brought but that these had all been lost in the ships which foundered on November 14th. The system of recording and accounting was so complex and ineffective that the assertion was almost impossible to disprove. In actual fact, of course, the genuine losses

255

of stores were disastrous. One vital item of supply that disappeared entirely was forage for the horses. In those days the supply of hay was what the supply of petrol is to an army to-day. With exceptional providence Mr. Filder had collected during October three week's supply of forage in his store, or on shipboard at Balaclava, and there is no doubt that the hurricane did destroy the lot. When the grass on the Upland became covered with snow there was absolutely nothing for the horses to eat.

Thus started the purgatory of the Crimean winter, not gradually nor even swiftly, but instantaneously. One day had been reasonably mild, the next was positively arctic. The trenches, in which the men were kept all night on picket, half filled with nearly freezing water. The snow heaped and drifted and thawed, then heaped and drifted again. Men kept their boots on because if once they took them off they could never get their swollen feet back into them. Starving horses stampeded searching for food, and when they died, as they nearly all did, their bodies were left to putrefy where they had fallen. If life was to be kept going at all and the army was not simply to perish to a man the link between Balaclava and the Upland had to be maintained, and the journey, on foot, carrying rations and any other necessaries of life that could be salvaged from the shambles in the harbour, became an unceasing travail for every man in the army. Every single man, if he was still fit to stand, had to play his part in this system of human transport, even if only to secure what he needed for himself, and after spending most of the day and all his remaining energy struggling through the snow to Balaclava and back he still had to face picket duty. What animals there were that were still alive—mules and mere skeletons of horses—carried an unceasing stream of sick men down to the harbour, sliding and falling in the mud along the unmade track which had served well enough during the dry weather but which was now useless for any sort of wheeled vehicle. When Raglan lost the use of the Woronzoff Road after the Battle of Balaclava he had gone so far as to admit the need for another road to link the Upland with the harbour, but the problem of finding labour to make one had been too irksome and he had abandoned the idea.

By the end of November eight thousand men, more than

a third of the army strength that still survived, were in hospital. By January this number was to increase to thirteen thousand—more than half. And most of the men sent from the Crimea to Scutari, as if not amply discomfited by frostbite, starvation, pleurisy, pneumonia, gangrene and all the manifold ills that exposure and neglect can induce, were to be hastened on their way to the grave by the miasma of dysentery, typhoid and even cholera germs that were waiting to pounce on them in the Barrack Hospital. Three-quarters of the men of the British army who died in the Crimean war died not at the hands of the Russians, nor even from illnesses contracted on service, but from the diseases they caught in hospital. In three months nine thousand men died in the Barrack Hospital alone. By February more than twenty-two thousand men of the British army had become casualties—nearly as many as the whole army that landed at the Old Fort—but not more than a third of these had been caused by the enemy. Replacements, as they came streaming from England, succumbed almost immediately. As Delane of *The Times* had predicted, if the army perished before Sebastopol another would be raised to take its place. But even so, by January 1855, the Guards Brigade was reduced to three hundred men, the Scots Fusiliers were down to seventy-eight and the 63rd Regiment had disappeared altogether.

In the Barrack Hospital, Miss Nightingale struggled with the deluge, in her own sphere virtually alone. To read of what she, the gentlewoman brought up in luxury, accomplished almost unaided in the dreadful conditions in which she had to work is almost incomprehensible. She was as exposed to the fevers and infections as anybody else; she lived through the winter in perpetually damp, unheated quarters sharing the common, almost indigestible food. When convoys of new patients arrived she would be on her feet, directing, assisting, comforting, for twenty-four hours and more. Then she would go to her room to deal with the purveying of the hospital which she had now taken over in its entirety, continually interrupted by all the details of administration that were invariably referred to her. She wrote long reports to Mr. Herbert. She dressed many wounds herself, and spent hours on her knees on the hard stone floor tending men for whom no beds could be provided. For throughout January and February there were more than two thousand patients in the Barrack Hospital. As often as she could—and it seems almost unbelievable that she ever had the time—she stood quietly beside a man while he was being operated on and she had some intangible influence that helped him to relax and bear the excruciating pain, for of course there were no anæsthetics. If she knew that a man was dying, and that there was nobody else with him, she sat with him that he might not die alone, and so long as he lived all the other pressing, unceasing calls on her time were deferred. It is said that during the unrelenting turmoil of the winter she sat quietly and soothed the last moments of more than two thousand men. And although her days were filled, almost beyond human capacity, with the incessant work she did and with her spontaneous acts of loving humanity, she would still make the round of the whole hospital every night—the beds, crowded into as many lines as space would allow in the wards and corridors, stretched for four miles—so that she could be seen by every one of her restless, unsleeping, suffering patients and that they would know that she was watching over them. One of her nurses later said, "As we slowly passed along the silence was profound; very seldom did a moan or a cry from those deeply suffering fall on our ears. A dim light burned here and there. Miss Nightingale carried her lantern which she would set down before she bent over any of the patients. I much admired her manner to the men—it was so tender and kind." It was a manner that, wherever she went, silenced the bawdy talk and the swearing, not in a spirit of priggishness nor even a tone of admonishment. It was the simple British soldier himself who spontaneously recognized the respect due to a woman, particularly to one who seemed to him to have all the attributes of an angel. Miss Nightingale herself has written: "Never came from any of them one word nor one look which a gentleman would not have used; and while paying this humble tribute to humble courtesy, the tears come into my eyes as I think how, amidst scenes of loathsome disease and death, there arose above it all the innate dignity, gentleness and chivalry of the men—for never, surely, was chivalry so strikingly exemplified —shining in the midst of what must be considered the lowest sinks of human misery, and preventing instinctively the use of one expression which could distress a gentlewoman." And it was no cheap sentimentality that prompted a soldier to write, "What a comfort it was to see her pass even. She would speak to one, and nod and smile to as many more; but she could not do it all you know. We lay there by hundreds; but we could kiss her shadow as it fell and lay our heads on the pillow again content."

And so from the unlikely ingredients of the Barrack Hospital grew the legend of the Lady with the Lamp. Florence Nightingale was but a single individual among the tens of thousands involved in the affairs of the Crimean War and it is easy enough to overstate the relative importance of the part she played. In her own personal story also the Crimean War was but an episode in the pursuit of her ultimate achievement in creating a proper medical service for the British Army. But the light of her lamp shone beyond the tragic beds of the Barrack Hospital and pierced the conscience of the British public, so that they, and not the patient soldiers, rose up at last against the monstrous callousness of the authorities. When Florence Nightingale left Scutari she said, "I stand at the altar of the murdered men, and while I live I will fight their cause." It was not the Russians whom she was indicting as the murderers.

15

THE British public had importuned their leaders clamorously
enough to send their soldiers off to war. Now, when they
really learnt what war meant to the soldiers they turned
round and blamed the leaders. As Russell started to taste the
tremendous power he was wielding through *The Times* his reports
grew more ambitious and now he attacked the whole strategy
and conduct of the war, and particularly the part played by Lord
Raglan. As had never happened before, but as was to become the
enduring practice for evermore, the daily problems of war were
discussed and settled by millions of people at their breakfast tables.
The people cried out in anger at what they were told and the
House of Commons echoed the cry, although it allowed no sense
of urgency to interfere with its Christmas and New Year recess
during which over two thousand soldiers died in hospital. When
Parliament reassembled on January 23rd its mood was directed
not so much at speeding the prosecution of the war as at finding
someone to blame for what had happened, and a member named
Mr. Roebuck moved the appointment of a commission to enquire
"into the condition of our army before Sebastopol, and to the
conduct of those Departments of the Government whose duty it
has been to minister to the wants of the Army." The motion
so alarmed poor old Sir John Russell, the President of the
Council, that he resigned before it was even put to the House.

Mr. Roebuck was a lawyer and apt to be long-winded, but on
this occasion he felt ill and had to retire from the House immediately after he had read the motion and before he was able to speak
to it. Mr. Disraeli suggested from the opposition bench that this
was probably the best expedient to ensure the motion's success.
It was in fact carried by a majority of a hundred and fifty-seven
and as it directly implied a censure on the administration the

government had no option but to resign and the Pembroke Lodge dinner party of seven months before was out of office. Nobody seemed particularly keen to take their places and the Queen had some difficulty in finding a successor to Lord Aberdeen. She asked three men, one after the other, to form a government and they all declined, but the public, illogical as ever, had made up its mind that it wanted Lord Palmerston who had been loud in his demand that Sebastopol must be taken at all costs even at the time when there had been no need to pursue the war any further. In effect he was as responsible as anyone else for the situation, but nobody seemed concerned about that now. So Palmerston became the Prime Minister although he was to have little personal influence on affairs in the Crimea, and the allied armies were to remain on the Upland, looking down on Sebastopol but still as far away from taking it as ever, for another seven months.

The Duke of Newcastle's successor as Secretary of State for War was Lord Panmure, a mere youngster of fifty-three, who had actually been a soldier for twelve years although he had seen no active service, and Kinglake has described him perhaps a little severely as savage, churlish, rough-tempered and impatient of contradiction. Not that that prevented people from contradicting him nor even forcing him often to change his mind. When Roebuck's commission of enquiry started its investigations and began to probe into departmental activities—while men still died on the Upland—Panmure said testily, "It is impossible to carry on the government until the House puts the commission down," which was an ungracious reaction to the mood of those who had created the commission and had swept him into office at the same time. However, he was not alone in suffering the feeling of frustration that was brought about by the commission probing into everything the government was doing. Four of his present colleagues, including Sydney Herbert, had been ministers in Lord Aberdeen's government—they had remained in office mainly because it had been difficult to find anybody willing to replace them. These four soon found that interference by the commission made their positions impossible and so they resigned. Not so Panmure, who had changed his mind about the commission within a few days. He now explained, "It is useless to resist the storm. We must try to guide it," and remained in office.

Inevitably Lord Raglan was the main target for popular attack. Panmure, comfortably ensconced in the War Office without any first-hand knowledge of conditions in the Crimea, set to work to drive the attack home. He might with some reason have criticized Raglan for an appalling lack of strategic sense, or for his constitutional reluctance ever to plan ahead. Instead, Panmure merely railed against the poor state of health of the army—for which Raglan could hardly be held to blame—and accused Raglan quite unjustifiably of neglecting his soldiers, saying, "It would appear that your visits to the camp are few and far between, and your staff seem to have known as little as yourself of the condition of your gallant men." It was clear that the criticisms were mere echoes of Russell's reports. The only suggestion of any kind that he made for the better prosecution of the war was that Raglan should recruit a corps of scavengers in Constantinople and bring them to the Crimea to clean up the camps. Such was the measure of the man who had been brought in to correct the dreadful shortcomings of the British army's planning and administration. Enclosed with his censorious despatch he sent a private little note to Raglan which hardly reflected the crusading determination of a reformer. "I have most reluctantly come here," he said, "not that I expect to do any better than my predecessor, but because I want to protect as far as possible the interest of the army, and to stand between you and those who are so angry at all that has happened."

In the course of a long and dignified reply which completely refuted all Panmure's allegations Raglan remarked, "Your lordship appears satisfied that your irresponsible informants are more worthy of credit than I am." He might have found Panmure more difficult to answer if the Secretary of State had probed into his strategy or his tactics which are, after all, the chief responsibilities of a general. But the people were seeking a scapegoat, not for the strategic blunders, about which they understood nothing, but for the shocking privations which Russell told them that their soldiers were suffering and which were so much easier to comprehend. If Raglan was not to be the scapegoat then it must be someone close to him and Panmure's choice fell on General Airey who was known to have considerable influence over the com-

mander-in-chief. But Raglan resisted Airey's removal as strenuously as he had defended himself, and Panmure was forced to
relent once again and to defer any decision until he had received
a report from a certain General Simpson whom the government
was sending to the Crimea to investigate the capabilities of the
whole general staff. That was the least the government could do
to satisfy the public lust for rolling heads. General Simpson must
have been something of a disappointment because he waited four
months before reporting and then said, "There is not one of them
whom I would wish to see removed"; but the government had
at least to make a gesture so they recalled old Sir John Burgoyne
who was just beginning to show some usefulness now that siege
warfare was the accepted strategy. Otherwise the Peninsula
veterans still held their commands and in the British army no
fresh minds were brought to bear on the conduct of the war. On
June 1st, more than four months after the old Government had
fallen, Panmure wrote grudgingly to Raglan saying, "You shall
hear no more from me as to your staff."

Spurred on by Parliament's obvious hunger for enquiries the
government appointed, in addition to Roebuck's commission,
two separate parties of commissioners whom they actually sent
out to Scutari and the Crimea. The members of the first party
were called the Sanitary Commissioners, and Miss Nightingale—
who should have known—said they saved the British army.
These people not only enquired, they acted, which was more than
any of the other commissions did. At Scutari they opened up
drains and cleaned out sewers, and in the Crimea they even
persuaded the soldiers to boil the water before drinking it. The
other party of commissioners went to the Crimea to enquire into
the running of the commissariat and the issue of stores, a system
that was as clogged as the drains. Of course poor old Filder came
in for most of their strictures, but when they had finished their
enquiries they made the tactical mistake of dragging into their
report accusations of carelessness in handling stores against the
Earl of Lucan and the Earl of Cardigan and certain other officers.
The brothers-in-law were never happy to accept criticism however mild, and although they were both already deeply involved
in litigation over more serious aspersions made against them they

demanded a Court of Enquiry into the findings of the enquiry. The court was convened in all solemnity under the Judge Advocate General in the great hall of Chelsea Barracks and sat uninterruptedly from April 3rd to July 4th taking over again the whole of the evidence which the commissioners had heard in the Crimea —while all the time the war dragged on. The court duly absolved the officers mentioned in the commissioners' report from all the charges made against them and found that everything that had happened in the Crimea could conveniently be blamed on the Treasury.

Mr. Roebuck's parliamentary commission hardly achieved much more. Having asked twenty-one thousand questions it solemnly pronounced as the essence of its findings that no provision had been made by anybody for a winter campaign, and that the main cause of the calamities that the British had suffered were lack of information when deciding on the expedition and lack of forethought when planning it, which was precisely what everybody had known when the commission had been appointed. The commissioners were not so rash as to name any specific offenders and thus they cheated the public of the happy satisfaction of a witch-hunt; but they did have the grace to declare that "the patience and fortitude of the army demand the admiration and gratitude of the nation."

Throughout the winter, while the various commissioners were setting about their enquiries to little practical effect, the war still went on on the Upland. The Russians in Sebastopol were perhaps a little better off than the allies on the plateau above them for they were comparatively sheltered from the biting gales that swept down from the steppes of the Ukraine and they had at least the amenities of a town. Consequently they were able to maintain an artillery fire on the allied positions which added its persistent contribution to all the other discomforts. However, the new government in England had at last recognized that the whole existence of the army on the Upland depended on communication with Balaclava harbour and materials were sent out to start building a proper road, and in time a railway line was actually laid as well. By March a Land Transport Corps had been formed and mules—even camels and dromedaries—were shipped over, from Constantinople. But these developments took many months and meanwhile the soldiers on the Upland continued their agony. It was not until February 13th, four months after *The Times* had first launched its appeal, that a tide of relief started to flow in and the schooner *Erminia* of the Royal Yacht Squadron, sailed by her owner Lord Ellesmere, entered Balaclava harbour with the first fruits of the Crimean Army Fund—flannel shirts, brushes and combs, meat, ale, wine—belated gifts from a conscience-stricken public. Thenceforth the worst privations of the campaign were to be progressively dissolved. But while all this energy was being directed at making the soldiers a little more comfortable nobody in Britain was concerning himself at all with a plan to beat the enemy.

Soon after the allies had landed on the Crimea a large force of the Turkish army had been brought over from Bulgaria to garrison Eupatoria, which had fallen into allied hands so bloodlessly, and Omar Pasha himself commanded in the town. The arrangement served to sweeten the Turkish general while conveniently detaching him from the other allied commanders, for although prejudice against the Turkish army was to abate a little before the war was over, it died hard, and the French particularly were as contemptuous of their allies as ever. To the Russians the allied occupation of Eupatoria had long been a source of irritation because the Tartar inhabitants of the town had few scruples against trading with their country's enemies and the Eupatoria district had contributed in no small degree to the salvation of the allies when they were in their worst straits during the winter.

On February 17th Prince Menshikov ordered the local Russian commander, General Wrangel, to surround and attack the town, but Wrangel bluntly refused to do so because he regarded the operation as too difficult. Menshikov, who was still probably a little uncertain of his position, accepted the refusal weakly enough. However, a few hours later Wrangel's second in command, General Khrouleff, went over his senior's head and told Menshikov that he would undertake to launch the attack if he could be given the troops he wanted, and Wrangel obligingly gave them to him although he still refused to take any responsibility and thus created a command situation which was somewhat unique. At daybreak on the seventeenth General Khrouleff assaulted the town and by half-past ten he had lost eight hundred men and the rest of his troops were in flight; he had no option but to agree with Wrangel that the operation presented insuperable hazards, and Eupatoria was left to the allies.

When the news of this shameful episode reached St. Petersburg the Tsar immediately relieved Menshikov of his command, and a long, confused career had come abruptly to an end. The legend is that the Tsar then lay down and died of humiliation, but the more likely report has it that, still the indomitable inspector of troops, he went out on a cold, blustery morning and contracted congestion of the lungs. It is possible that he was so depressed about the situation in the Crimea that he had not the will to recover, and on March 2nd he died.

From the beginning of 1855 the main influence on events in the Crimea itself began insidiously to pass over to the French. Louis Napoleon was becoming impatient that the qualities of military genius which he was convinced he had inherited from his uncle were being so disastrously wasted. Moreover, if the Second Empire was to be properly consolidated on the splendid pattern of the First, the Emperor must show what a great general he was. Louis Napoleon at least deserves credit for having worked out a strategic plan for finishing the war which was more than anyone else had attempted. Raglan, although constitutionally opposed to planning in detail, had now certainly adopted a definite course of action, but this amounted to nothing more imaginative than the bombardment of Sebastopol until the town should be so reduced to ruins that the success of a final assault would be assured. In the event this was what was actually to happen, although the process of reducing Sebastopol carried just as devastating a reduction of the strength of the allied armies. But Louis Napoleon's theory, which had considerable validity, was that Sebastopol would be much more easily taken if first it was completely invested, which implied surrounding the town and cutting it off from the line of communication with Russia through Bakshiserai. Only thus could the garrison be prevented from continuing to obtain those apparently inexhaustible supplies of men and materials that negatived any effect of the allied siege.

Louis Napoleon's plan, which he had worked out in detail, amounted in effect to Raglan's previous flank march in reverse; while certain holding forces were to be left on the Upland, the Bakshiserai road would be cut and the allies would work round to the north side of Sebastopol harbour, which was the very position from which St. Arnaud had been so eager to extricate himself. But the nub of the new plan was that Louis Napoleon, the Emperor of the French, would emulate his uncle and would himself lead this great Army of Diversion, as he was pleased to call it, to a resounding victory.

After St. Arnaud had died Colonel Trochu seems to have disappeared into some historical limbo, and in January, Louis Napoleon sent out to the Crimea in his place, as "aide-de-camp of the Emperor on mission to the Army of the East" a certain Marshal Niel. Niel's duty was to keep an imperial eye on Canrobert just as Trochu had kept an eye on St. Arnaud. The Emperor had decided that all the efforts of the French army were henceforth to be reserved for his grand new plan and consequently Canrobert was not to be allowed to commit his forces to any direct attack on Sebastopol, although there would be no objection to his implying to Raglan that that was just what he intended to do. Marshal Niel was an officer who had not been involved in the Emperor's somewhat unorthodox accession to power and he was prepared to follow the practice, unfashionable in the French army at the time, of penalizing military inefficiency even in the face of political influence. His first action when he arrived at the French camp was to remove from command of a division a certain General Forey—whose military distinction had been limited to capturing the sitting members of the National Assembly in Paris on December 2nd three years before—and to replace him by a General Pélissier who had been given no part in the revolution at all. This change of command was certainly to have a happy effect on the final outcome of the war, for Pélissier was a general with rare qualities of leadership and resolution, but invidiously enough for Louis Napoleon it was ultimately to seal the doom of his own private plan.

Following the first bombardment of Sebastopol on October 17th, Colonel Todleben had worked wonders with the town's defences and now they ran in a continuous semicircle from the Redan on the east to the Quarantine Bastion on the west. The main strongpoints on which the October bombardment had concentrated were what were known as the Flagstaff Bastion opposite the French lines and the Redan which was overlooked by Mount Inkerman, but Todleben had now built a more formidable redoubt called the Malakoff and this had become virtually the strongest point in the line. Canrobert promised Raglan that he would open a new bombardment on the Flagstaff Bastion on January 1st while Raglan undertook to attend to the Malakoff, and it was implicit in their agreement that an infantry attack would be made by both armies immediately after the bombardment, although of course no details had been planned. But Canrobert, with Marshal Niel's eye on him, was true to his Emperor's trust and he managed to put off the bombardment for three months—in the event it was not opened until April 9th —and even more successfully to avoid launching any attack to follow it up.

The April bombardment—which opened on Easter Monday and found the Russians momentarily unprepared because they were all in church—differed from the one day's bombardment in the previous October only in that it went on for ten days and allowed the allies to pump fifteen times as many projectiles into Sebastopol; they fired a hundred and thirty thousand rounds and the Russians replied with eighty-eight thousand. Against allied casualties of a few hundreds, six thousand Russians were killed— in fact the Russian losses during 1855, until the fighting ceased, made even the British deaths in hospital look puny, averaging two hundred and fifty a day for months. Otherwise the bombardment took the allies no nearer the capture of the town although when it ceased on April 19th the Flagstaff Bastion had been almost entirely reduced by the French—but it was the Russians who attacked. Confused fighting went on for days, the Russians making lodgments close to the French and British lines, the allies driving them off again, and both sides suffering appalling losses. On the twenty-fourth a truce was declared so that the mounting heaps of dead between the lines could be collected, and the soldiers of Britain, France and Russia mingled freely together in

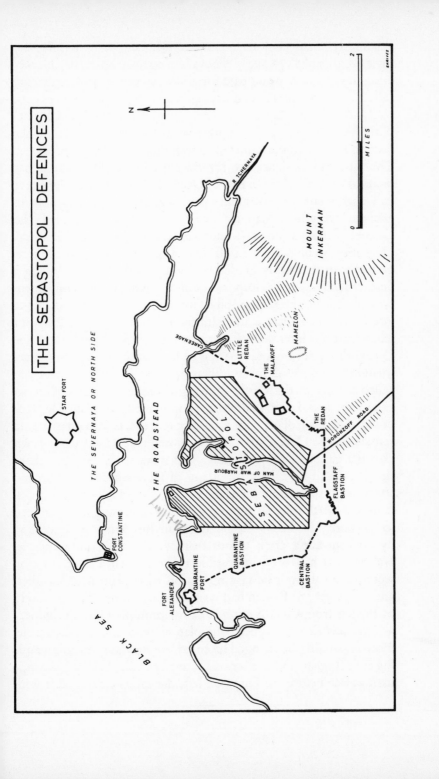

apparently unaffected friendliness until they were recalled by their commanders to apply themselves once again to the bloody business they were being paid for. Later, when similar truces were called, a greater intensity of feeling had been generated by events.

On April 16th Louis Napoleon crossed the English Channel with his recently wed Empress to pay the courtesies of the Second Empire to the Court of Queen Victoria at Windsor Castle. The visit had its delicacies, for Britain had not been altogether inclined to applaud the events of December 2nd. But the Emperor had a tremendous plausibility and apparently he was able to explain everything happily away to the satisfaction of the Queen, because a few days later she was to confide in her diary, "My impression is, that in all these apparently inexcusable acts, he has been invariably guided by the belief that he is fulfilling a destiny which God has imposed on him," which was a convenient way of shifting the responsibility for murder. Encouraged by the good relations he had made with the English Court the Emperor announced his intention of going to the Crimea himself, and the Queen thought how brave it was of him although the announcement caused some alarm in military circles. A council of war was called in one of the Castle drawing-rooms, the Prince Consort presiding, and Louis Napoleon propounded his plan. He proposed that Canrobert should command the troops that would remain on the Upland, that Raglan would take a field army down into the valley of the Tchernaya and menace the Russians from the flank, and that the great Army of Diversion, sixty thousand strong with their Emperor at their head, would fall on Sebastopol from the north side. Without previously disclosing his intentions to anybody, he had been building up his Army of Diversion by concentrating fresh troops from France in Constantinople. Naturally it had been impossible to keep such a concentration secret, even though he saw no reason to explain it to his allies, and on April 3rd Raglan had written to Panmure, "Why a body of French troops is collecting at Constantinople I cannot divine."

Panmure first denounced the plan as wild and impracticable. Then apparently he changed his mind, for he was soon commending it to Raglan, and at a second council of war, held at Buckingham Palace before the Emperor left, the cabinet adopted it with only one reservation—that the Emperor himself should not take part in it, for even in those days it was widely believed that the business of commanding armies should be left to the soldiers. Louis Napoleon was not at first to be deflected, but after he had returned to France he began to realize how great was the opposition to his going to the Crimea, even in his own country, and to save the imperial face he found a convenient political crisis which positively demanded his continued presence in Paris. When Panmure sent details of Louis Napoleon's plan to the Crimea, Raglan's only comment was, "It appears very complicated," which was sufficient to discourage the British general from concerning himself with it any further.

Unfortunately for Louis Napoleon, Niel had unwittingly destroyed any hope that the Emperor's grand strategy would be pursued when he had promoted Pélissier to a high command. Pélissier was a stocky little man of sixty-one and one of the few French generals of the day with a firm will and a simple belief that the purpose of his profession was to attain military success. He was so vehement about this purpose that not even the most politically minded officers felt disposed to deter him. When the Russians made dangerous lodgments on the hills close to the French lines, Canrobert, faithfully observing his Emperor's injunction that no French troops should be committed to action, had declared that to recapture the positions would not be to any advantage. Pélissier, without consulting his commander-in-chief attacked them, and Canrobert found himself unable to voice disapproval; Pélissier even went further and attacked some of the Russian defence works and when on one occasion he secured quite a notable victory Canrobert was obliged to make excuses about it to the French government. For the first time Lord Raglan found himself in sympathy with a French general who shared his own simple purpose of prosecuting the war, unscientific as that prosecution might be.

And it was just at this time that Raglan was also to enjoy an entirely unsolicited accession to his strength in the shape of fifteen thousand Piedmontese troops who, without any unnecessarily formal preliminaries, had landed at Balaclava and had put themselves at the British general's disposal. The Piedmontese had no quarrel with the Russians at all. Their quarrel was with Austria who was not even a belligerent in the war. But Count Cavour was pursuing the unification of Italy with single-minded relentlessness and he nicely calculated that a peace conference would be certain to follow hostilities in the Crimea and that those countries which had actually been engaged in the fighting would have the greatest influence at the conference table. One of the most convenient features of the war was that Austria, the stumbling block to Cavour's ambitions, had carefully refrained from active involvement, and Britain and France would be in honour bound to uphold against Austria the claims of a brave people who had fought and died at their side. Of all the purposes in history for going to war this was surely one of the most original, and unlike most war aims it was entirely successful. When the Piedmontese first arrived in the Crimea there seemed little prospect of fighting, but in the end they were to meet the Russians in a satisfying battle in the Tchernaya valley and to fight their way successfully to the conference table and to the vindication of Count Cavour's somewhat unique method of diplomacy.

On the Upland, Louis Napoleon's plan with its suggestion of investing Sebastopol seemed to have sparked off some unprecedented thoughts about strategy. The Emperor's idea, which was manifestly sound, was to invest Sebastopol as closely as possible and thereby cut the Russian line of supply at a point where it was reduced to a single road into the town—as Eupatoria was still in allied hands the road thence could be disregarded. The road to Sebastopol through Bakshiserai was formed of the junction between two lines of supply, one coming from the north across the Perekop isthmus, the other from the east through the seaport of Kerch on the eastern tip of the Crimean parallelogram. Here, at this tip, a narrow strait separates the Crimea from the rich lands of the Caucasus and ships can also sail from Kerch across the inland Sea of Azov to the ports at the mouth of the Don. Of these two lines of supply to Sebastopol the route through Kerch was certainly the more important. It offered comparatively easy contact with Taganrog near the mouth of the Don—a city that had once even aspired to the hope of becoming the capital of Russia—and the road to Kerch was far better than that across the

Perekop isthmus, so that the garrison depended on this eastern route more than on the route from the Ukraine.

Raglan's remark that Louis Napoleon's plan was much too complicated reflected his rooted aversion to manœuvring troops to predetermined positions, an exercise which he was ever careful to avoid. Nevertheless, it was probably the Emperor's plan that started him thinking about cutting the Russian line of communication, for he conceived in his own mind what he considered the more straightforward idea of sending a seaborne expedition to the Kerch peninsula. This would certainly mean cutting only one of the lines, and Sebastopol would still be in open communication with the Ukraine, but the attraction of the scheme was that it needed no tactical planning as it merely implied sending a flotilla of ships loaded with troops who would have to find a convenient place to land just as they had done when the allies had first come to the Crimea. Pélissier, with his lively imagination, encouraged the idea; Admiral Lyons, who had now taken over from Dundas the command of the British fleet, positively inflamed it. Even old Sir George Brown, to whom Raglan proposed to give command of the troops, approved. Canrobert did his best to uphold his Emperor's trust by telling Raglan that there were twenty-seven thousand Russians on the Kerch peninsula—which was as good a guess as any even though it proved to be grossly exaggerated—and that the expedition would be doomed to failure. However, Pélissier had already become a tremendous influence in the French camp, and on May 3rd—the very day when the mails arrived from England bringing the decision made at Buckingham Palace to adopt Louis Napoleon's plan—Canrobert was driven by weight of opinion to consent to the embarkation of nine thousand French infantrymen in Kamietsh Bay, while at the same time three thousand British troops embarked at Balaclava. Lyons, who had never shared Raglan's scruples against misleading the enemy, sailed his flotilla towards Odessa and waited until night had fallen to turn and double back round Cape Kherson on an easterly course.

It may be that Canrobert consented to embark his troops knowing full well what the next development was going to be. The new-fangled underwater telegraph was just at that time probing its way across the world and a cable was actually being laid along the bed of the Black Sea to link the French and British ports in the Crimea with Varna and thence with the capitals of Europe. For the first time in history British and French generals, fighting wars in remote parts of the world, were to be in immediate and frustrating contact with their governments. It was one of the most revolutionary factors ever to affect the conduct of war, and henceforth the day-to-day decisions, which had long been the happy prerogative of the generals, would be made by the politicians. The knowledge that this cable link would soon be completed had reconciled Louis Napoleon in no small measure to his detention from the Crimea, for now he would be able to control the war just as effectively and much more comfortably from Paris. When the service was put into operation on May 4th —the day after the Kerch expedition had sailed—the Emperor wasted no time. The very first message Canrobert received contained orders to send every ship he could lay hands on to Constantinople to embark the French Army of Diversion.

Canrobert told Raglan with some satisfaction that he had no option but to obey the Emperor's orders and that consequently he must recall the flotilla and send the French ships to Constantinople. He also mentioned that the Emperor had instructed him to take his, Louis Napoleon's, place as the generalissimo in command of all allied troops in the Crimea in the execution of the great strategic plan. Louis Napoleon had certainly mooted some such unblushing proposal when he had been in London, but as everybody had disapproved of his going to the Crimea at all the need to disabuse him of the belief that the proposal would be accepted had not arisen, and as Raglan had dismissed the whole strategy as too complicated and had no intention of interesting himself any further in it, he too took no notice of Canrobert's extraordinary presumption. In any case he was too annoyed at the fate of the Kerch expedition to have any anger left over for anything else. Canrobert sent a fast despatch boat with orders recalling the French ships and with it Raglan was obliged to send a message leaving the decision to Sir George Brown as to whether the British part in the expedition should continue on its own. The suggestion that three thousand men might proceed with an operation for which twelve thousand had been sent is indicative of the shallowness of the planning that had preceded it. Sir George Brown can hardly be blamed for deciding to return, and on May 6th all the troops were back in the Crimea.

But an emperor's wishes cannot be treated with complete disregard and a week later, while it was still undecided where the French troops from Constantinople were to land, the great plan was discussed—although with some asperity—at a series of councils of war in the Crimea. Omar Pasha came from Eupatoria to join the discussions because it was part of the plan that the Turkish army should be brought round to the Upland there to constitute, with a few French formations, a holding force to keep the Russians occupied while the British and the new French Army of Diversion were to undertake some complicated adventures on the enemy's flank. But Omar Pasha had other views. Encouraged by his success against the Russians at Eupatoria he proposed to bring his army south, following the route of the allied march from the Old Fort, to attack Sebastopol from the north side— a move which would have deprived the French of that very opportunity which Louis Napoleon was relying on to achieve his spectacular victory. But in any case both Raglan and Pélissier were entirely opposed to the plan. They both favoured concentrating allied resources on besieging Sebastopol from the Upland, although for different reasons: Raglan because any other strategy would, as he had complained, be too complicated, and Pélissier because he sincerely believed that only a properly planned attack from the long-prepared positions on the Upland could be launched with a certainty of success.

At the second conference it was clear to Canrobert that he would not be able to convert his colleagues to acceptance of the Emperor's plan and that consequently he had failed the trust placed in him. Impulsively, with all the Frenchman's sense of drama, he produced the dormant commission and placed it in Pélissier's hands charging him to take over the French command. But Pélissier somewhat robbed this theatrical gesture of its effectiveness by reminding Canrobert that the dormant commission could only be used if the commander-in-chief were incapacitated and that the French government might well want some say in a change of command. Canrobert, rather than that he should have to confess to Louis Napoleon that he had failed to convert the others to the plan, wrote to his Emperor, "My health and my mind, fatigued by constant tension, no longer allow me to carry the burden of an immense responsibility. I ask the Emperor to leave me a combatant's place at the head of a simple division," and Niel followed this up with a hurried cable imploring the Emperor to accept his resignation without hesitation. So Canrobert was relieved of the French command and Pélissier was promoted in his place. Every experience throughout the war, starting with the scourge of cholera among his troops in Bulgaria, had progressively discouraged Canrobert, until at last the spirit that had brought terror to the streets of Paris had itself been completely crushed.

Within a few days of taking over the French command Pélissier had agreed with Raglan on how they would prosecute and finish the war. Pélissier brought to the councils of the allied generals a degree of executive ability that had so long been lacking. Raglan had all along been purposeful enough in his intentions, but as a paradoxical legacy from his apprenticeship to the Duke of Wellington he had shown no capacity for putting them into effect. On May 22nd, only six days after Canrobert's resignation, Pélissier cabled Marshal Vaillant, the Minister of War, that he had made two important decisions with Raglan and together they intended to put them into immediate effect; they were about to attack the Russian outposts in the Sebastopol defences and a second expedition to Kerch was actually in course of being embarked. Vaillant replied hysterically to Niel, "This news to-day is great trouble! What? Generals and admirals, and not one of them has thought it his duty to consult the Emperor on affairs of such importance!"

The Emperor himself felt constrained to add his own expression of concern. If he were not careful his authority would soon be usurped by his new commander-in-chief in the Crimea. But the cable he sent to Pélissier somehow lacked the Napoleonic touch. "I have confidence in you," he conceded, "and do not pretend to command the army from here. However, I must tell you my opinions and you ought to pay regard to them." It seemed to Pélissier now that he had nothing to fear from this man whose stature was revealed as less than imperial and he replied, perhaps a little undiplomatically, that he had abandoned the Emperor's plan "without regret," explaining, "I am determined not to fling myself into the unknown; but to shun adventures and to act only on sound knowledge, with all the enlightenment needful for the rational conduct of an army," which was not a particularly tactful way of telling the Emperor that he thought nothing of his strategy. The message caused some embarrassment in the war ministry, whose members had the unenviable task of transmitting its contents to the Emperor, and Vaillant asked Niel to tell Pélissier to moderate his mode of expression. But despite that Niel had been the instrument of Pélissier's sudden promotion he was equally powerless in the new commander-in-chief's hands and he was soon replying plaintively to Vaillant, "At yesterday's meeting General Pélissier imposed silence on me with indescribable harshness." And so it was that at last the allies had acquired a leader with a spirit of offensive determination whom neither politicians nor even crowned heads, nor their sycophants, could deflect from his purpose.

Nevertheless, with all Pélissier's ability, and with Raglan's newly found confidence in an association between them, the second expedition to Kerch was an unqualified success not because of any particular competence on the part of the allies but thanks to an appalling stupidity shown by the Russians. The first expedition had offered ample warning of what was in the allies' minds, for Admiral Lyons's feint towards Odessa had been but a token homage to security and next day the flotilla had been clearly seen from the Crimean coast moving eastward. And although the expedition's sudden withdrawal had seemed inexplicable at the time this did not necessarily imply that another more determined attempt might not be made later. The allies had in fact gone out of their way to present the Russians with an obliging disclosure of their intentions and Prince Gortchakoff, the new commander-in-chief, took a definite counterstep, despite that it turned out to be ill-advised. Apparently the undistinguished part which General Wrangel had played in the Eupatoria affair had in no way shaken Gortchakoff's confidence in him, for he now moved him to Kerch to take over the defence of the town and the straits. Wrangel had nine thousand troops at his disposal—Canrobert on the previous occasion had found it convenient to estimate the local Russian strength at three times that number—sixty-two heavy guns and a squadron of fourteen naval vessels. Properly handled, this defensive force could well have shown a formidable opposition to an allied landing even though this time the French and British troops numbered fifteen thousand. But as soon as Wrangel heard that another expedition was on the way, and without knowing how big it was, he withdrew the whole garrison from Kerch on the frightened assumption that the allies might land and cut it off from the rear, and he destroyed all the guns and all the vessels of the naval squadron before a shot had been fired. Consequently the expedition was to achieve a success which, for its want of tactical planning, it hardly deserved. The allied squadron passed into the straits on May 24th without any opposition, the troops landed and destroyed all the supplies for Sebastopol that they could find, and the Navy sent its shallow-draught vessels into the Sea of Azov there to deal effectively, and with little difficulty, with the swarms of unarmed transports plying between Kerch and the Don ports on whose activities the very life of Prince Gortchakoff's army depended. In one of war's greatest anti-climaxes, the whole objective of Louis Napoleon's inspired strategy to cut off supplies from Sebastopol had been achieved without firing a shot. Certainly the road through the Ukraine was still open but the garrison in Sebastopol was now so enormous—in May it amounted to a hundred and twenty thousand men crowded inside the tiny perimeter of its defences—that there was no possibility of keeping it adequately supplied. When Wrangel gave up Kerch without a fight he determined the fate of Sebastopol and the outcome of the war, although nearly four months were still to pass before the town was finally to be taken by the allies.

The spring and the early summer had transformed the Upland, and the grass and the flowers were growing again until it was difficult to believe that the country had but recently been a wilderness of death. But the Russians, straitened by the pressure of the siege and the reduction of supplies, withdrew from the

Balaclava plain and the Tchernaya valley, so that on the south side of Sebastopol harbour the allied ring closed more tightly round the town. Even so, Louis Napoleon was still importuning Pélissier to adopt his plan and move round to the north side, and early in June he had the temerity to send a positive order. However, it had only been the day before when Pélissier had agreed with Raglan that they would jointly make an ambitious attack on the Sebastopol defence works, so that on this occasion when Pélissier flagrantly disregarded the Emperor's order he was able to blame circumstance rather than to have to admit positive disobedience. On June 6th, at three o'clock in the afternoon, five hundred and forty-four allied guns opened a bombardment, and next day the Mamelon—a prominent hillock not more than a hundred yards away from the main Russian redoubt—was assaulted and taken by the French. It was a bloody battle, for now there was not even a pretence of science in the fighting. Grape-shot, canister, round shot, musket balls, Minié bullets, bayonets, pistols—all were used with joyous indiscrimination and ghastly effect. And the casualties in the battle that day gave the clearest indication of how the initiative in the war had passed to the French, due to the tremendous accession of new strength to the French army and to General Pélissier's aggressive influence. The French casualties were five and a half thousand compared with less than seven hundred among the British. The capture of the Mamelon marked a signal victory, for it brought the allies to a position overlooking the town considerably farther forward than they had penetrated before. But the victory brought no reaction from Louis Napoleon until a week later when he cabled to Pélissier saying that before he could congratulate him he wanted to know what had been the cost. When the casualties were reported to him he said ungraciously—but possibly with some justification—"I wish you to observe that a general action that could have decided the fate of the Crimea would have cost no more."

By now Louis Napoleon's interference with Pélissier was beginning to weigh down even the general's buoyancy and he was driven to cable to his Emperor, "In the situation the complete execution of your orders is impossible. It is to place me, Sire, between insubordination and discredit. I pray your Majesty either to free me from the straitened limits imposed on me, or to permit me to resign a command impossible to exercise at the end, sometimes paralysing, of an electric wire." Louis Napoleon may have fancied his strategic ability but he had not the calibre of leadership to recognize that he must either remove Pélissier from his command or cease undermining his authority, and he settled the problem simply by disregarding it. On the seventeenth Pélissier telegraphed, "I have waited for an answer to my important despatch but have received none, and the combinations settled with our allies are taking their course. To-morrow, at daybreak, in concert with the English, I attack the Redan, the Malakoff, and their dependent batteries. I have firm hope."

The allied attack on the Redan that followed was a failure. The date of the attack had been deliberately chosen for June 18th—perhaps a little inauspiciously for the French—because it was the anniversary of Waterloo, the theory being that a joint victory by the British and French on that day might efface some embarrassing memories. As if to disprove the possibility of such an unlikely outcome Pélissier chose that occasion to inscribe two blemishes on his reputation as a sound general. First, on the day preceding the attack he summarily dismissed Bosquet from the command of his division, not on grounds of incompetence as a general but because Bosquet had retained in his possession a plan of the Malakoff taken from a dead Russian officer. For Bosquet to have failed to pass the plan to his commander-in-chief was a stupid omission even if it had not been deliberate. His duty clearly was to take the plan to Pélissier and his failure certainly deserved some disciplinary action. But where Pélissier erred was to prejudice the success of an impending attack by summarily removing a commander who knew intimately the ground and the men who were to be engaged, and by replacing him by a general—General d'Angely, the commander of the Imperial Guard—who had only just come out to the Crimea and was given but a few hours before the battle to acquaint himself with what he could of the complicated details of the battlefield and even of the disposition of his own troops within the intricate siege works.

And then to crown this indiscretion Pélissier, on the morning of the attack, made one of those abrupt departures from the agreed plan, such as his predecessing French generals had so repeatedly and so blithely indulged in. On the seventeenth a heavy bombardment had been directed on the objectives of the next day's attack and Pélissier had agreed with Raglan—following that careful consideration and discussion that was now being directed so remarkably to all the allies' moves—that the bombardment would be reopened at dawn the next morning and that the attack would be made two hours later. On the evening of the seventeenth Pélissier sent a message to Raglan—almost in the faithful tradition of St. Arnaud—saying that he intended to disregard the agreed plan and to attack at dawn without any preliminary cannonade, and as had happened so often before, Raglan was compelled to comply with the summary, last-minute whim of his allies. The concentrated bombardment of the day before had successfully warned the Russians that an attack was pending and as their nightly repair of the devastation of the previous day had become a routine they were quite ready for an attack the next morning, and they were immensely relieved that no preliminary bombardment had flattened out once again their hastily repaired defences.

Twenty-five thousand allied troops were mustered for the assault, but no real attack developed because the rifle and musket fire exchanged between the two sides was so deadly. Cancellation of the bombardment had completely thrown out the time-table and by eight o'clock only local attacks had been made and each attack had been driven off by the Russians. So Raglan and Pélissier decided to call the whole thing off. Including the casualties suffered during the artillery exchanges the day before, five thousand allied soldiers had been killed or wounded. Eight months before, the allied generals had funked an attack which at the time might well have finished the war and which they estimated might cost five hundred casualties. Now thousand upon thousand continued to mount up. It was on the occasion of this unsuccessful attack that Pélissier revealed the inner spirit of ruthlessness on which his generalship was founded: when it was reported to him that two of his subordinate generals had launched the assault prematurely—one of the main causes of the failure—

and that they had both been killed in battle later in the day, he declared, "If they were not dead I would send them before a court martial." No wonder that Niel had commented to Vaillant, "It is not an eagle we have set up in Canrobert's place but a vulture."

Ten days after the allied failure to capture the Redan, Lord Raglan died. He was sixty-seven now and despite what Russell had written about him he had shared in full with his soldiers the privations of the Crimean winter, for winter showed no respect for rank. And whatever may be said of Lord Raglan's imperturbability and his tendency to avoid decisions, no man with his particular quality of human understanding and with his load of responsibility could have lived through so tragic a crisis and not have suffered deeply himself. For some months now he had shown in his bearing, soldierly as it remained to the end, the measure of his personal distress.

On June 26th he fell ill and it was clear that he had been beset by that scourge that had carried away so many thousands of his soldiers. Mercifully the cholera that attacked him was in but a mild form and he was spared the indescribable torture that so many had suffered, but it was too severe to be combated by a man nearing his seventies. After he was struck down he lived only for two days and on June 28th he died, and after his death the vulture Pélissier stood beside his bed and cried like a child.

Much has been said—it has been said here—of Raglan's ineptitude as a general, and what has been said might well infer a far greater responsibility for the criminal mismanagement of the Crimean War than does in fact rest on him. Of course, of the responsibility for going to war at all in the first place he can be wholly absolved. That was not a soldier's decision. Of the responsibility for the decision to land on the Crimea—which was in itself the cardinal act of criminality—he can also be acquitted, for even if he had refused to take the British army to the peninsula, there is no doubt, and there was no doubt at the time, that the Government would have found someone else to do it. And although when the fighting started he committed error and stupidity after error and stupidity it is doubtful if any other British general of the day would have done any better. Before the present century, when staff colleges and command courses have promoted the conduct of war to a professional science, commanding any army in war was largely an empiric exercise—unless of course the commander happened to be a Marlborough, a Napoleon or a Wellington.

But it is no crime not to be a genius. Fitzroy Somerset, Earl of Raglan, was certainly no genius; in fact he was a bad general, but he was a good man in the true, unaffected sense of the word. He was a sincere and kindly man with no conceit and no arrogance, and although he was inept as a commander in battle he had one of the great qualities of a leader—he could inspire undiluted affection and respect. He lost a lot of battles, but he won a lot of hearts.

On Raglan's death command of the British forces passed to General Simpson, who had come out to purge the staff and instead had won their confidence. Throughout July the allied trenches crept forward nearer and nearer to the town until the foremost French lines were within twenty-five yards of the Malakoff. Naturally, even within the limited capacity of the weapons of the day, the casualties on each side that resulted from such close and sustained contact were enormous. The fight for Sebastopol had now become almost hand to hand, and so it continued for two long months. Now that Pélissier was in command of the French some redisposition of the forces had taken place and he was not as concerned as his predecessors to keep his troops on the safer side of the Upland. He moved a large part of his army across to the right so that it faced the Malakoff as its target on the eastern end of the Russian defence line and the main British attack was now concentrated on the French left, aimed at the Redan.

The Russians were to make one last effort to break through the encircling grip that was now so obviously closing on them. Alexander II, the new Tsar, who was a weak man without even his father's conceit, was still feeling his way and was hesitant to make decisions, so he instructed Gortchakoff to call a council of war in Sebastopol. On August 9th the council decided, albeit by a bare majority, to take the offensive although they were unable to agree on how or when. So it was left to Gortchakoff to make the decision and he ordered an attack to be made on August 16th in the Tchernaya valley although he left the details somewhat in the air. Clearly he had in mind a repetition of the tactics of the previous October when the Russians had become masters of the Balaclava plain and had almost succeeded in cutting off the British from their harbour. Circumstances had later forced them to withdraw from the plain and from the Tchernaya valley, and now eighteen thousand French troops were camped on the Fedioukine Hills and the French right was supported by nine thousand Piedmontese.

Gortchakoff mustered a force of sixty thousand men, with three hundred guns, but he had still not made up his mind whether to attack the French or the Piedmontese right up to the morning when this formidable army was due to march out of Sebastopol. However, one of his divisional commanders made it up for him by leading his division up the Tchernaya valley and launching an unplanned and ill-conceived assault against the French, who were waiting for such a gratuitous opportunity to swoop down from the hills. Inevitably, because even overwhelming numbers must be handicapped when trying to attack up hill against prepared defences, the Russians were driven off with tremendous slaughter, and within a couple of hours they had lost nine thousand men. For the Piedmontese this was just the chance they had been waiting for, and, relieved to see the French striving so successfully, they joined them enthusiastically in the fight, suffering two hundred casualties and thereby qualifying themselves for consideration at the conference table. The French lost fifteen hundred killed and wounded, but they had the satisfaction of knowing that any Russian threat to break the ring of the siege had been surmounted for ever.

For the Russians in Sebastopol the end had clearly come. They were making an heroic effort to reply with their guns to the tremendous weight of bombardment that was now being poured upon them almost incessantly. They had spent night after night repairing the damage of the previous day, removing the dead and wounded, and next morning they would stand to their defences, all the gaps in the ranks filled up, awaiting yet another onslaught and serving their own guns still with considerable effect on the allies. But the cost had been high, and bankruptcy—human and material—stared them in the face. The cemetery on the north side had already earned the name of the Grave of the Hundred Thousand. Just before Tsar Nicholas had died it had been reported to him that the Russian war casualties had already exceeded two hundred and forty thousand. Not all these had been suffered in Sebastopol and in the battles preceding the siege, for even more frightful had been the toll taken of troops merely marching to the Crimea. Through the winter, thousands upon thousands of reinforcements from Russia had struggled over the wind-swept steppes, toiling along in the snow, ill-nourished against the cold, lying shivering in the open, night after night, sleepless though exhausted. Of every three of these marching soldiers two had lain down and died beside the road. And of those who survived and reached Sebastopol, and lived to see the spring and feel again the blessed warmth of the sun, eighty-one thousand were killed in action during the six months from March to August 1855. Such was the measure of human slaughter that arose from the disputed possession of a single town.

Of the town itself there was practically nothing left, in fact possession of the ruins which remained on the shores of the harbour was now little more than symbolic. Where any discernible sign of a building still stood—and most buildings by now were heaps of unrecognizable rubble—it had been reduced to a broken, gutted, lifeless shell. Of gardens, squares, avenues, even passable roads, there was nothing left. Except as a battered stronghold for a hundred thousand men, Sebastopol no longer existed.

On August 17th the allies opened yet another concentrated bombardment and Gortchakoff decided at last that Sebastopol must be abandoned. "There is not a man in the army," he wrote to the Tsar, "who would not call it folly to continue the defence any longer." Admiral Nachimoff had been killed not two weeks after Lord Raglan had died. He had been convinced of defeat from the day when the allies had moved round to the south of the town and had long resented a fate that had kept him in a high position fighting a hopeless cause. Todleben had been wounded and taken to Russia, and Gortchakoff was left with few of the more stalwart spirits who had faced the opening of the siege when Menshikov had left them on their own. The parapets of the defence works even where they had not been blasted away by allied gunfire were drying up in the heat of the sun, splitting and crumbling and becoming largely ineffective. The thousands of troops who were still crowded into the trenches and in the fortresses of the Malakoff and the Redan were packed in solid masses in caves which had been scooped out under the parapets, and these men, waiting to be called to resist an allied assault, were now virtually cut off from support from the rear. The gunners, exposed in the batteries, fell daily by their hundreds and their bodies piled up in putrefying heaps, for even the nightly exercise of repairing and re-manning the defences, and carrying away the day's casualties, was now beginning to go by default.

On September 5th came the greatest allied cannonade of all and it lasted for three days. From the Upland it was difficult to believe that anything or anybody in the town could survive it. But the patient Russian masses held their positions under the cataclysmic rain of shot, and the heaps of dead and dying mounted up while the guns in the redoubts still replied forcibly enough. On the eighth at noon the Union Jack and the Tricolour were hoisted on the Mamelon, where Pélissier now had his headquarters not a hundred yards from the enemy lines, and the definitive attack on Sebastopol was launched at last. General Macmahon led the French to the Malakoff and General Codrington the British to the Redan.

The French had but twenty-five yards of ground to cover to the objective of their attack. They carried planks to bridge the Russian trenches and ladders to climb the parapets of the redoubt. The Russian soldiers, waiting in their thousands in the burrows beneath the parapets that had been prepared for just this eventuality, rose up to meet the French assault, and every trench, every mound, every firing-step was fought for by both sides in a spirit of conclusive desperation, each position taken, re-taken and taken again without any tactical finesse, each man concerned with nothing else than his immediate personal ascendancy. The struggle went on for four hours and cost the French seven and a half thousand casualties.

Codrington's assault on the Redan launched by the Light Division at the same time as the French attack, gallant enough as it was, failed entirely. The space between the British trenches and the enemy stronghold was much wider than that which the French had had to cover so that the Russians were able to pour an almost impenetrable fire into the advancing infantrymen. Some of the forward troops, led by a Colonel Windham, actually entered the enemy's works, but the Colonel found he was not being supported so he doubled back himself to try to procure reinforcements and when he came forward to the front again he found, not very surprisingly, that his men—or at least those who survived—had withdrawn. Two thousand five hundred British were killed or wounded and the Redan still remained in Russian hands. But the day had cost thirteen thousand Russian casualties and the French were in the Malakoff. On September 8th, 1855, Pélissier's soldiers repaid to Britain with generous interest the debt that St. Arnaud had incurred on the Alma.

In the midst of the shambles that was all that was left of the great arsenal and fortress of Sebastopol the Russians were contriving an exceptional piece of engineering, and by the evening following the allied assault they had completed a pontoon bridge across the harbour. By daybreak the next morning Sebastopol was empty; every able Russian had crossed to the north side, and wearily in their tens of thousands they dragged themselves up on to the steppe out of the range of the allied guns. Two of the ships in the harbour were on fire, and as the sun came up and the last of the Russian soldiers retreated across the bridge the allies started to smash the southern end of the pontoon and to begin the final destruction of the Russian fleet. During the night the magazines in the redoubts and on the harbour wharves had been blown up one by one, set off by delayed fuses placed by the Russians before they had left. Next day, the pits made by the explosions offered convenient mass graves for the thousands of bodies that the allies found piled up in the defences and in the ruins of the town. The Malakoff and the Redan, fortresses which had defied bombardment for months, were an indescribable shambles, witness of unbelievable heroism and unspeakable suffering by the conscripts of the Tsar. Two days later, in a great vault in one of the forts, the allies found two thousand men who had been lying wounded and immovable at the time when the rest of the garrison had retreated. For over forty-eight hours these forgotten men had lain helpless in their agony, with no food nor water, and when they were found less than five hundred were still alive.

At an appalling cost of human life and suffering on both sides—the total casualties in killed and wounded exceeded three hundred thousand—Sebastopol had been taken and the objective for which the British and French crowds had so long clamoured had at last been attained. Nobody, either in the crowds or among their leaders, had looked beyond that immediate objective, probably because for so long it had in itself seemed so unattainable. Now it began to dawn on everybody, with a sense of shocking disillusionment, that nothing at all had been settled by what had been achieved. What was left of the Russian army, and that was formidable enough, had crossed the harbour and had climbed the heights to the north and the east of the town and now it stood overlooking the allies, as viable as ever—perhaps even in better circumstances than before. Certainly it still had its problem of supply but with Sebastopol no longer to defend the material demand was enormously reduced and the road from the Ukraine was still open.

Thrashing round blindly for some way of winning this perverse war, and remembering the easy success of the Kerch expedition, the allies launched another combined operation, this time on the port of Nikolaieff at the mouth of the Dnieper, the river that empties into the bay on the northern shore of the Black Sea in whose western sweep Odessa lies. The operation was successful in itself because the town was but lightly defended, but Nikolaieff was too far from the supply route from the Ukraine for its occupation to have any marked effect. Louis Napoleon indulged in a new flight of strategic fancy and proposed a major invasion of Russia using Nikolaieff as a springboard. He proclaimed that his purpose was to cut off the Crimea entirely from the rest of Russia, but there seemed to be little enthusiasm among the allies to start an entirely new war somewhere else and this time he could get no support for his plan. In Britain it was believed that it would be simple enough for the allied armies merely to emerge from Sebastopol and drive the Russians out of the peninsula; as it was almost exactly a year ago since the campaign started, and as winter would be bursting on the Crimea again in less than six weeks, public memory seemed to have alarming limitations. Probably the most creditable action by the allied generals in the whole war was the inaction in which they now indulged in the Crimea.

As soon as Russia had been driven out of Sebastopol, as a year before she had been driven out of Silistria, Emperor Francis Joseph of Austria, true to character, threatened to join the allies. But it was clear to Britain and France by early 1856 that a virtual stalemate had arisen in the Crimea, and now that Louis Napoleon had the Battle of the Tchernaya and the capture of the Malakoff as battle honours for his Empire even his military ambitions seemed at last to have been satisfied. So on February 25th, with Austria reluctantly excluded and Count Cavour conspicuously invited, a peace conference was called in Paris and Russia took in it an equal part with the powers who had tried but failed to drive her out of the Crimea. Even so the harbour works in Sebastopol, the forts, anything that remained of the arsenal and dockyard, had been destroyed by the allied engineers so there was little immediate prospect that Russia might again enjoy her naval power in that part of the world—which was probably why she showed at the conference a surprising readiness to agree that warships of all nations should be prohibited from entering the Black Sea. Nevertheless, she did show some resistance to a proposal that she should be permanently excluded from the Danubian principalities, but the western powers at least were adamant that there were to be no more threats to Constantinople and the proposal was carried. Somehow, in the press of wider international problems, the matter of the keys of the Church of the Holy Sepulchre in Jerusalem was neglectfully overlooked and the real cause of all the disturbance was left unsettled—which is the traditional outcome of most wars.

The Treaty of Paris was signed on March 30th, 1856, and by this instrument the naval dockyard of Sebastopol, which had been physically destroyed anyway, was for ever abolished. For ever lasted no more than fourteen years, for when the Germans entered Paris in 1870 the Tsar showed an unusual astuteness by sending a note to France frankly repudiating the treaty, knowing full well that the French were hardly in a position to take exception. Nor, in the current circumstances in Europe, were the British. So Sebastopol rose from its ruins, until in 1890 the most powerful man-of-war of the Russian fleet, built, armed and manned in the dockyard, was launched by Alexander III—the last but one of the Tsars—and with a disturbing significance he christened the ship *Sinop*.

By the time peace was signed another winter had passed over the Crimea. But this second winter was no more of an ordeal for the British soldier than any sojourn in a frostbound, wintry land. For there was no fighting, the camps were now well hutted and the troops revelled in warm clothing and adequate rations. Britain had at least learned one lesson, even though it had cost tens of thousands of lives to teach it.

The winter passed, and peace and spring came at the same time, which was as it should be, and in the Crimea the flowers and the grass grew again. For the last time, the soldiers marched down the road to Balaclava harbour, the road of a hundred thousand dreadful memories. Then, when the soldiers had sailed away, silence fell on the Upland and on the Balaclava plain, and the echoes of all the horror, all the misery, all the slaughter, all the shameful blunders, grew fainter and died away, and at long last one more of the world's unnecessary wars had come to an end.

Bibliography

The Invasion of the Crimea, Vols. I-VIII. A. W. Kinglake. *William Blackwood, 1863-1887*

Turkey and the Crimean War. Rear-Admiral Sir Adolphus Slade, K.C.B. *Smith, Elder & Co. 1867*

Historical Record of the Seventh, or Royal Regiment of Fusiliers. W. Wheater. Printed for private circulation, Leeds, 1875. (Kindly lent by Mr. W. V. McAllister, of Nyamandhlovu, S. Rhodesia.)

The War in the Crimea. General Sir Edward Hamley, K.C.B. *Seeley & Co., Ltd. 1891*

The Crimea in 1854 and 1894. General Sir Evelyn Wood, V.C., G.C.B., G.C.M.G. *Chapman & Hall, 1896*

A History of the Coldstream Guards. Lieut.-Colonel Ross of Blandensburg. *A. D. Innes & Co., 1896*

Life, Letters and Diaries of Lieut. General Sir Gerald Graham, V.C., G.C.B. Colonel R. H. Vetch, C.B. *William Blackwood, 1901*

From the Fleet in the Fifties. Mrs. Tom Kelly. *Hurst & Blackett, Ltd., 1902*

The Panmure Papers, Vols. I and II. Edited by Sir George Douglas, Bart., M.A., and Sir George Dalhousie Ramsay, C.B. *Hodder & Stoughton, 1908*

The Life of Sir William Howard Russell, C.V.O., Ll.D., Vol. I. John Black Atkins. *John Murray, 1911*

Memories of the Crimean War. Douglas Arthur Reid, M.A. *St. Catherine Press, 1911*

At Home and on the Battlefield. Letters from the Crimea, China and Egypt, by Sir Frederick Charles Arthur Stephenson, G.C.B. Collected and arranged by Mrs. Frank Pownall. *John Murray, 1915*

The Second Empire. Philip Guedalla. *Hodder & Stoughton, 1922*

With the Guards We Shall Go. A Guardsman's Letters in the Crimea. Mabell, Countess of Airlie. *Hodder & Stoughton Ltd. 1933*

Lord Palmerston, Vol. II. Herbert C. F. Bell. *Longmans, Green & Co., 1936*

Florence Nightingale. Cecil Woodham-Smith. *Constable, 1950*

The Reason Why. Cecil Woodham-Smith. *Constable, 1953*

Voice from the Ranks. A personal narrative of the Crimean campaign by a Sergeant of the Royal Fusiliers. Edited by Kenneth Fenwick. *Folio Society, 1954*

Roger Fenton, Photographer of the Crimean War. His photographs and letters from the Crimea, with an essay on his life and work by Helmut and Alison Gernsheim. *Secker & Warburg, 1954*

Index

Abdul-Mejid, Sultan, 77
Aberdeen, Lord, 27, 93-4, 261
Acton, Lieutenant, 243
Afif Bey, 17-18
Agamemnon, H.M.S., 174, 182, 193
Ahmed III, Sultan, 77
Airey, General, 129-30, 135, 171, 211-13, 223, 235-7, 262-3
Albion, H.M.S., 193
Alexander I, Tsar, 45-7, 52
Alexander II, Tsar, 283
Alexander III, Tsar, 290
Alexander, Fort, 192
Ali, Mohammed, 19
Alma, River, 112, 126, 131, 135-6, 142, 148, 155-8
Alma Tamack, 138
Alonville, General d', 222
Angely, General d', 280
Apostol, Sergey Muraviev-, 50-1
Arab Tabia, 80-1
Arethusa, H.M.S., 58-9, 193
Argyll and Sutherland Highlanders (93rd Regiment), 195, 201
Arnold, Lieutenant, 82-3

Bakshiserai, 167-8, 171, 181, 186, 266-7, 272
Balaclava, 111, 173-7, 195-8; Battle of, 199, 200-8, 222, 224; 225, 232, 242, 247, 255-6, 264-5, 271, 273, 279, 290
Balchick Bay, 90, 102, 104
Barrack Hospital, 248-59
Barrier, the, 228-9, 233, 238, 240
Bashi-Bazouks, 78-9
Belbek River, 112, 126, 163-8, 173-4, 179, 181
Bellerophon, H.M.S., 194
Bent, Capt., 82-3
Bentinck, Brig.-Gen. Sir Henry, 153

Bergh, Hubert de, 198
Berthelot, 176
Bosquet, General, 87-9; at Battle of Alma, 132-51; at Battle of Balaclava, 217; at Battle of Inkerman, 232, 241; dismissed by Pélissier, 280
Bouat, General, 137-8
Bourlouk, 141-2, 145, 149
Britannia, H.M.S., 84, 90, 191
Brown, General Sir George, 71, 85, 98, 99, 111, 119, 120; at Battle of Alma, 146-8, 184, 232, 235; to Kerch, 273-5
Bruat, Admiral, 100
Bulganak, River, 112, 126, 128, 131-2
Bullard, Lieutenant, 82
Buller, General, 233
Burgas, 87
Burgoyne, Sir John, 70-1, 80, 111, 123, 164-6, 184-6, 263
Burke, Lieutenant, 82-3
Butler, Captain, 80-1

Calamita Bay, 113
Calthorpe, Colonel, 224
Cambridge, Duke of, 68-9; at Battle of Alma, 153-5; at Battle of Balaclava, 200, 210; at Battle of Inkerman, 234-8
Campbell, Brigadier-General Sir Colin, at Battle of Alma, 136, 144, 153; at Battle of Balaclava, 195-202
Cannon, General, 82-3
Canrobert, General, 111, 138, 150-1, 156, 166; assumed French command, 176-7; before Sebastopol, 183, 189, 191, 201; at Battle of Inkerman, 229-32, 241-4; at siege of Sebastopol, 254, 267-74; resigns command, 275-6

Canrobert Hill, 196-200
Caradoc, H.M.S., 106, 111, 113
Cardigan, Major-General the Earl of, in Bulgaria, 91-2; at River Bulganak, 127-130; at Battle of Balaclava, 196-224; accused of mishandling stores, 263
Careenage Ravine, 187, 226, 233
Cathcart, Major-General Sir George, before Sebastopol, 182-3; at Battle of Balaclava, 198, 200, 210, 222; at Battle of Inkerman, 232-7
Caton, 57
Cattley, Mr., 254
Cavalry Division, 168
Cavour, Count, 272, 289
Chapman's Battery, 187
Chasseurs d'Afrique, 201, 222
Church of the Holy Sepulchre, 13, 17, 289
Clarendon, Lord, 13, 26, 32
Codrington, Brigadier-General, at Battle of Alma, 146-154; attacks Redan, 286
Coldstream Guards, 35, 41-2, 101, 154
Constantine, Fort, 111-12, 192-3
Constantine, Prince, 45-50
Crimean Army Fund, 265

Dannenberg, General, 230, 244
Dardanelles, 18-19, 21, 23, 29, 71-2
Daubeny, Colonel, 240
Delane, John, 98, 257
Disraeli, Mr., 260
Dnieper, River, 288
Dobruja, 75-6, 79, 91
Dock Ravine, 186
Duberly, Captain, 203
Dundas, Admiral Sir Dean, 56, 60, 83, 98, 100, 105, 182; bombards Sebastopol, 190-4, 273
Dragoons, 1st (The Royals), 207
Dragoons, 4th Light, 215-16
Dragoons, 5th, 202, 207
Dragoons, 13th Light, 215
Dragoon Guards, 4th, 202, 207
Dryad, 198

Egerton, Colonel, 233, 239
Ellesmere, Lord, 265
Elliott, Lieutenant, 202-6
Erminia, 265
Eupatoria, 108, 113-15, 265-6, 275
Evans, General de Lacy, 144, 231

Federoff, Colonel, 225-6, 229
Fedioukine Hills, 196, 210-11, 220, 222, 224, 284
55th Regiment, 240
Filder, Mr., 253-4, 256, 263
First Division (infantry), 142-3, 153-4, 210, 233
Flagstaff Bastion, 187, 268
Forey, General, 267
Fourth Division (infantry), 126, 173, 236
Francis Joseph, Emperor, 22, 33, 84-5, 289
Furious, H.M.S., 55-6
Fury, H.M.S., 100
Fusiliers, 7th, 152-3
Fusiliers, 1st Royal, 43

Galatz, 76
Gallipoli, 43, 70-4, 80, 85-7
General Hospital, 247
Giffard, Captain Henry, 61
Gladstone, Mr., 94
Gordon's Battery, 187
Gortchakoff, Prince, on Danube, 83-5, 91; at Battle of Alma, 151, 155; in Sebastopol, 160, 178, 241; defence of Kerch, 277-8; at fall of Sebastopol, 283-5
Grach, Colonel, 79, 80
Great Ravine, 186
Grenadier Guards, 154
Grudzinska, Johanna, 46
Guards Brigade (infantry), 153, 155, 234, 238, 244, 257
Guirgevo, 82-4

Hamelin, Admiral, 100, 104, 190-3
Hardinge, Lord, 40, 223
Heavy Brigade (cavalry), 128; at Battle of Balaclava, 196, 202-8, 223

Herbert, Sydney, 248, 257, 261
Highland Brigade (infantry), 136, 153-5
Hinde, Lieutenant, 82
Home Ridge, 228-9, 233-4, 238-40, 242
Hussars, 8th, 215
Hussars, 11th, 215, 220

Inkerman, Mount, 173, 225-44
Inniskilling Dragoons, 202-3, 206-7

Joinville, Prince de, 58

Kadikoi, 174-5, 195-6, 201-2, 207
Kaffa, 106
Kamara, 196
Kamietsh Bay, 177, 184, 273
Kamishlu, Lake, 117
Kamsatch Bay, 177, 184
Katcha, River, 100, 112, 126, 160-1, 163, 173-4, 182, 191
Kerch, 272-4, 276-8
Kerkinitsky Bay, 108
Kherson, Cape, 108, 110, 111, 177, 273
Khrouleff, General, 265-6
Kinglake, A. W., 17, 43, 97, 158, 174, 178, 194, 239, 261
Kiriakoff, General, 151, 161
Korniloff, Admiral, 167, 178-81, 183, 185, 188
Kourganie Hill, 142, 154
Kvetzinski, General, 151

Lancers, 17th, 209, 215-16
Land Transport Corps., 264
Light Brigade (cavalry), 91-2, 128, 186; at Battle of Balaclava, 203, 208, 210, 212-24
Light Division (infantry), 98, 142-3, 146, 148, 286
London, H.M.S., 193
Lucan, Lieutenant-General, the Earl of, on the Bulganak, 128-9, 130; on the flank march, 168-72; at Battle of Balaclava, 198-224; accused of mishandling stores, 263

Lyons, Vice-Admiral Sir Edmund, 100, 102, 103, 105, 107, 111-12, 115-16; bombards Sebastopol, 190-4; to Kerch, 273, 277

Macintosh, Colonel, 165, 177
Mackenzie's Farm, 168, 170-2, 186
Macmahon, General, 286
Mahmoud II, Sultan, 77-8
Malakoff, the, 183, 268, 280, 283, 286-7
Malta, 43, 62, 70-1
Mamelon, the, 279, 286
Marmora, Sea of, 71
Marseilles, 89, 249
Maude, Colonel, 170-1, 195-6
Maxse, Lieutenant, 174
Mayow, Colonel, 220
Menshikov, Prince Alexander, to Constantinople, 20-5; 75; at Battle of the Alma, 136-8, 141-2, 149, 151, 159; at defence of Sebastopol, 160, 166-8, 171, 178-81, 185-6; at Battle of Balaclava, 195; at Battle of Inkerman, 230, 244; failure at Eupatoria, 265-6
Meynell, Lieutenant, 82-3
Michael, Grand Duke, 230, 244
Miloradovich, General, 49
Mogodar, 30
Moldavia, 27, 75
Moller, General, 178-9
Moltke, Captain, 77
Moniteur, Le, 157-8
Monto, Colonel, 175
Morris, Captain, 209, 215, 217

Nachimoff, Vice-Admiral, 178-9, 285
Napoleon, Prince Jerome, 69, 140-1, 143, 238
Napoleon, Prince Louis, prepares for war, 15-16, 22, 25, 28, 33; receives Raglan, 64-9; announces victory on Alma, 157; strategic plans, 266-7; visits England, 270; during siege of Sebastopol, 271-280; more plans, 288-9
Nasmyth, Lieutenant, 80-1

Nesselrode, Count, 27, 33
Newcastle, Duke of, 93-9, 193, 223, 248, 261
Nicholas I, Tsar, prepares for war, 16-20, 26-28, 34; Decembrist revolt, 45-53; during Crimean campaign, 148, 157, 159, 210, 229-30, 244; death, 266
Nicholas, Grand Duke, 230, 244
Niel, Marshal, 267-8, 271, 276-7, 282
Nightingale, Miss Florence, 245, 248-9, 251-4, 257-9, 263
Nikolaieff, 288
Nizam, the, 77-8
Nolan, Captain, 144-5, 212-16, 218, 221
North Valley, 196, 199, 200-2, 210

Obelenski, Prince, 49
Odessa, 21, 25; bombardment of, 54-61, 102, 163, 182, 273, 277
Ogilvy, Colonel, 82
Oliphant, Mr., 165, 177
Omar Pasha, 69, 70, 73, 76, 80, 88, 265, 275
Orlov, Count, 27
Osten-Sacken, Count, 57, 163
Osten-Sacken, Madame, 61

Paget, Lord George, 199, 216, 220-2
Palmerston, Lord, 94, 261
Panmure, Lord, 261-3, 270-1
Paris, Treaty of, 289
Paskevich, Prince, 79, 82-3
Paul, Tsar, 46
Pélissier, General, 267, 271, 273, 275; assumes command, 276-87
Pembroke Lodge, 93-7, 261
Pennefather, General, 231-44
Perekop, isthmus of, 108, 272-3
Pestel, Paul, 47, 50-1
Prince Consort, 42, 270
Prut, River, 27, 75-6, 78-9, 85

Quarantine Bastion, 268
Quarantine Fort, 192

Quarry Ravine, 228, 233, 238, 240
Queen, H.M.S., 57-8, 194

Radziwill, Prince, 219
Raglan, Field-Marshal Lord, 40; career of, 62-3; goes to Paris, 64, 68-70; goes to Turkey, 72-4; moves to Varna, 86-9; despatch to, 96-9; prepares to invade Crimea, 100-7; invades Crimea, 111-18; marches south, 124-33; at Battle of the Alma, 135-58; advances on Sebastopol, 161-76; bombards Sebastopol, 182-90; at Battle of Balaclava, 199-224; at Battle of Inkerman, 232-44; at siege of Sebastopol, 253-54; Panmure attacks, 262-3; death, 282-3
Redan, the, 187, 189-90, 268, 280, 282-3, 286-7
Redcliffe, Viscount Stratford de, 21-5, 31, 70, 73-4, 249
Retribution, H.M.S., 30, 61
Richelieu, Duc de, 54
Rodney, H.M.S., 194
Rodolph, Mount, 187, 189, 225
Roebuck, Mr., 260-3, 263-4
Russell, Lord John, 93, 260
Russell, William Howard, 246, 248, 260, 262
Rustchuk, 82, 84
Ryleyev, 48, 51

St. Arnaud, Marshal Achilles, career, 64-7; meets Raglan, 69-70; goes to Turkey, 72-4; moves to Varna, 86-91; prepares to invade Crimea, 100, 104, 106; invades Crimea, 113, 116, 124-5, 131-4; at Battle of the Alma, 135-44, 157-8, 162-7; death, 176.
Samson, H.M.S., 58
Sandbag Battery, 229, 233-6
Sanspareil, H.M.S., 193
Sapouné Ridge, 200, 202-3, 210, 225, 232, 241
Scarlett, Brigadier-General, 128, 202-6, 221, 223

296

Scots Fusiliers, 43, 154, 257
Scots Greys, 202-3, 206-7
Scutari, 71-2, 85, 88, 246-7, 249, 250, 253-4, 257, 259, 263
Second Division (infantry), 142, 143, 145, 226, 228, 231-2, 238-9
Selim III, Sultan, 77
77th Regiment, 233, 239
Severnaya (Star) Fort, 164, 167, 181
Seymour, Sir Hamilton, 20, 27
Shegog, Trumpeter, 204-6
Shell Hill, 226, 231-2, 238, 241-2
Shelwell, Colonel, 220-2
Shumla, 76, 79, 80, 83, 92
Silistria, 76, 79-84
Simpson, General, 263, 283
Sinop, 29-31, 178
Sinop, 290
63rd Regiment, 257
South Valley, 196-212
Strangways, General, 239

Taganrog, 45, 272
Tarkan, Cape, 106, 111, 113
Tchernaya, River (and valley), 110, 172, 186, 195, 225-6, 228, 231, 236, 270, 279, 283-4
Terrible, H.M.S., 58
Third Division (infantry), 161-2
Tiger, H.M.S., 58, 61
Times, The, 80, 81, 98, 157, 194, 208, 246, 257, 260

Times Fund, The, 248-9, 252-4, 265
Todleben, Colonel de, 178-80, 183, 185, 267-8, 285
Tractir Bridge, 173-4, 186
Trochu, Colonel, 86-8, 114, 131-4, 267
Trubetskoy, 49

Unkiar Skelessi, Treaty of, 19, 23, 25

Vaillant, Marshal, 69, 71, 276-7, 282
Valley of the Shadow of Death, 186-7
Varna, 80-2, 85-91, 101-3, 130, 274
Vienna Note, 28
Ville de Paris, 104, 106
Vladimir Regiment, 151

Walachia, 27, 75, 85
Ward, Mr., 253
Wellington, Duke of, 37-40, 51, 63, 99
West, Lord, 242-3
Westmorland, Lord, 33
Windham, Colonel, 287
Wood, Sir Evelyn, 123
Woronzoff Road, 186-7, 195-6, 210, 212, 224, 256
Wrangel, General, 265-6, 277-8

Yalta Mountains, 110
Yea, Colonel Lacy, 147-8, 152-5

Zouaves, 91, 104, 140, 156